STALIN'S DRIVE TO THE WEST, 1938-1945

STALIN'S DRIVE TO THE WEST

1938-1945 *The Origins of the Cold War*

R. C. RAACK

STANFORD UNIVERSITY PRESS

STANFORD, CALIFORNIA

Stanford University Press
Stanford, California
© 1995 by the Board of Trustees of the
Leland Stanford Junior University
Printed in the United States of America

CIP data appear at the end of the book

Stanford University Press publications are distributed exclusively by Stanford University
Press within the United States, Canada, Mexico,
and Central America; they are distributed exclusively by Cambridge University Press throughout the rest of the world.

Original printing 1995
Last figure below indicates year of this printing:
05   04   03   02   01   00   99   98   97   96

To the memory of my uncle,
Ralph Daniel Names (†1940),
who bought a boy books
about the world beyond

ACKNOWLEDGMENTS

I AM GRATEFUL to many people and institutions for the many forms of support they have given me over many years of research, writing, and historical filmmaking. Particularly, I thank the International Research and Exchanges Board and its many helpful coworkers, past and present, in the United States. It has made possible the scholarly exchanges that gave me time and opportunities to accomplish the research upon which much of this study is based. I am especially grateful to the dedicated archivists I have so often encountered in my many research stands. Many of them have saved for years material that might have been, might still be, politically unwise to save. I am likewise thankful to the many thoughtful and resourceful librarians who help keep the materials and assist the scholars who so need their help. The Bibliography contains a list of the archives, ranging geographically from Moscow to California, that I have consulted. I express particular thanks to the Public Record Office, London, for the use of PRO documents referred to and quoted from, and hereby recognize the Crown copyright of same.

Professor Jerald Combs of San Francisco State University read and commented on the entire manuscript in the light of his expertise on United States foreign policy for the period. My friend and longtime colleague Professor John D. Walz, of California State University,

Hayward (now emeritus), was always ready to supply helpful criticism and information based on his fine understanding of Russian history. Professor Lech Trzeciakowski, of Adam Mickiewicz University, Poznan, likewise a friend of many years, gave a good bit of time to preparing a critique of those sections of the manuscript dealing with Poland. Professor Norman Naimark of Stanford University most generously gave me a helpful critique of Chapter 5, in which the Red Army comes to Germany. Another friend of many years, R. Arnold Ricks, recently retired from Bennington College, suggested appropriate improvements for several sections. Brian George of Oakland, California, tendered sound advice on the basis of his years of editorial experience. George "Duff" Wyllie of San Francisco gave me a civilian historian's critique that was thoroughgoing as well as thoughtful. Karen Usborne and Lesley Cunliffe, of London, both authors in their own right, gave much proper advice when it was asked. Shirley Taylor, my Stanford Press editor, helped to transform ponderousness into prose, as did Bert R. Hearn, of San Diego, who gave the penultimate text careful reading. It is appropriate for each and all of them to disown the flaws that remain, for only the author is responsible for what he has included, concluded, and neglected.

I am additionally eager to pay respect to many colleagues and other professors who, over many years, have persisted in striving for the perhaps seemingly modest rewards deriving from the substantial effort that leads to solid scholarship. They have helped set for me the model of the scholarly professor I have tried to be. I cannot name them all here, but they will know, if and when they read these words, who they are. My deepest thanks to them all for being the people they are.

R. C. RAACK

CONTENTS

Illustrations follow page 72

STALIN'S DRIVE TO THE WEST, 1938-1945

INTRODUCTION

JUST A FEW years ago, former Soviet President Mikhail Sergeevich Gorbachev, as part of his domestic program of *perestroika* and *glasnost'* and to encourage public discussion of current Soviet affairs and history, officially reopened domestic discussion of Stalin's role in bringing about World War II. Gorbachev's purpose was evidently not to clarify history, however, but rather to ward off burgeoning criticism of the Soviet past by reconfirming the official version. In the course of his review, he praised Stalin for his conduct of the war, and, by implication, for his handling of wartime diplomacy. Since then, many Soviet (and post-Soviet) historians have been extremely cautious about revealing any history that is unkind to the image of the Kremlin's past international conduct. Some seven years after Gorbachev's apparent encouragement of openness, historians still await free access to what is stored inside the long-closed Soviet archives.[1]

President Gorbachev, perhaps naively, evidently wished to stabilize domestic and Warsaw Pact politics on the inexact history leading to the positive view of the Soviet past he then outlined. His explanation of the coming of World War II and of the ensuing Cold War—the original issues of which are inextricably bound up with wartime diplomacy—was that foreign dangers forced Stalin to undertake his early wartime collaboration with Hitler: Stalin had to make the Nonaggression Pact with the Nazis in August 1939 in order to defend "the world's first socialist state."

This version of one of the central events of the Stalinist period and recent world history was certainly not Gorbachev's own invention. It was the old Communist line, purveyed by implication at the time of the Pact by Stalin and his helpers and then by his party successors. But it was also, in many respects, the version accepted by important Western statesmen, including Winston S. Churchill and Franklin D. Roosevelt, to their own and to their nations' extreme diplomatic disadvantage during World War II. For it was the Nazi-Soviet Pact that first set the conditions for Soviet political and territorial advance westward across Europe as far as the Elbe River in central Germany in 1945.

Many commentators then as well as historians since have tried to justify the subsequent long-term occupation and bolshevization of central and east central Europe as unintended or defensive, and the occupation meant to be temporary. Both the occupation and bolshevization continued, some have argued, because Cold War developments magnified Stalin's fears of the West and made Soviet retreat impossible. But, in fact, when the Red Army march westward did stop in 1945, it was only because the occupying armies of the Western Allies had set up camp across the middle of defeated Germany. Stalin's dream of further conquest did not end: indeed, Stalin's successful drive to the west in 1944 and 1945, which was the result of Soviet diplomatic machination and military victory both before and during World War II, was a threat to the Western powers some perspicacious statesmen had anticipated as early as the late 1930's.[2]

The secret agreement behind the Hitler-Stalin Pact, whose historical existence batteries of Soviet historians for years tried to deny,[3] permitted Hitler to initiate the destruction of Poland and the rest of Europe he had not already secretly deeded over to Stalin. With Stalin's agreement, Hitler was certain of the Soviet Union's benevolent neutrality in the war he would soon begin, and he was also reasonably confident of Soviet collaboration in the invasion of Poland. Once Poland was out of the way, Hitler and Stalin followed that dismal triumph by sealing in later negotiation alternative plans for the ultimate destruction of Lithuania, and by arranging a new division of Poland between themselves. At least implicit in their original scheme was their mutual agreement to bring bloody con-flict all along the path of the original "cordon sanitaire," from Fin-land to Romania.

With their attacks on Poland in September 1939 the two dictators launched World War II. Hitler perhaps did not expect exactly that outcome when they first made their deal; but Stalin did. Indeed, the war in the West was the very result Stalin most happily saw coming from his undertaking with Hitler. With their Pact, Hitler gained the opportunity to seize some of the lebensraum to the east he always said he wanted for a greater realm for his own people, and he also won the space he needed for the vast concentration camp that he planned for the extermination of undesirable "races."

Stalin's gains from the Pact were more immediate, in that he could at once lay hands, "defensively," as the Soviet description then repeatedly suggested, on limitrophe lands immediately to the west of the Soviet Union running from Finland to Romania. Not the least of the Soviet gains was the subsequent strange apologia, issued on Stalin's behalf by many Westerners, including such unlikely fel-lows as leading members of the British Conservative Party and War Cabinet, that these moves were defensive, and even helpful to the Allied cause. Encouraged by these apparently cheaply purchased successes, Stalin's hopes for a far vaster expansion of Soviet power to the west, whenever circumstances proved favorable, took free flight. Even plans for Bolshevik world revolution directed from the Kremlin seemed suddenly plausible in the superheated atmosphere of easy victories just won.

This, in brief outline, was the beginning of this still poorly and strikingly misunderstood, albeit central, episode of contemporary history. Many facts, masses of them newly available from former East Bloc archives, at last make clear the connection of the war's origins with the Soviet *Drang nach Westen* of 1944–45. Also per-haps for the first time, we can now see the postwar consequences of the pact of August 1939 between the two dictators, which united them in bringing down the European house established at Versailles in 1919, and then created the political and geographical chaos that resulted in the Cold War. The events of 1939–45, therefore, lead us directly to the events of most recent times.

The wartime disputes between Stalin and his Western allies origi-nated over nothing less than the redisposition of the territorial and governmental results of the Nazi and Red dictators' original territorial deals. Such controversies inevitably found no diplomatic resolution in the alliance first defined by Churchill's early, incautious, commitment of British support to the Soviet Union. That commitment was ratified by an equally incautious Roosevelt, who preferred to conduct his own diplomacy with Stalin from the standpoint of his unfounded assumptions, and without consultation with his Secretary of State. Owing to wartime circumstances, these diplomatic failures went uncorrected, thereby setting the precedent for maintaining the secrets of the Westerners' failed diplomacy.

The early origins of the Cold War described here differ greatly from those accounts, prevalent in such Western, and more than abundant in American, historical literature, of a kind of sudden, surprising, late wartime or early postwar upwelling of Cold War antagonisms.[4] These antagonisms have often been attributed in such accounts to a variety of causes, most often Western in inspiration, whereas in truth the results were taken for the cause. History, to be sure, is not an exact science. None of the human sciences is, whatever the claims of some ardent practitioners. Indeed, a large part of the historian's methodology, itself little more than the search for and the reflective comparing of different sources, has already been suggested above in passing. Yet, in spite of history's evident methodological simplicity, it can be more or less exact, depending, if not exclusively, first, on the availability of sources, and second, on the completeness of the historian's research in the sources that are available. One thing is sure: good history, whatever the other qualities from which it derives, can only be founded in historical fact. The historian's initial task is, therefore, to cast the widest possible, tightly webbed net for appropriate historical sources. Recent political changes inside the former East Bloc now make that task for the period of World War II relatively easy compared with what it was just a few years ago.

The following history is the first, to my knowledge, to undertake to account for the coming of World War II and the Cold War on the basis of the large number of recently published sources, and even more recently opened archival materials, deriving from behind the former Iron Curtain. It is also solidly fixed in Western archival searches, and in Continental, British, and American monographic historical reporting. Just as critical to the soundness of the history told is the ambient color provided by details and background information found in some rather unusual unpublished archival materials, including films and photographs that have recently been opened for study in Poland, the former German Democratic Republic, and even in the former USSR, as well as in Western countries. For a number of reasons, few East Bloc, or Western, historians have ever consulted, either singly or as a whole, many of the archival sources used in this study, especially the audiovisual evidence. The author had the opportunity to view these widely dispersed historical materials from a background understanding gathered from the many readily available and much consulted Western sources and writings, as well as from Western audiovisual materials. Thanks to even the limited glasnost' of recent years, the Soviet and post-Soviet popular press, and to a lesser extent the historical journals, have increasingly been filled with fascinating and helpful histories. Many of these accounts have been full of recriminations directed to a number of past Soviet leaders, most notably to Stalin, so that, quite suddenly, the list of attributions and accusations of Soviet criminal complicity and behavior has lengthened enormously. At the same time, however, as noted earlier, there has been an obvious effort in Moscow to make certain that the new attacks and revelations, when founded on substantial local archival sources, were in no way directly connected to the crucial foreign policy events of Stalin's time.[5]

Yet even the beginnings of this guarded candor, although for some time only highlighting the domestic crimes of Stalin and his unusual associates, significantly bolstered the otherwise abundant evidence of Stalin's crimes. In particular, the more recently opened archives of the former East Bloc strikingly show the extent of Stalin's ideologically driven appetite for foreign adventure.

It is not so strange, then, that the role of the Soviet *vozhd'*, the secretive, duplicitous, paranoiac, murderous, and self-glorifying Stalin (to sum up manifold descriptions of him in current Soviet literature), in bringing on the Cold War, is still largely obscured, even in recent histories. The "pock-marked Caligula" (as Boris Pasternak is said to have called him), whom his critics at home now charge with at least 20 million domestic deaths, was praised by many contemporaries as the "great Stalin." As dictator of all the Russias, he left no aspect of life alone but presumed to be the self-ordained critic of music, film, theater, literature, architecture, and science. In the Kremlin, he served as the disarming host of midnight suppers, drinking bouts, and command showings of popular films for nonplussed foreign and other guests.[6] Afterward, as morning drew on, he just as felicitously moved to consult the dossiers of candidates for exile and death presented to him for judgment.

This man and his only slightly less imponderable contemporary in destructive achievement, Adolf Hitler, held total charge of the destinies of millions in their lands and abroad. Viacheslav Molotov, Stalin's close associate and foreign minister of the Soviet Union, belatedly, but proudly, confessed how "everything was snuggled in Stalin's fist and mine."[7] As for Hitler, few have doubted his central command in wartime Germany, given the strong basis in fact on which the conclusion rests. Yet even he has had his defenders, though some have perhaps had in mind, like Stalin's defenders, a purpose different from the most exact reconstruction of history.[8] The other makers of wartime and postwar diplomacy, Stalin's temporary Western allies in the anti-Nazi crusade, were, as Western statesmen, subject to eventual public challenge and to the vagaries of democratic politics, and therefore had to try to deal rationally and responsibly with their downright improbable dictatorial counterparts.

Of course the work of the democratic leaders of those days in dealing with both Stalin and Hitler could be founded only on what they could perceive behind the dark glass of official secrecy. Because their responses to Soviet and Nazi behavior were skewed by lack of information and by faulty information, it was not surprising that many erroneous assumptions were made about the existence of local political forces; Stalin's baffling changes of pace and direction were not judged to be simply the turns of a single man acting on his own.[9] Thus Stalin's skill at drawing the iron curtain continued to leave Western diplomats frustrated. But historical memory of this bafflement, even in some continuing institutions such as the British Foreign Office (its fully staffed equivalents in France, Poland, and the Baltic states, for example, largely ceased to exist shortly after the war began) seemed to vanish when most needed. Although this was in large measure attributable to rapid wartime personnel changes and to confusion sown by internal friends of the Soviet Union, whatever was supplied to the record was insufficiently regarded by political higher-ups.[10] Many of these conditions were also operative in the United States, where latent disputes sometimes resulted in divergent policy alternatives.

The Western wartime leaders were, after all, politicians daily preoccupied with a hundred topics. They came to their posts equipped with historical experience and learning, filters through which information about the wartime choices they were required to make had to pass. Not untypically, these leaders had formed opinions based in part on their own experiences, their own perceptions, perhaps emotionally colored, and also on what information they received from their wartime advisers. But President Roosevelt, as is well known, was notorious for rejecting or evading the advice of experts better informed on foreign matters.

Similar lacks of information have skewed many earlier histories of these events. All too many anglophone history writers on the subject have not bothered to take into account information that was well formulated in works on Stalin by competent Western scholars like George F. Kennan and Adam Ulam.[11] Kennan, writing from wartime Moscow, offered Charles Bohlen in Washington a relatively restrained analysis of Soviet behavior and intentions. "Soviet political aims in Europe," Kennan wrote in January 1945, "are not . . . consistent with the happiness, prosperity or stability of international life in the rest of the Continent"; of the Soviets, he said, to attain Europe's weakness and disunity, "There is no misery, and no evil, I am afraid, which they would not be prepared to inflict, if they could, on European peoples."[12] More recent studies of Stalin by Robert Conquest and Robert Tucker and also by Walter Laqueur, recounting recent Soviet reporting on Stalin, have essentially confirmed the findings of the earlier Stalin scholars.[13] Where the account that follows differs somewhat when dealing with Stalin as a personality from what these writers have told falls in the stress placed on the ideological force, personal rigidity, and frequent irrationalism that stand out in Stalin's actions.

The same historians who for years ignored reporters like Kennan and Ulam on Stalin also missed the important German materials on the period, and the revelations that over the years have appeared in Czech, Polish, and Russian. Many of these are now being belatedly confirmed by abundant testimony in the Moscow and Soviet historical press. One cannot but conclude that many historians, like some wartime politicians and diplomats (and some of their advisers), have deliberately chosen not to look at Stalin as he really was. Some of the most confused, uninformed, indeed, downright incorrect historical reporting on this subject has come from historians of the United States, historians who, it bears noting, for years almost took over the presses and lecterns occupied with Cold War historiography on the west side of the Atlantic. There is no question that a great deal of this work has been both highly politicized and also provincial, based only on domestic research.[14]

It ought to be self-evident to all historians that the history of one nation's international relations cannot, even by historical reporters possessed of the best will, be described exclusively from the sources produced by that nation, or even by those of one coalition of nations. Imagine an effort to describe exclusively from their own documentation the by now exhaustively reported history of the contribution of the French, or the Germans, or the British, to the origins of World War I. Obviously, the history of the origins of World War II and the subsequent Cold War cannot be completed from records in the United States National Archives or the British Public Record Office, or from the two together, yet many authors, particularly American, not only have limited their research in that way but also have gone on to presume for and to impute all too unconditionally to foreign, nonanglophone, statesmen humors, stimuli, and responses to documented American (or Western) behavior having little to do with evidence found in the actual historical record. This purblind approach at best ends with history seen in a convex mirror, distorted out of its wider international and chronological contexts, with results taken for their causes.

Readers of history behind the once formidable Iron Curtain have had a far different problem in that they have been denied information and access to information that has been available in the West for years. It is hardly surprising that now, after so many years of reading state histories, Russian readers have an urgent and still unsatisfied demand for historical truth about the events of the Stalinist era. Curiosity's genie, *pace* Mr. Gorbachev and others who even now try to keep Stalin's secrets, cannot be put back in the bottle.

The misinformation deriving from all this faulty historical reportage on the coming of World War II and the Cold War has had a profound effect on popular thinking. It permeates many widely circulated history textbooks at secondary and university levels, and, until just recently, the entire East Bloc press.[15] The same misinformation still infects much of the Western and Eastern press. Bad history has all too often driven out good, and is all too often still repeated or implied in historical and political opinion broadcast in the English-speaking world and on the European continent. On key international issues, it still sometimes radically twists both journalistic and political thinking. In short, whether intentionally or in ignorance, journalists and politicians still champion policies that are based on wildly mistaken historical premises. One has only to listen to debate on past foreign policy issues, not only in the anglophone world but elsewhere, to realize how many false notions about the history of the coming of World War II and the Cold War still exist, in spite of all the revelations from what used to be called the East Bloc. Stalin himself could hardly have wished for a different outcome.

Erroneous histories of the wartime years, abundant in East and West, therefore represent something more than grist for a professorial *Federstreit* or for the academic conference room. These authors have not just misreported historical events; they have misconceived the background of yesterday's events, and, more significantly, the events of today. The need to keep the real story in sight in contemporary history is one of the historian's responsibilities to those outside academe. The latter must develop and evaluate policies on the basis of the clearest possible understanding of the past nearest to us.

The dispatch of the present widespread historical confusion, the settling of this important contemporary historical business, fixing Stalin's important diplomatic and military place in the history of World War II and the early Cold War, is an overdue undertaking. Most histories of the times, some focusing on the coming of the real war and others on the origins of Cold War, have overlooked this clear connection of events. The historical task here requires a pulling together of what is to be found in a mass of disparate materials bearing on what was occurring simultaneously in places as widely separated geographically as Finland, the Baltic states, London, Moscow, Washington, D.C., and even the Far East.

Although the present study takes an international approach, the focus has been kept where it belongs: on the work of Hitler and Stalin, and later, on Stalin and his Western allies, on the demolition of traditional Europe, and on the effort to reconstruct it during and after the war. The original center of wartime and early Cold War events was central and east central Europe, the lands where Hitler and Stalin effected their first cooperative work of destruction and where the wartime disputes at the level of the Big Three and their foreign ministers centered, and it is there that the geographical emphasis must fall.

The world has now turned to a new phase of East-West history. Those politicians, historians, and journalists who, for whatever reason, have long denied us a factual recounting of this vital period of Soviet and Western diplomacy, the years from Munich to Potsdam, must now confront an end to the befuddlement that still pervades our sense of the central historical events of the century. We owe a thorough clarification of these times to readers everywhere, and not the least, perhaps, to the Muse of history, Clio, and to all that she means as a symbol of the quest for historical truth. We owe it to history itself, to reconstruct the past not as some have wished it to be, or as too many have described it to be, but as the sources show it to have been.

Much material has yet to be made available from East Bloc archives. Given the kind of purposeful political direction that still governs certain key record centers, it may be perhaps many years before all the details are available and assimilated, and many monographs and articles that tell more of the story than is currently available will eventually be written. This account is necessarily incomplete, but what is unfinished here will be finished, and corrected, by others later. Still, the essence of the history that follows should superannuate countless earlier histories of the coming of the War and Cold War.

1

STALIN TAKES THE REVOLUTION
ONE STEP WEST

PRAVDA AND *Le Journal de Moscou*, the latter in 1938 the international voice of the Soviet foreign ministry, in mid-February of that year reported one of Joseph Stalin's rare public statements linking foreign and domestic policy, couched in the form of a response to an inquiring letter by one of his Soviet *concitoyens*. The fact that Stalin gave this public testimony tells us that the Soviet leader wanted to tell the world outside his nation something. But what? For the interpretations of his remarks afterward supplied by vitally interested observers and government analysts in other European capitals could not have been more varied.

The Times of London reported that Stalin was saying, on the one hand, that the subversive clique in Moscow most recently tried and executed as enemies of the people had opposed the "victory of socialism in one country." Yet he had, on the other hand, noted that the "victory of socialism in our country is not final." He then went on to suggest actions by the proletarians of other countries to help make the revolution more secure in the Soviet Union, and to propose that Soviet workers should assist the workers abroad. British diplomats in Moscow and in the Northern Office of the Foreign Office, and elsewhere, reporting and commenting on Stalin's statement, differed widely in their interpretations but in general they discounted the speech as being anything of vital importance.

By contrast, the Nazi propaganda organ, *Völkischer Beobachter*, noted that the contents of the report must be a shock for Western would-be friends of the Soviet Union who favored a rapprochement of the USSR and Russia's former allies of World War I, Britain and France, against Germany. Indeed, as Dr. Goebbels's Nazi organ told it, the report proved that the Soviet Union had in fact never abandoned the Trotskyite policy of world revolution and remained, as always, a danger to all other states. A highly placed Polish press commentator with likely connections in the foreign ministry in Warsaw took the same point of view in *Gazeta polska*: the Poles had never held the illusion, so common in the Western states, that Stalin had ever truly renounced support of international revolutionary activities. The Polish point was now clearly reconfirmed.[1]

There is reason to believe that Stalin expected his remarks to produce the confusing results they did; certainly the wide variations in interpretations were not unusual, for the steady cacophony of misinformation and disinformation emanating from Moscow in the months before the start of World War II more often than not baffled rather than enlightened contemporary observers outside. From today's vantage point, it is not unreasonable to conclude that the apparent babble of voices at that stage of Soviet history was a deliberate ploy to maintain a level of confusion that was meant at least in part to keep Moscow's diplomatic doors open to all comers.

Historians have generally agreed that Adolf Hitler, Benito Mussolini, and the political leaders of the Japanese empire wanted a second World War, or were, at least, willing to take the risk, because they urgently wanted what they thought they probably could not get without a war. Less by far is known of Joseph Stalin's contribution to bringing on the conflict. His often inconsistent words and actions of the prewar days have long puzzled historians and have led to major misunderstandings of his international politics. But newly opened archival sources prove that Stalin, quite as much as Hitler and Mussolini and the Japanese, wanted the war, and, if in a different way, had a part in beginning it.

Stalin was evidently by nature, and certainly from experience, cautious. In the late 1930's, he was far less confrontational than his contemporaries in the European war party. Furthermore, although he had held power about fifteen years when he opened his grand

diplomatic and military tour de force by joining Hitler in the
of moves that led directly to World War II, he had only a n
background in the conduct of foreign affairs, and very little k
edge of foreign places. Stalin moved toward conflict with the world
outside after years of waiting patiently for the right circumstances
to advance his extraordinary plans. When he went to war in 1939
against two neighbors to the west, Poland and Finland, his goals
were to expand the borders of the giant Soviet state and to project
its influence farther to the west. In the Polish war, his caution, secrecy, and characteristic duplicity manifested themselves in astonishingly effective efforts to ensure that Hitler and the Germans were
blamed for Soviet territorial expansion westward. He also successfully led many to believe that his moves to the west were defensive
even in the Finnish war that followed.

In the later days of war, and in the immediate postwar years, as
opportunities for expansion were opened before him, he consistently acted to conceal his aggressive moves and to avoid direct confrontation with powerful foreign states. Again, he took advantage of
opportunities in both Europe and Asia to advance Soviet power only
where there was an absence of serious opposition, or where he had,
in effect, the tacit agreement or the prospect of ineffective hostile
response from states that might thwart his advances. Stalin's clumsy
and unsuccessful attempt to blockade Berlin in 1948, and the direct
military assault of the Korean War of 1950, both central events of
the Cold War, clearly showed a change to more direct confrontation.
But if by the late 1940's Stalin's approach had changed, he still kept
to his expansionist plans.

Stalin was a man captive to several traditions. They underpinned,
and, at the same time, in their odd variety also served to confuse
both contemporary and historical observers of his behavior in foreign affairs. Nearly all the territories he initially undertook to seize
in Europe, beginning in 1939, had once belonged to the Russian
tsars. Stalin as a young revolutionary no doubt feared as much as
hated the tsars and their imperial authority; yet fear and hatred do
not necessarily obviate the secret admiration of success or pride in
and understanding of the dimensions of the once mighty tsarist empire. Stalin had had no serious formal higher education and he knew
little about the broader perspectives of European culture and civilization. Although he himself was a Georgian, it was the Russian na-
tionality he praised and prized most of all. "Russianness" was one

of those legacies to which he was captive. Tsarist expansionism was another. Bolshevik dreams of world communism, V. I. Lenin's dreams, were yet another.

Self-anointed to carry out the purposes of the founder of the Soviet Marxist ideology, politics, and diplomacy, Stalin succeeded to Lenin's radical domestic and international program. "We pledge to you, Comrade Lenin, that we will fulfill your commandment[s] with honor," he vowed, rededicating himself in 1940 to the most powerful of the legacies to which he faithfully clung.[2]

Lenin's was far more a Soviet than a Russian program, and Stalin had to try to realize it in circumstances far different from those that Lenin had faced. The Leninist Russian program, like that of the tsars, was internationally expansionist, but whereas the tsars were locally expansionist by tradition, the Bolshevik program was driven by often unspecific Marxist-Leninist ideological precepts having global application. These were steadily coined and recoined, and endlessly repeated in hortatory slogans and propagandistic media fantasies advocating the violent creation of a new and better world based on the Soviet model. Stalin's original political plans were therefore militant, and, like Lenin's, recklessly violent. By 1924, Stalin had written and adapted for a postwar world his own compendium of Lenin's radical interventionist politics to achieve international Marxism. Stalin's restatement negated the notion of noninterference in the internal affairs of other states, yet, not so oddly, given his own modus operandi, he often, as in the case of his remarks of February 1938, seemed to suggest a lack of interest in Trotskyite internationalist adventurism, stressing his preoccupation with completing the Marxist-Leninist program in the USSR. Stalin was publicly separating himself from the exiled Leon Trotsky and the Bolshevik faction that advocated international social revolution by military means, generally considered to be the most aggressive Bolshevik stance in international affairs. Many Westerners in high places, not only then but in early postwar years, accepted Stalin's ambiguities as disavowals of Trotskyite adventurism. Even when he engaged in flagrantly expansionist foreign adventures, he often successfully disarmed his real and fancied domestic enemies and fooled both friend and foe.[3]

In fact, Stalin was, we can now be certain, effectively a Trotskyite (who, ironically, saw to the murder of this once much revered disciple of Lenin, one of the fathers of revolutionary internationalist thought). This is confirmed by long-concealed documents that reveal the extent of Stalin's international plans: first, a Red military thrust to the west of Europe, that to be followed by a vast expansion of the Soviet system carried out by the Red Army. His moves along the western front in 1939 and 1940 were therefore only the first of an intended series. They virtually duplicated, *mutatis mutandis*, the schemes Lenin had in mind with his invasion of Poland in 1920.[4] Yet, again it must be stressed, Stalin was extremely cautious as a tactician; though he had bold international plans, he absolutely lacked the public, manipulative bravado and flamboyance of Hitler and Mussolini. His secretiveness, his reflectiveness, his carefully maintained serenity covering an agile mind, helped him, during the negotiations of World War II, to appear to eminent Western statesmen and others as a sincere, plausible, and reasonable partner in international affairs.[5]

To Stalin, in the circumstances of the Soviet Union before the war, necessity dictated caution. To outsiders, the Soviet Union's reality was hidden in its vastness and remoteness, behind heaped-up layers of outrageous propaganda underscoring its alleged triumphs and military prowess. But after twenty years of Soviet power, Stalin, the USSR's unchallenged chief, still wielded too few resources to confront even modestly strong outside states, or groups of states. For all its immense dimensions and manpower, Stalin knew that his empire was frail and impoverished.[6] Still, in the circumstances, the solution to this problem of weakness could be found in his experience of deftly seizing all power for himself in the confused Russian domestic conditions after the 1917 revolution, when for years he could not confront his rivals directly. His carefully prepared subterfuges and schemes and his tactical willingness (and extraordinary mental ability) to deny one day what he had said the day before had then regularly paid dividends in personal and political triumphs.

Stalin's caution extended to a well-considered concern not to leave behind any documents that might firmly establish previous positions. Experience of success with one method obviously predisposes a person to repeat the technique in anticipation of another success. Stalin would patiently employ his earlier successful maneuvers in the long struggle for total power. One of them was, of course, to conceal his aims in words. But "his element," as one of his best biographers summed it up, "was fighting, struggle against enemies, and vindictive triumph over them."[7] Stalin's method in intraparty battle was to gather allies patiently, first from one side, then from another, telling each group what they wanted to hear and assuring them of his support, playing them against each other and bringing about their destruction, and so on in turn, moving from one set of opponents to the next. Much of the diplomatic history of World War II and Stalin's dealings with foreign allies and enemies is enlightened by understanding his ways, native or learned.

Stalin's constant struggle for greater power at home and abroad was founded on ideological dogmas as he interpreted them, and on the same techniques of calculated deceit and subtle manipulation that had brought him his earlier successes. Those were his greatest skills, to be reused when the occasion required, and probably often when it did not. Since Stalin's ultimate foreign goals for his rambunctious Soviet Russian state were patently neither conservative nor modest, he was bound to meet opposition someday. In fact, in the summer of 1939, the giant Soviet state ("one sixth of the earth," as its partisans east and west proudly considered it) could count no limitrophe state, except perhaps war-ravaged China (and China only because it was the Soviet Union's de facto ally against imperial Japan), among its friends.

Stalin's main prewar preoccupations, in the late 1920's and mid-1930's, had been domestic. In those years he had ruthlessly forced the industrialization and collectivization of the Soviet state, following his interpretation of Marxist-Leninist doctrine. By 1939, even before his visibly grand foreign triumphs in the aftermath of the Hitler-Stalin Pact, he had found not only a taste for diplomacy and foreign maneuver but also a confidence in his ability to win international power and influence, and soon. Both he and Viacheslav M. Molotov, his Foreign Minister from early May 1939, often spoke of this urge for international power as a kind of manifest destiny, as if Russia's hour, the predicted eve of international revolution, were imminent. The Russian Revolution that Lenin had pioneered in Petrograd, provincial Moscow would carry west.[8]

To be sure, it was not Stalin, for years domestically mired in his obsessive quest for power at home, who first embarked on the scheme to turn the European and Asian world order upside down. Hitler, and then Mussolini, were the ones who upset the European balance of power established by the Treaty of Versailles, and they both blustered unremittingly for propaganda effect at the Soviet Bolshevik state. Indeed, Hitler had founded his domestic career on campaigns against Jews and Bolsheviks, who were regularly linked in his outpourings as the chief enemies of civilization. During this period, the Soviet Union, spiritually a galaxy light-years removed from its European neighbors, was wholly absorbed in revolutionary rebuilding, and wasted by the crude extravagance of the reign of terror that Stalin pursued to destroy his opponents and strengthen his power at home. Hitler's *Anschluss* with Austria in 1938, soon followed by the destruction (obligingly participated in by Hungary and Poland as well) of the Czechoslovak multinational state, began the demolition of the existing territorial order. In April 1939, the Italians joined in by occupying Albania.

It is now clear that Stalin, his state on the eve of war still virtually without friends among nations, was desperately seeking some form of accommodation with Hitler to forestall, or make impossible, a German attack on the USSR. Hitler made no secret of his desire to expand Germany's frontiers in the east. Stalin, well aware of the weakness of his state, then needed time to turn his newly created and dearly bought industrial strength to the tasks of rearming. The experience of the Spanish Civil War had shown that most Soviet arms were not equal to those of the Germans.[9] Stalin no doubt remembered that the Germans had earlier brought the tsarist, and then Lenin's government to its knees. The Germans, toward the end of World War I, had secured the cession of vast Russian-controlled territories to Germany in the Treaty of Brest-Litovsk. Great Britain and France had not been able to prevent this in 1918; Stalin therefore had no reason to believe that an alliance with them against Hitler would be any more effective than the Dual Entente was against the Kaiser on the Russian Front in World War I. Such skepticism was even more justifiable in view of the fear of and hostility toward the Bolshevik state then rampant among certain influential groups in the Western powers. Many Westerners indeed thought that conflict between Germany and the Soviet Union was the best hope for avoiding their own war with Hitler. The two pariahs might, it was often hoped out loud, knock each other out.

For years before, veiled in the ambiguities of Soviet propaganda, the notion of a European collective security agreement, primarily directed against Hitler, had glimmered in Moscow's carefully controlled media. But in the light of what we now know of Soviet behavior in 1938, and of the signing of the Hitler-Stalin Pact and the German-Soviet Treaty of Friendship in the fall of 1939, the Soviet

Union's many prewar testimonies to the need for collective security against fascism must be seen as little more than emotional preparation for conditions devoutly unwished in Moscow. Although these hints of collective security never slowed the efforts of the Kremlin-directed Communist International (Comintern) to foment domestic strife in other nations, particularly in Europe, the official propaganda line from Moscow was intended to encourage the hope in the democracies that Hitler could be stopped by the prospect of a formidable East-West alliance. However, it now seems evident that if Stalin actually was interested in any kind of collective security with the West, he would have brought his diplomacy to bear on achieving it only after Hitler had forced him to abandon all hope for a German connection. And forcing that abandonment, it is clear, was not Hitler's intention.

Stalin had had an alliance with Czechoslovakia since 1935, one part of the incomplete scheme of collective security against the Germans and their potential allies that was put together primarily by the French and the small states of east central Europe that had gained territory as a result of the Treaty of Versailles and ancillary post–World War I treaties. This alliance pledged the USSR to help the Czechs militarily in the event of a foreign attack, but only after France had fulfilled its own obligation, also dating from 1935, to help. In 1938, Hitler's loud demands, reinforced by wildly articulated threats, for German-populated territory within Czechoslovak borders led to the Sudetenland crisis, which, under terms of the treaties, could have required the direct military involvement of both France and the Soviet Union.

Fearing a general war, France and Great Britain were suddenly driven to great efforts to satisfy (the word "appease" was used later) the German demands for Czech territory that had a German-speaking majority. Neither France nor Great Britain was militarily, or spiritually, prepared for a conflict, whatever the cause. Yet during the many months before the crisis was resolved, and war finally averted, with the agreement at Munich in late September, Stalin did not initiate any close diplomatic or military conversations with his potential Czech and French partners in war, and he consistently responded in most general terms to their requests for helpful information about his plans. To be sure, many citizens and members of the government in Czechoslovakia at the time were, in any case, terrified that if the Red Army ever came west, it would never go home. Keeping the Comintern-rattling Muscovites as far from "Europe" as possible was a fixed principle of diplomacy among most of the governments there.

The Czech president, Edvard Beneš, was worried about the prospect of domestic conflict in the event of war, probably because some Czechoslovak citizens, given a choice, would sooner keep the Reds (including the Moscow-loyal local Communist party) at bay than keep hold of territory with a largely disloyal German majority. In Czechoslovakia at that time, the Czechs were well outnumbered by their potentially disloyal minorities: Germans, Hungarians, Slovaks, and others. President Beneš would also later admit, albeit only privately, that although the Czech generals were ready to fight, as were loudly vocal segments of the population (especially the Communists), the long neglected military forces were unprepared for a major conflict. Of course those who then feared the coming of the Red Army and any empowering of the domestic Communists could not then have known how valid their fears were.[10]

In any event, leaders in Paris, Prague, and London, and military attachés in Moscow, noting the well-known weaknesses of the Red forces, were wholly pessimistic about the prospect of a successful Soviet intervention on the Czechs' behalf. Stalin by 1938 had wasted his armies and their commanders through years of ruthless purges. The purges still continued. Western and German military observers, who were well informed on the catastrophic disruptions and dislocations that had occurred in the Soviet military forces, were inclined to believe that any help Stalin could have given the Czechs would have been very limited—perhaps, as President Beneš, recalling Stalin's limited help to the Spanish Loyalist government, later indicated, only air support and an international brigade. Though Beneš privately considered the Red Army weakness an excuse for not calling on Moscow's aid after Britain and France had made it clear that they were not going to intervene to help the Czechs keep their unruly Germans, it seems very unlikely that Stalin really wanted to help the Czechs at all.[11]

In fact, throughout the Sudeten crisis, in the months before Munich, Stalin never made a real effort, except in words, to encourage the resistance of his potential allies by a show of strength against Hitler's demands, as he could well have done had he been prepared, and prepared to act. In one bizarre episode toward the end of the crisis period, the Soviet Foreign Commissariat threatened the Poles, who were then making their own territorial demands on Czechoslovakia, with diplomatic retaliation.[12] But the Germans were never officially challenged, either over their threats to the Czechs or over their previous annexation of Austria. One wonders why there was such reticence, given the high level of moral dudgeon that Soviet Foreign Minister Maxim Litvinov was displaying before the League of Nations and elsewhere on behalf of the Czechs. Was Stalin truly hanging back because of Soviet military weakness, or was he deliberately not getting involved because he did not want to discourage Hitler from attacking Czechoslovakia, and thereby provoking a German confrontation with the West? Also, was he afraid of frightening the German people away from their faith in the Führer with a threat of Soviet intervention on behalf of the Czechs? Soviet intervention would have brought home to Germany the dreadful prospect of another two-front war and would have revived the traumatic memories of the events of 1914–18. If we trace Stalin's hopes in the Czech crisis of 1938 back from the existing record of his secret Trotskyite programmatic leitmotif of war and revolution that took definite form just a year or so later during the Polish crisis of 1939, we can infer that in 1938, as in 1939, Stalin very much wanted a general war in the West, though without his participation, with the British, French, and Germans bogged down in a reciprocally debilitating conflict over Czechoslovakia. It was just such a war that his quick agreement with Hitler, manufactured in not entirely dissimilar circumstances in the summer of 1939, was clearly designed to encourage.

A European war in 1938, which the Czech crisis then portended, would have given the Soviets, weak as they were, and preoccupied as they were with a formidable Japanese enemy at their Siberian back door, the hegemonic position in east central Europe. Undeniably they held the overwhelming mass of potential force in that area. To the west, the Poles, who in 1938 still appeared a greater military force than they proved to be in 1939, might possibly have remained neutral in a German-instigated war over Czechoslovakia. But no one even then could be certain that the Poles, either alone or in collaboration with their Romanian friends, could long block Soviet expansion westward. Nor was it at all certain that they could, or would, resist any Muscovite march on the small and nearly defenseless Baltic states.

If the Germans had been wholly preoccupied with war in the west, and with the Czechs, in 1938, one can speculate that the Poles, disregarding danger from the Soviets on their east (for they were among those most riskily discounting the Soviet military), might have been unable to withstand the temptation to blackmail Germany with the threat of invasion—and perhaps actually to invade their otherwise preoccupied neighbor. The Poles, too, had expansionist dreams, some directed toward lands to the west, and they had no solid reason to be especially friendly to the Germans, however much that seemed part of their foreign minister's long-term policy. But whether the Poles remained neutral or invaded Germany, thereby bringing about more European chaos and weakening their own eastern border, Stalin could see that war in the west of Europe was certain to enhance Soviet power in the east.

Stalin, then, had everything to gain, as Lenin thought he had in World War I, by encouraging every possible imbroglio between the Germans and the Western Allies, and then sitting back for a time to profit from what developed.[13] Even failing an outright war over Czechoslovakia in 1938, Stalin could still harvest the propaganda rewards of his public support for the small Slavic-run, ostensibly democratic, state. He could build his reputation as a man of peace, an antifascist, ostentatiously giving whatever aid he could manage to the Czechs, separated as he was from them by strips of Polish and Romanian foreign territory, and from German armies by the bulk of Poland, meanwhile sending over to Prague, Paris, and London a steady flow of propaganda encouragement to stand fast against the Nazi tyrant. In effect, the Czech crisis offered him at the very least the prospect of winning the same kind of accolades, opportunities, friends, and rewards he had garnered from his early, well-propagandized, but very carefully limited involvement in the Spanish Republican battle against fascist General Francisco Franco and his Nazi and Italian friends.[14]

Hitler's adventurism had therefore handed Stalin an amazingly favorable, though dangerous, diplomatic situation and the prospect of a general European war. Given Stalin's expansionist aims, he could not fail to try to exploit the situation. He knew that an agreement with Hitler, a détente and some mutually advantageous territorial arrangements, could settle, at least for a time, the looming rivalry between himself and the powerful Germans over control of east central Europe. Moreover, in encouraging the possibility of a German alliance, Stalin might also have wanted to ensure himself a choice of bids in potential future negotiations, with the Germans on the one hand, and the Western Allies on the other, which might force these rival suitors to offer more in return for his cooperation. Yet the mass of evidence suggests that, though he continued his delicate, at first long-distance, flirtation with the West well into the summer of 1939, and even into direct talks over a dowry of expected help and other secret conditions of mutual assistance, he had long since decided that he had a great deal more to gain from an arrangement with Hitler than from an arrangement with the West against Hitler. And a German alliance, an arrangement in which he had, to be sure, always publicly disavowed any interest, is what he at last got in August 1939.[15] It came after months, even years, of frantic signals to Berlin.

These signals out of Moscow suggesting a German-Soviet rapprochement did not pass entirely unnoticed by Western diplomatic observers. Some of them were even read in Washington. One Briton in the Moscow embassy concluded a February 1939 report analyzing the dismissive attitude in Moscow toward solicitous approaches by the Western powers: "Possibly the rats are thinking of leaving the ship and therefore assume, or affect to assume, that it must be sinking."[16] The fact that the "rats" were then still assumed to be aboard the Western ship of collective security testifies to how deftly Stalin had sent many more signals to Berlin right past the Western diplomatic community. It also helps to establish how effectively Stalin's propagandists and diplomats had built up the ambiguous façade for both the Allied capitals and Berlin.

What Stalin ultimately got from the pact with Hitler was a buffer zone of new territory in the West, with something like the reconstitution of the former tsarist borders in east central Europe. That was probably what he had had in mind long before. He accomplished the task in 1939 by splitting with Germany the lands of the states that lay in between. Eventually he could either add to the Soviet Union some of the lands he took as other "republics," or simply add them to existing "republics." Such territorial expansion clearly fitted his traditional concept of Russia's grandeur. He also had asked for Hitler's intercession with his Japanese friends to call off their threat to the Soviet Asian areas, and had further suggested that Japanese expansion be turned away from the Soviet far east to southeast Asia, toward the vulnerable Western colonies and dominions. Such Japanese moves, when they came, created even more international mayhem. The defense of those areas by the West during the war with Japan, once it came, drastically reduced the strength of the Western Alliance in the European war against Germany. Not so oddly, though, 22 months after the war broke out, it became, manifestly to Stalin's surprise, Stalin's war against Germany as well.

Looking at the world through Soviet eyes in 1939, assuming the baggage of experience and experience-conditioned sentiment that was Stalin's, recalling Hitler's earlier shrieks of anti-Bolshevism, watching as he wrecked the European status quo and terrified the Western European democratic peoples (so few they were then) with wild threats of destruction from the air and strong hints of secret weapons of mass effect, we can understand why Stalin wanted that accommodation with Hitler. Such an accommodation would give Stalin the time he needed for rearmament, and it guaranteed a buffer of Soviet-occupied territories and new Red lands to the west to reestablish the forward momentum of the stagnated international revolution. For Hitler, of course, accommodation offered a chance to bring down the whole traditional European house to the west of Soviet borders. Stalin shared the same goal. Somewhere in this mix of expectations, too, there must have existed a certain spiritual bond between the two revolutionary fantasists who wanted to remake the European demographic, social, political, and geographic map. Stalin, at any rate, at least for a time, apparently saw Communists and National Socialists someday coming together, and the Germans more likely than the Western "imperialist" nations to take on "socialism," as Stalin defined it. Farfetched? Stalin, making revolutionary dreams into expectations, seems not to have thought so.[17]

In the suddenly intense diplomatic pace of the spring and summer of 1939, as Hitler moved forward to war against Poland, Western diplomats, become firm, issued to Poland an almost unconditional guarantee of support. The German dictator upped the level of his coqueterie with Stalin's agents and began receiving increasingly less coy responses; then, following the early negotiations through diplomatic intermediaries, Hitler sent his best salesman to Stalin's door with a clear proposal and attractive conditions, which in their generosity no doubt even surprised Stalin himself.

For months, Western Allied emissaries in Moscow had been conducting what amounted to a full-court press for better relations and military conventions. The British and French governments had finally become convinced that only a strong coalition of powers could stop Hitler from running amok all over Europe. Since June, their representatives had been sitting patiently in Kremlin anterooms and slowly working through tedious negotiations with Stalin's agents. Their design, fully exposed in the Western press, was to create an up-to-date version of the Entente of 1914–18 that would unite Britain, France, and the Soviet Union in a solid force of collective security against Nazi Germany. Then, one day in August, while the emissaries were still haggling with Stalin's demanding, undoubtedly stalling, delegates, the German foreign minister, Joachim von Ribbentrop, flew into Moscow secretly, bringing Stalin Hitler's sensational offers.

What the Westerners had not been able to achieve in months of talks Ribbentrop got in one day. The Hitler-Stalin Pact was signed on August 23, the evening of Ribbentrop's arrival. Stalin, having got what he wanted from Hitler, and even more, telephoned his military negotiator to close down the act that had held the long discomfited Westerners in Moscow.[18]

Now, once again, we see why the schedule of Stalin's foreign policy preferences in 1938 can almost certainly be read back from his expectations of what would come of the August pact with Germany. Stalin was convinced that the new world war predicted by Marxist-Leninist doctrine had already begun. Accepting Hitler's offer set the spark to ignite the flame of world revolution.

The first recorded revelation so far available of the great dimension of Stalin's scheme of war and revolution dates from the early summer of 1940, when Foreign Minister Molotov and one of Lavrentii Beria's henchmen in the People's Commissariat for Foreign Affairs (the Narkomindel) excitedly announced the program, once as a major part of a five-hour harangue, for the information of a would-be collaborator from Lithuania. Following Soviet reoccupation in June 1940, of most of the lands that had once belonged to the tsar, Molotov sought to overwhelm this stupified candidate, Vincus Krėvė-Mickievičius, for a place in one of Stalin's new Baltic satrapies with a jubilant forecast of a grand Red Army march west bearing the revolution even farther, and of a great battle to be fought hundreds of miles to the west near the Rhine to ensure its final triumph. It seems obvious that Stalin and Molotov, and probably others in the inner circle of the Kremlin, had been busy inflating these no doubt long held fancies with immediate expectations, for the scheme went very much beyond sitting back to await a breakdown of capitalism in the aftermath of the new European war.[19]

Hints of this scheme had already been put out in discussions with Comintern chiefs in the fall of 1939, and its major aspects were being mooted in more remote Soviet diplomatic circles as early as 1940, and widely leaked. It seems likely, therefore, that it had been much discussed, and—so it appears—triumphantly announced by Molotov for political underpinning and for the psychological relief that conspirators find in sharing secrets with a widening circle of intimates. Indeed, because Molotov was usually no less secretive, and certainly no less conspiratorial, than Stalin, the fact that he incautiously broadcast wild expectations to at least one other party, who eventually relayed it to others, says something about the dimensions of the hubris already abroad in the Kremlin after the Soviet victories to the west, in 1939 and 1940, and the military victory in the Far East over Japan in 1939.[20] Stalin, who was himself sometimes given to odd outbursts, may have been no more tight-lipped. And because the Soviet domestic party information system depended on the word of the leader being passed down through party echelons from top to bottom, it was certain that many were going to know before long what the vozhd' originally had broadcast. It is well known that much drinking went on in Stalin's ambiance, following which words doubtlessly also flowed, but with or without alcohol, agreeing with the vozhd' was most certainly politically correct, as was passing down his genial thoughts; and the chorus of yeas doubtlessly sustained him and others of the inner circle, and some others far beyond, in their revolutionary hopes.[21]

The German-Soviet pact did bring a temporary resolution of Germany's demands for more territory in east central Europe, and it was even more advantageous to the Soviet Union. It also guaranteed Stalin the major force in the east of Europe that he wanted, if, and when, France and England were to confront Germany over its threatened attack on Poland. It also brought him much, beyond these tangible gains, by way of promise to fulfill his grandest imaginings. It is unlikely that Molotov was not blurting out what he truly foresaw in the future when he told what he and Stalin, and perhaps more than a few others outside the inner Kremlin circle, by then had firmly in mind.

He anticipated a long war, and predicted revolution to follow: when war came, the combatants in the West would squander their resources on each other. Following Marxist-Leninist analysis, they would stay with the imperialist conflict until home fronts moved to the verge of collapse. The Soviet Union, meanwhile, would encourage the continuation of the war by helping the Germans just enough to make certain that the conflict was prolonged to the bitter end.

No doubt Stalin and Molotov had in mind the final scenes in this picture of the war to come, tableaux from inside defeated Russia in 1917 and from defeated Germany in 1918, when they signed the pact with Hitler. In such politically disrupted landscapes, so Molotov predicted, Soviet-spread anti-war, anti-imperialist, revolutionary ideology, violently refurbished by the discomforts and discontents of war, would soon flame up in working-class heads all over Europe. The proletarians of the industrialized Western nations would turn against their "imperialist" governments. Soldiers, perhaps even whole armies, would revolt, as many did in 1917 and 1918. The Red Army, finally prepared and armed to the teeth, could be rushed westward into combat in support of the "revolution" in weakened Europe. The Bolshevik sword would be carried even farther, to help local revolutionaries finish off any European powers that still survived. It would tame both these European survivors and any other state (such as the United States—a "swamp," Molotov called it, "whose [prospective] entrance into the war does not worry us in the slightest") that opposed Red Army control of the European land mass. The West, unified under the Communist International, would be red: "The Soviet system," Molotov said, ". . . shall reign everywhere, throughout all Europe."[22]

That was the plot, a fantasy of war, with military slaughter on the Rhine, Marxist-Leninist law, and World War I precedents combined, that lay behind the Kremlin's breathtaking vision of the future. It was, indeed, so exciting and exhilarating a vision that the obvious risks of the undertaking could easily be brushed aside. In any case, after the years of purges, there was probably no one left to point out the risks.

Stalin's international servants in the Comintern were also swept up in his risky adventurism and the tactical requirements involved. It was their task, as true believers (among them perhaps a few cowed into silent submission by years of Muscovite purges), to develop a political line to explain and support Stalin's turn into Hitler's camp. They quickly took up their difficult task under Stalin's and Molotov's direction in the late summer of 1939. They had to work out a political and propaganda format that could give the Communist parties abroad a plausible explanation of the sudden diplomatic accord between Hitler and Stalin and of its wide-ranging consequences. Some of the record of their internal discussions, now at last available, provides more than conclusive support of the truth in those historically heretofore much neglected reports of Molotov's unusually candid outburst of prognostication. The record tells how zealously Comintern agents, in the hothouse atmosphere of Muscovite exile, set about following Kremlin direction, though that meant twisting their minds to invent formulations absurdly at odds with former commitments of partisan faith, and formerly accepted facts.

The tactical line the Comintern operatives developed during the period of the Hitler-Stalin Pact, from 1939 to 1941, went as follows: Germany, once the *Hauptkriegsbrandstifter*, larded in past years with all the opprobrium tricked out in the languages of low buffoonery that necessarily agile Soviet propagandists could devise, was now to be treated with understanding as the Soviet Union's friend and defender. The British and French, by contrast, were now to be identified as even more dangerous, the greatest enemy devils in the Marxist-Leninist netherworld. They had succeeded, according to the new line, to the roles of "inflamers of war," and main "imperialist" aggressors of World War II. Working out these new ideological precepts in detail, the Comintern *apparatchiki*, always following Stalin, declared that the capitalist masters of France and England had a secret goal beyond the war with Germany they had declared over its invasion of Poland. Their ultimate war goal was not to limit German expansion but to destroy the Soviet Union. Before embarking on this formidable task, they first had to destroy German power, now the USSR's forward bulwark against "imperialism." Hitler, the Comintern thinkers concluded, had seen through the corrupt Western purposes. By signing up with Stalin, he had shown that he would not be used by the "imperialists" in the way that the Poles, who had leagued with Britain and France, had been used. Following this line, then, loyal party members and sympathizers the world over were obliged to give their support to Hitler's Germany, which was defending the USSR, and to undermine the Western Allies wherever possible. The Pact had relieved Germany of the necessity to fight on more than one front and had defeated the British blockade in advance, so that Germany could more than effectively serve as the Soviet bulwark against the London and Paris imperialists.

All this was the party line for the comrades and others who would take it in, some gullibly, some, most certainly, with misgivings. Behind the party line lay the purpose of the propaganda. Molotov had expressed it cynically: "Today we support Germany, but just enough to keep her from being smothered before the miserable and starving masses of the warring nations . . . rise against Hitler." Thus Stalin's foreign policy of genius, his "policy of peace" praised to the skies by some Comintern insiders.[23]

To Stalin, following Lenin, the long war to come meant also that European-dominated colonies all over the world would seize the occasion of their masters' wartime weakness to revolt—as many colonies had long threatened to do, and as Soviet Russian ideology encouraged them to attempt. Encouraging Japanese adventurism in colonial Asia had to have been part and parcel of the plan to create the conditions for revolutionary discontent there. What the Bolsheviks could not begin by way of world revolution in the weakened state of Soviet power in the immediate post–World War I years, Stalin would help them to attain. The pact with Hitler was the first step in carrying out Lenin's testament in Europe in the new "imperialist" war; the Third World War, to follow, would spread the Communist system around the world.[24]

The Hitler-Stalin Nonaggression Pact of the summer of 1939 came, when written, to have a secret attachment establishing "spheres of influence." Discussion of this euphemistically titled section of the document was initiated by Stalin. In effect, it set by mutual agreement rather than by conflict new geographical limits for the hegemony of each power. It offered Stalin the immediate opportunity he needed to protect his rickety empire, while at one and the same time it won back most of the former tsarist territories that the young Bolshevik state had had to forfeit after World War I. Beyond that, Stalin encouraged the coming of war to the west by implying his indifference to German territorial demands on Poland, whose borders Britain and France had guaranteed. Secretly, Hitler and Stalin agreed first to divide Poland between them by means of war, not one against the other, but both against Poland. Having prospectively made off with most of the territorial swag in the negotiations with the Germans, as he would later in fact—in the short run, even taking prizes at the ultimate expense of Hitler—Stalin, at the signing of the Pact, grinned like the cat who swallowed the canary. Fortunately a German photographer was on hand to record the historic moment. Stalin had won both time and territory, and had helped to start the war he wanted.[25]

In the West, on the highest levels at least, there had been little belief that any pact between Hitler and Stalin was a real possibility. In Warsaw, in Whitehall, and at the Quai d'Orsay, the signing brought consternation and confusion. Stalin may already have received secret information from some of his highly placed agents in Western capitals about the nature of the Western guarantees to Poland, and he perhaps knew that the Western Allies had only thought to guarantee Polish independence against the Germans. It was likely that the Western powers, obsessed with the old German menace and remote from and unsure about the Soviet Union, and wholly confused about Stalin's aims, would shy away from making another declaration of war on behalf of their Polish ally when the Soviets intervened in the war against the Poles. It was therefore essential for Stalin to obscure as best he could the circumstances of the Soviet attack, as the quick success of the German blitzkrieg against Poland soon made it easy to do. The Poles themselves were at first baffled by the sudden arrival of the Soviet armies on their territory on September 17, 1939.[26]

The Hitler-Stalin Pact (or Molotov-Ribbentrop Pact, as it is just as often called) cleared the way for the Germans to deal with the Poles, as they were determined to do, without interference from the Soviets. It ended the hopes of the British and French that Hitler could ultimately be forced to compromise his megalomaniacal demands. Up until August 23, Western diplomats had clung to the one imponderable, the unknown response of the Soviet Union in the event of a German invasion of Poland; this imponderable would have existed even in the absence of any agreement between Stalin and the West. The possibility of a two-front war, as it might ultimately have become even without a formal Anglo-French-Soviet alliance, would have revived for the Germans the specter of their traumatic disaster of 1914–18, a possibility that even Hitler feared, telling in his obsessive monologues his dread of replaying the German defeats of World War I. Stalin, ignoring in his zeal prospects of any other outcome to Hitler's war than the latter's holding the *Wehrmacht* along the agreed line in Poland and a slaughter to exhaustion along the Rhine, was clearly delighted to relieve Hitler and the Germans of their historical fears, and to help tip the scales toward a German war with the West.[27] The Hitler-Stalin Pact also contained secret provisions for an exchange of matériel and supplies. The Germans could therefore embark on a war knowing that in the likely event of a British naval blockade (again recalling World War I), they would still be amply provisioned by the Soviets in both food and oil. In return, the Germans were to assist the Soviets with armaments and technology.

Molotov and Ribbentrop drew a firm line of demarcation for their respective conquests far to the west of the middle of prewar Poland. That line would then no doubt represent the future border between the two aggressor states. The line passed down the Vistula River through the center of Warsaw. The capital itself was to be divided between the two dictators.[28] In addition to taking the western part of Poland, the Germans implicitly got a free hand to deal with Lithuania, assigned to their sphere of influence in the secret agreement. The Soviets were given a free hand in the other Baltic states, Latvia and Estonia, in Finland, and, more ambiguously, in Romania, part of which, like the three small independent Baltic states and Finland, had once belonged to the tsarist empire.[29]

Since the Soviets had not been systematically preparing for war at quite the pace of the Axis powers and were still poorly staffed, armed, and equipped and plagued with serious problems of internal transport, they could not coordinate their attack with Hitler's even had they wanted to do so. Hitler had chosen September 1 for the beginning of his undeclared war.[30] Therefore the Poles were already reeling under the German onslaught and the Nazi armies were deep inside the country when the Soviet armies crossed the eastern Polish border on September 17. In some cases the Soviets, whose propaganda broadcasts from the outset of Hitler's war had justified the German attack, suddenly announced their arrival by radio, loudspeaker, and leaflet as friends coming to help save the Poles from the Germans. In some cases they proclaimed themselves revolutionaries, the liberators of the minority nationalities in Poland, and of peasants and workers in general, from the Polish lords, factory owners, and landlords. Some of the few Polish organized troops still on the eastern border, or military units yet intact falling back eastward from the battle with the Germans, fought against them. But there was little in the way of central command left to organize a new defense front in Poland, whose government took note of the hopelessness of the situation and of its own vulnerability in retreat not very many miles from the entering Soviet armies, and went over the border into neighboring, neutral Romania.[31]

The Soviets had carefully considered the nature of their surprise attack, which came when the Western Allies, France and Britain, were already ruing their connection with the doomed Poles. The ill-prepared Westerners had done little to help the Poles, and the swift effectiveness of the German air and ground blitzkrieg in any case made any opposition futile. The Germans and Soviets were in control of the mass of Poland so quickly that even an Anglo-French assault on the German "West Wall"—which the Western Allies were quite unprepared to mount—could not have saved the Poles. But such an assault certainly would have conjured a lively, and irrepressible, historical memory among the frightened Germans once the Red Army began to move westward.

The Soviets had carefully planned their propaganda description of their attack on Poland. (Stalin checked the notes himself, and made sure they took the exact line he wished expressed.) It was really no more or less than what President Franklin D. Roosevelt later condemned elsewhere, saying, less than a year later, in 1940, when the Italians attacked France from the rear, "The hand that held the dagger has plunged it into the back of its neighbor." But Roosevelt, more considerate of the Soviets in 1939 at the time of their attack on Poland than of Mussolini later, forswore public condemnation of Stalin.[32]

Perhaps Roosevelt actually believed the Soviets when they publicly portrayed their attack on Poland as a rescue mission—a coming to the aid of the White Russians and Ukrainians in Poland, whose brethren in the Soviet republics were called upon to save them in the "collapse" of the Polish republic.[33] But Mussolini's excuse for the attack on France in 1940 to seize some partly Italian populated areas was hardly different, and the far different response Roosevelt made to Soviet excuses in 1939 seems in retrospect to have been an early sign of his diplomatic unwillingness later on to confront Stalin's wartime misbehavior.

Though Hitler and Ribbentrop had only lame excuses for their destruction of independent Poland, they allowed the Soviets to justify their attack on Poland as implicitly defensive against the Germans. Stalin was meanwhile secretly recommending to Hitler that no rump Polish state be established in the aftermath of the war. (Mussolini was privately recommending just the opposite, hoping to encourage Britain and France to make the quick peace with Germany that Hitler himself evidently expected.) Stalin, quite obviously, wanted to keep Germany in the war and Europe in turmoil while he picked up the additional territories he had been promised, and the longer the war, the firmer his hopes that the conflict he foresaw would permit him to realize his plans for all Europe. His words to the West, put out through *Pravda* and some naively cooperative Western news agencies, were that England and France had caused the war and had rebuffed both Germany's efforts to stop it and the USSR's efforts to end it quickly.[34]

Stalin was lucky to be so remote from Roosevelt and the Western leaders. Many of them were, like him, in any case viewing matters from the perspective of their experience in World War I.[35] And Roosevelt, in spite of all the abundant bad news about the terror from the Soviet Union, long persisted in his strange willingness to view the Soviet Union in a far more favorable light than he wanted to cast on Hitler's Germany. Germany, of course, was a European state where he had once been and therefore knew more or less, and against which he had once organized military forces. Like Churchill, who had noted that he saw World War II as a continuation of World War I, Roosevelt may have been looking at the events of 1939 from a 1914 point of view. It should be said also that, as of 1939, no one in the West really knew the scope and ruthlessness of Stalin's purges and ethnic "cleansings." Though the mass of Hitler's crimes against the peoples of Europe were, ultimately, quite as horrible and much sooner visible, they had not yet been executed.[36]

Hitler had originally feigned in attacking the Versailles treaty to want back only the territories that had German populations or had been taken from Germany in the aftermath of World War I—because they were German, he said, playing upon the widespread guilty reconsideration of the Versailles settlement. When he got Austria and the Sudetenland without war, these victories only increased his confidence that the "decadent Westerners" would never fight. Stalin must have understood Hitler's clever evocation of righteous indignation in dealing with the democracies, in particular with the Anglo-Saxons, for whom the word "fair" not only existed but also seemed to make diplomatic sense. In the secret agreement on the territorial division of east central Europe, Ribbentrop and Molotov had agreed to divide Poland along a line running right through its capital, Warsaw—a move that certainly would have heavily underscored the Soviet Nazi cooperative land grab for what it was. The prospective division of families, the easier highlighting of the Polish disaster via the bifurcation of the entire urban social and economic infrastructure of its capital—all would have come to light much more easily across a more permeable border. Likewise, Stalin's excuse for the Soviet September offensive against the hapless Poles, that is, the need to rescue the White Russians and Ukrainians from the Germans, would have been seen to be quite fraudulent if the Soviets had simply annexed the large bulk of the Polish population, the central Polish homeland, and the eastern half of Poland's capital. Finally, and Stalin and Molotov certainly must have been aware of this, the dubious border known as the Curzon Line, which had been invented by some of the state-making Western allies in the aftermath of World War I as a possible eastern border for the reborn state of Poland, could be approximated for its propaganda value in a new partition. This could only be done, however, if the Soviets were to abandon Poland west of it to the Germans.[37] Thus Stalin, with his mind on the future, could say to the West, in the perhaps likely event that it defeated Hitler, and then chose to challenge the Soviets on their ill-gotten gains, that he was only taking back what some in the West, with their weak knowledge of east central European history and geography, had already conceded as rightfully Russian—as if Russians were somehow delegated by Heaven to superintend the earthly destinies of White Russians and Ukrainians.[38]

Because the Baltic states and Finland and part of the territory of Romania that Stalin ultimately took had historically been under tsarist control, they qualified to some sympathetic observers as legitimate prizes under a strange notion of justified territorial expansion. But who in the West, in any event, knew where Ukrainia and White Russia began, and "Great" (or was it "Red"?) Russia or Poland stopped, even if "ethnic" lines could possibly be drawn on a map? Winston Churchill was just one of the major players who never seemed to be able to figure out that remote geography and demography.

Beyond all these intricacies lay the very serious failure of the Western press to try and find out the truth about Stalin's Russia. If Prague and Warsaw were "faraway places" in the eyes of prominent

Westerners, Moscow was remote indeed. The Western press neither regularly nor responsibly sent in to Moscow reporters capable of getting at the truth, nor did they send in reporters who, failing to get near the truth by being systematically denied all access to the reportorial field, would be ready to proclaim that the worst had to be believed and reported in the light of that very denial of access. In the long run, the Western press was frequently an all too willing helper to the Soviet leaders in their need for propagandistic obfuscation. So it had been in the past, even before the war, so it would be again during the war when reportorial clarity and truth were vital.[39]

On the other hand, Hitler and his foreign minister, Ribbentrop, were so mightily pleased with their wild pact with Stalin that they lost sight of details, some of them major.[40] By permitting the Soviets to negotiate a description of their intervention in Poland as being a defense of fellow Slavs, Hitler and Ribbentrop helped focus all the West's righteous-minded obloquy heaped on aggressors on the geographically nearer Germans, to their enormous propaganda disadvantage. What would France and Britain (and the United States, for that matter) have been able to negotiate, by way of working their populations up into the now necessary overheated, warlike states of mind, if it appeared that the world's loci of evil—then Germany, Italy, and Japan—had to be further extended to include the Soviet Union? There would have been little reason to continue a war against Hitler in the middle of Europe if his power after defeat were certain to be replaced by that of Stalin's Russia.[41] If Hitler hoped the quick success of his blitzkrieg against Poland would bring the British and French to abandon the war on behalf of an ally that had vanished, he certainly misplayed his hand when he connived with the Russians to justify their actions there.

Thus when Stalin, on Ribbentrop's second visit to Moscow in late September 1939, proposed a renegotiation of the demarcation line that had been arrived at in earlier talks, he must have had their first rash diplomatic blunder in mind. Apparently with little trouble, and certainly with little or no forethought from either Ribbentrop or the Führer, he readily got the Germans to treble their mistakes.[42] Stalin's proposal, quickly accepted by Ribbentrop after Hitler's thoughtless telephoned OK, was that the Germans trade Lithuania, which had originally been assigned to them under the secret land deal, for that part of central Poland between the Bug and Vistula rivers. This included the eastern part of Warsaw that had been assigned to the Soviets. Hitler reserved for himself only a small part of Lithuania that bordered on German East Prussia.

It is hard to say which country, Poland or Lithuania, was the unluckier in the secret swap. Stalin had won for himself a free hand in all the Baltic states, while Hitler was saddled with the majority of the unruly Poles, though with only half the former Polish territory. Moreover, Stalin could save himself from having to decide what to do with the Poles in the territory he was swapping, Poles who had always been troublesome subjects of the tsars. He would, as we shall see, set out to destroy as a national group the significant number of Poles whom he did collect, but he would have had to work that destruction on several million more, including most of those in the Polish heartland (a project Hitler himself was eager to complete), had Hitler not thoughtlessly consented to his proposal. Certainly he would have had a difficult time covering up the deliberate depopulation of part of Warsaw and central Poland—much more difficult than covering up the mass deportation of Poles from his new eastern Polish territories.

Lithuania is, and was, a geographic wedge pointed at the main centers of Russia, Leningrad and Moscow; its eastern border is approximately one hundred miles closer to them than the border in Poland ultimately agreed upon by Stalin and the Germans. Since Hitler even in the fall of 1939 had to have had in the back of his mind an eventual showdown with Bolshevik Russia, the trade of Lithuania to Stalin testifies not only to his insouciance but also to his lack of concern for his beloved German people, whose sons would some day have to take those miles one by one. In this exchange, Stalin clearly showed the extent of his caution and guile, and the firmness of his ideologized will to round out the traditional tsarist borders and fulfill Lenin's plans for Europe and beyond. But it was his good fortune that the Germans were such blunderers.[43]

Among the Western Allies at the end of September 1939, speculation abounded, but there was no real knowledge of either of the two secret territorial divisions. Apparently no one noticed later on that the two published maps (on the front page of *Pravda*) did not correspond to the actual division. Stalin's march into Poland, originally denied even as a possibility by British Foreign Secretary Halifax, was soon considered thoughtfully defensive, even beneficial to the West. The Western Allies could still focus their hostility and fear on the much nearer Germans. Certainly Stalin had booked marvelous diplomatic and military victories at little cost so far except to those who would have to suffer his regime. His next moves in the Baltic states and his consolidation of power in Poland were to be effected with equal skill.

2

STALIN FIGHTS THE WAR —
OF DEFENSE

WE HAVE to assume that at least two possible courses of action arose in Stalin's mind when he learned of the British and French declarations of war on Germany following its invasion of Poland on September 1, 1939. It seems likely that he was somewhat surprised that the Western powers would follow through on their pledges to Poland (though, as we know, they did so unenthusiastically). We must also assume that, in spite of all the Soviet agents in the highest positions in Britain and France, Stalin may not have known that the two Western nations were poorly prepared and quite unwilling to come to the aid of the Poles, except with token force. This fact the British and French would only establish over the next two weeks of the German attack eastward, while Stalin was continuing feverish preparations for his own approaching invasion of Poland.[1] Stalin certainly would have been alert to the possibility that the Germans might decide to expand farther eastward if the opportunity presented itself (which it readily did), and, that being so, he would have been working full speed to create both offensive and defensive battle forces, the former to attack the Poles, the latter to deal with the Wehrmacht if that became necessary. Stalin's position then was one of extreme danger, because he had to count on Hitler's not moving farther east, beyond the agreed demarcation line, if only because he had a war he had not quite expected going on to the west.

Moreover, Stalin was much taken up with drafting the ideological rationale for his sudden volte-face after implying for years that he was attached to the West. All that urgent discussion in the Kremlin and Comintern with respect to keeping the ideological ranks solid in the face of the ensuing shock to both leaders and rank and file, especially in Communist parties abroad, took up much valuable time. Meanwhile, military developments forced quick decisions.

Stalin, in the absence of clear evidence of Western intent toward the war in Poland, would have to organize his own moves to deal with the possible responses of the Western powers. The arrangements he had worked out with Hitler for keeping the Soviet attack secret, and the elaborate efforts he made in collaboration with Hitler to describe the Soviet invasion as defensive of Soviet "brotherly" peoples, are evidences of how concerned he was to play for favorable opinion outside the Soviet Union. Depending on outside responses, he wanted to be able to decide whether to advance or withdraw, and to maintain control of possible developments. By mid-September, after the last-minute negotiations with Hitler, Stalin must have known that the whole idea of Western military aid to the Poles was hardly more than a façade. He may well have received information from his agents in the Western governments about their secret agreements with the Poles and the limitations of help they were prepared to give. For propaganda purposes, however, he still had to make the coming Soviet assault on the Polish rear sound like an anti-German move.

To make this propaganda convincing, Stalin needed, and got, Hitler's help. We have already seen how the Soviets cleverly undertook to help the Germans put themselves totally in the wrong, and then subsequently renegotiated new borders they could rationalize for those who wanted, or needed, to believe in them. Molotov's and Stalin's initial mistake, setting the Lithuanian salient to point at the heart of the Soviet Union, was then, luckily for them, undone. But they had not shied away from its creation, so overpowering was their need, so strong their desire to join Hitler in the destruction of Europe's prewar order. Their original, flagrant aggression, taking well over half of Poland and a major part of its capital, was covered up. The real nature of the Soviet war against Poland was cleverly concealed in these renegotiations. The move of the border from the central Polish Vistula River eastward to the Bug simply appeared to put the British-concocted Curzon line in place, oddly flattering British foresight and expertise.

With the Western Allies now engaged in a semblance of war with Germany in the west of Europe, Stalin had to move quickly to take the fullest profit from his secret agreements with Hitler. He had to get his disorganized country into the war while the West was still bedazzled by the terrifying success of the Nazi blitzkrieg against Poland.[2]

At first, he was fully occupied, and in some considerable amount of fright, over the Polish situation and just what Germany's intentions really were.[3] His mistrust of the Germans to hold to their agreement on the division of Poland seemed for a time quite justified, for the German armies moved against the Polish army with breakneck speed well beyond the original Nazi-Soviet demarcation line of the Vistula into what was originally planned as the Soviet area of conquest. Yet Hitler in this case held true to his word. Once the Soviets had made their way across the eastern part of prostrate Poland to meet their German allies, German and Soviet field commanders and diplomatic representatives in Moscow carefully extricated the Germans from the Soviet-assigned areas.[4]

The new line of demarcation was finally settled with Ribbentrop and Hitler on September 28. The Germans then slowly withdrew to the west, parting after jubilant celebration with their co-victors, the Soviet commanders, and a grand parade of the two conquering armies at Brest (Brešć), in the center of Poland. The German troops in the east marched westward through newly erected victory arches courteously embellished by the Soviets with both swastikas and red stars. Poland's brief two decades of independence were over.

Stalin had already undertaken to force the two small Baltic states to the north, Estonia and Latvia, to accept Soviet bases—meaning, that is, to allow the stationing of Soviet troops on their territories. The move also of course meant that they would henceforth be hostage to the Soviets. Here again, Stalin, with his usual caution and guile, made it appear that he was only securing defensive stations against the Germans in the Baltic countries, implying that the two tiny states that had lost their former protectors, the British and the French (and, as well, the Germans), needed Soviet protection. Hitler had sufficient naval and air forces to control the only access the two Western powers had had to the Baltic Sea. But Hitler had for the time being abandoned the Baltic states and Finland to the Soviets. Since Sweden along with all the other Scandinavian and Baltic countries (including the Baltic states already, in effect, invaded by the Soviets) had earlier declared its neutrality, the smaller Baltic peoples were in a helpless position.[5]

Britain and France, where panicky public opinion could influence policy, feared the worst for their own countries as they learned, through the German propaganda machine, of the terrors of the blitz. Nazi Propaganda Minister Goebbels filmed, photographed, and broadcast all the German destructive success in Poland with a view to driving the civilian populations of Germany's remaining enemies to demand peace lest the same fate soon befall them.[6] Unlike Stalin, the Nazis deliberately trumpeted their brutalities, and by documenting the terrible destruction and suffering in Warsaw, they showed the European West how successful their program of total and ruthless war had been, and how great a threat it was. Even the work of Western photographers and cinematographers made effective Nazi propaganda.[7]

Within a few days after being turned over to Stalin, the Lithuanians suffered the same kind of treatment the Estonians and Latvians had suffered earlier. Their foreign affairs minister was summoned by Molotov to Moscow, where he was browbeaten and threatened until he had, on October 10, signed a treaty establishing his country as a "defensive" outpost of the Soviet Union.[8] Hitler remained passive in the face of this extension of Soviet armed power to the German border, obviously again carrying out his part of the secret bargain to the letter. Stalin had reason to be thankful to him for allowing him to expand Soviet power where tsarist power had once reached, and, at the same time, to establish a useful western glacis for his enormous state. With large Soviet garrisons on their territories, it was clear that the small countries would necessarily be beholden to Moscow and must therefore be careful not to offend their unwelcome protector.

What, then, were Stalin's additional plans for dealing with his new conquests and sphere of influence? For the nonce, the other European powers were distracted from his actions there by what soon became popularly known, because of the notable inaction of both sides, as the "phony" war, or *Sitzkrieg*. First of all, at the end of November, Stalin grasped the opportunity and organized the Soviet invasion of Finland. This country, another of the former tsarist Russian border territories on the Baltic, was the fifth independent European nation to be set upon by Stalin since his August 1939 agreement with Hitler. In the secret protocols of the Hitler-Stalin Pact, Finland enjoyed exactly the same status in the Soviet sphere of influence as the three smaller Baltic countries on Russia's border.[9] Like the invasion of Poland, the opportunity for this adventure developed suddenly. Stalin was not well prepared,[10] but he had to act hastily, as he had done against the Poles, for he was determined to secure his goals before the West reconsidered its position in the light of the rapid defeat of Poland. The British and French might possibly free themselves temporarily of their German problem by accepting the peace that Hitler seemed to be offering them following his new successes.[11] Such a peace would permit Hitler to turn his interest east.

The perceptive reader of *Pravda* in the fall of 1939 would have noticed a sudden change in emphasis. After the invasion of Poland, not one word of whose "liberation" had been breathed in the Soviet peoples' republics before it was under way, *Pravda* began noting the glories of the Soviet armed forces in almost daily front-page picture and press reports. This seemed not to be merely the propagandistic creation of a proper sort of local defense-mindedness suitable to the situation brought about by the declared war in the West; certainly it was an innovation, quite different from *Pravda*'s editorial policy the previous spring and summer, when Dr. Goebbels's thundering propaganda salvos anticipated the German attack eastward on Poland, in the very direction of the Soviet Union. Rather, it seemed clear that the Russians and other Soviet peoples were being worked up by means of the most simplistic, nationalistically pitched propaganda to patriotic fervor for a possible war with Finland.

By the middle of November 1939, a perceptive Soviet reader would have realized that relations with the Finns were degenerating. The Soviet government began to make demands on the Finnish government for concessions of garrison rights such as had been granted by the three smaller Baltic states, and this time the Soviets even demanded territorial changes in its favor. A great deal of this propaganda against the Finns seemed to be a Russian echo of the German public campaign of charges and limited demands directed against the Poles just a few months earlier. And like those charges and demands, the Soviet charges and demands were a smokescreen for far more ambitious plans. Molotov was later to say privately that Finland, too, would have to join the Soviet Union; it would be another advance toward the time when "the Soviet system . . . shall reign everywhere."[12] In other words, the real reason for the Finnish war, and the fundamental motive for all Stalin's moves westward was not simply to expand the Soviet state to former tsarist borders but to expand the Soviet system.

Before the annexation of eastern Poland, there were approximately 160 million Soviet citizens living in more than eight million square miles of territory, a state two and a half times larger in physical size than the next largest state on the globe. It possessed unimaginable physical resources, both developed and undeveloped. There were fewer than four million Finns. Finland was one of the Baltic states that, like Sweden and the other Scandinavian countries, had long before solemnly declared its neutrality in any war to come.[13] Since 1932, it had had a nonaggression treaty with the Soviet Union.

Quick to learn from the German example, the Soviets initiated an undeclared war against Finland with a faked border incident that repeated the form of the German provocations before the attack on Poland. Sudden terror bombing attacks against major Finnish cities, just as the Germans had made against Poland, followed. None of these attacks was reported in *Pravda*, or elsewhere, to the ever "peace-loving" Soviet peoples. With as much surprise as was possible, given the long period of threats, the Red Army began to advance against Finland along the long border. The end of November 1939 was hardly a favorable time in that northerly climate for the kind of undertaking Stalin was mounting, and the fact that he went ahead further suggests his feeling of urgency.[14] The Soviets added one new element to their scheme—one not used by the arrogant Hitlerites. This was the setting up of a group of Bolshevik Finns and their supporters as a People's Democratic Government of Finland in the first border town captured. Stalin intended this government to take over in Helsinki as soon as it was conquered, and meanwhile it was to gain support from the leftist elements inside the country.

Stalin quickly turned on the Soviet-style rhetoric, part of his "culture of enemy-invention," which in postwar years to follow became unwelcomely familiar to Westerners. The Comintern and propaganda minions had been busy since Ribbentrop's first visit to Moscow churning out new lists of enemies and revising old ones, creating new titles for them and former and future friends to suit the altered post–Nazi Pact situation. The Poles were now fascists, the

British and French were now imperialists and warmongers, the Finnish government in Helsinki was a group of marionettes. *Pravda* and the other Soviet organs screamed shrill and self-righteous invective at the Finns as they earlier had against the Poles: "Our people hates" the Finnish government; "Shame to the ['White'-Finnish] provocateurs"; "militarists"; perpetrators of an "imperialist policy"; "Drive these hangmen as far away from Finland as possible! Overthrow the entire bankrupt gang!"; Soviet patriots must strike "an annihilating blow at the Finnish incendiaries"; "Wipe the Finnish adventurers off the face of the earth!"; "The Soviet people repudiate with loathing [the] filthy insults of the international political sharpers. We know that our government's sole motive is . . . to underwrite the life and peaceful work of the states which are neighbors of the Soviet people." The focus of the propaganda bombast was the millions of Soviet citizens. *Pravda* showed photographs of citizens at mandatory political meetings all over the nation, standing in nearly rapt attention before factories and offices and gaping with manifest concern at speakers and even at loudspeakers as evident protocol demanded, listening to sections read aloud from the daily propaganda barrage of the Soviet press. All this emphasized that the goal of the Red Army was to "liberate" the Finns, the "pigs, reptiles, bandits, and warmongers," who would then be corralled and led in the proper direction by the new Soviet-backed "people's government."[15]

The Finnish campaign proved to be a disaster for the Red Army. The Finns stubbornly resisted liberation from the "marionettes," much, it appears, to Stalin's surprise. They were as well prepared militarily as they could be in the circumstances, in spite of the fact that the Reds were aided by German refusal to transship supplies to Finland from some of its friends, notably Hungary and Italy. The Red Army suffered incredible battlefield failures and losses against the tiny Finnish army and soon became an international laughingstock. It was again recalled that Stalin had recently purged (in fact the purges continued) the command of the army along with the rest of the Soviet leadership and population. Much of the Soviet failure was attributed to this disaster. (No one, except the Germans, knew that Stalin's purges of his own high command had been encouraged by false German information, carefully planted in Prague to be conveyed to Moscow, that the highest commander of the Red Army, Marshal Tukhachevskii, was a German agent.)[16] Ironically, the Soviets themselves made the dimensions of the failure even worse by their heavy emphasis on the army's military readiness, so that the usual willingness of influential Westerners to believe the Russians even on this subject spread the picture of total disaster. Western cinemas showed newsreel pictures of dead Soviet troops, frozen stiff, and masses of abandoned equipment; photos of the same came out in popular pictorial journals. Few Westerners had seen similar scenes of German dead (and there were many) from the fronts in Poland, partly because of the quick collapse there and the quick dispersal of the small Polish camera units, and partly also because of the failure of Western cameramen and news reporters to get close to the fronts.[17]

The widely broadcast, now publicly visible, debacle of the Red Army was mainly the result of poor military preparation and organization, and also of the general chaos that existed in the centrally dominated Soviet state. Stalin was not a military expert, and the decision to make a winter assault in order to take the prize while the taking appeared good was, given the level of Soviet preparations, extremely bad. Still, the Soviet disaster had the effect of encouraging Western populations to fight back: dictators could be bested. From what Westerners knew from the press and newsreel, four or so million Finns were effectively holding off countless millions of Russian bullies.[18] It was a story for the popular mind to encourage the bulldog breed in Britain as well as the French. Both nations helped to ostracize the Soviets by putting them, publicly shamed, out of the League of Nations. In the United States, where the people also liked a morality play, all gave sympathy (but little else) to the underdog. And all the Western publics wishfully thought out a suitable happy ending.[19]

Public opinion even helped carry British and French strategic thinkers, who still were dead set against a wholesale assault on the Germans along the much propagandized, supposedly impregnable, Siegfried Line, to think of a northern peripheral strategy to deal with the Germans. They even thought of bloodying the Russians they saw assaulting the West via the Finns. Some wanted to take a leaf from the dictator's book, to exploit the territories of the still neutral Scandinavian states, Norway and Sweden, for these goals.

Hence, in the earliest days of the Red Army failure in Finland, thoughts were born in both London and Paris (even the reputedly Soviet-friendly British ambassador in Moscow had decided by December 1939 that the Soviet Union was "in undeclared war against us"), and significant planning was done also, for attacks on the source and shipping lanes of Scandinavian iron ore and other important matériel being delivered to Nazi Germany. Most of it came from Sweden. Much was being transported safely to the Reich through neutral Norwegian coastal waters.

The planning went even further, encompassing direct British-French aid to the Finns via Sweden. A successful Western Allied effort to seize the Swedish mines, which would require an invasion via northern Norway, would also provide a direct route to supply the Finns from the north. And the Western Allies were thinking of, and reconnoitering for, possible air strikes against Soviet oil production areas on the Black Sea, which were the source of much of the oil supplied to the German armed forces. These forays would require the involvement of Turkey, Iraq, or Iran, all still technically neutral.[20]

Undoubtedly the Allies, who had immobilized themselves in confronting the Germans on the Western front, were simply trying to discover ways to get at them without a replay of something like the disastrous Somme offensive of 1916. Sufficiently oiled and provisioned by the Soviets and others, the Germans could almost ignore the British sea blockade, itself conceived in the spirit of World War I. Yet the Western powers, reflecting desperation in these plans, were ignoring the potential consequences of such aggressive actions in the realm of public opinion, for public opinion, as in the United States, which generally supported peace and neutrality, would surely have turned against the British and French after such attacks.[21] Public opinion had already been effectively directed against Nazi aggression in Poland and Soviet aggression in Finland. Now key Western Allied leaders rashly thought they might ignore the consequences of its possible redirection against themselves.

The word that the Finns could not hold out long against the Red Army soon muted serious government discussion in the West about intervention to help the government in Helsinki, but the threat of Western intervention, and the news of the proposed attacks on Soviet territory (word of which had been conveyed to the Soviet ambassador in London, Ivan Maiskii, and probably also by other British and French agents to their Kremlin boss) did bring Stalin to reflect on his prospects in the Finnish campaign. Rather than provoke an Allied attack that could lead to war with the West, he would call off the misbegotten Finnish "liberation." Even if the Red Army could break through on the Karelian front and capture the main southern Finnish cities, the Finns might fight a guerrilla campaign that could last for months and would certainly engage additional Western sympathies. Quite clearly, too, Stalin had no good reason to be confident in his army after its miserable performance in Finland. If he withdrew, he could use the time to rearm and reorganize to meet the wartime challenge sure to come in the west. In any event, he had to be ready to seize the opportunities for an advance in whatever direction the shifting, unpredictable fronts of the war he had done so much to bring about might offer.[22]

And, indeed, within a short time, the Red Army was much better equipped, to judge from a comparison of the weapons shown in films of the 1940 and 1941 May Day parades. Moreover, much of the equipment destroyed or captured by the Germans in 1941, in the first days of the invasion of the USSR, was subsequently to be replaced by the Soviets with far better equipment—new MiGs, Iaks, and Iliushins substituted for the old I-16; the T-34 for the BT-5 and T-26 tank. [23] One Soviet source, in Stockholm, Ambassador Aleksandra Kollontai, is said to have told the British in 1940 that, even with all his urgent preparation, Stalin still believed he could not be ready for war with the Germans until 1944. Later writers have suggested he had in mind a considerably earlier date.[24] Whatever way matters might go, Stalin would not lose sight of the prospect of the further advance to the west.

When the Red Army ultimately broke through the defenses along the Karelian Isthmus, Stalin allowed the Finns to make peace (March 12, 1940) on terms that would continue their national existence, though they lost considerable territory and surrendered the important Baltic base of Hangö, near Helsinki, which covered the sea approach to Leningrad. Stalin meant their independence to be temporary. At least for the time being, he had to put aside his People's Democratic Government for the Finns, which manifestly had had a purpose in his mind larger than the one it actually served in this 1940 resolution of the Finnish situation.[25] His Finnish underlings went back to their Moscow lodgings to join other Communist exiles plotting their own local revolutions in collaboration with the Comintern. Though departed from what remained of Finnish soil, the bolshevized Finns should not be forgotten, for their "government" was to become the very model of later Soviet creations elsewhere, as similar situations opened for Stalin in future years.

STALIN FIGHTS THE WAR — OF DEFENSE 47

Just as important, even with his concession of peace, Stalin had made an unforgiving potential enemy. One British observer in Helsinki expressed it: "The latent [Finnish] desire for revenge . . . will blaze forth in all its fury." So minded, they would seek an ally in war, should the occasion come, to reclaim their lands from the Soviets. Two years later, the Finns were at the gates of Leningrad, supporting the Germans in the siege in which so many Leningraders would starve and freeze during many months of enemy encirclement. Yet the citizens of Leningrad, it might be recalled, had turned out en masse in 1940 to welcome and cheer the "victorious" Workers' and Peasants' Red Army's return home after it had completed the "liberation" of eastern Finland.[26]

Stalin had made his move for peace just soon enough. Evidently he did not know through his agents what date Hitler had set for his march into two more of the neutral Scandinavian countries, Denmark and Norway—in the case of the latter, preempting the British and French attack on the iron ore routes and saving the Westerners the international embarrassment they would have reaped. The German assault on Norway in April 1940 turned into a battle for the northern ports of that country. The British, French, and some exile Poles, with the Norwegians now their allies, tried to hold these Norwegian enclaves not only as a front on which to battle the Germans but also as a foothold for an eventual attack on the Swedish mines.[27] But the German assault on the Low Countries a month later soon concentrated Western Allied attention elsewhere.

With the second new German blitzkrieg, this time against the Dutch and Belgians, previously neutrals, and the French, in May 1940, the Allied Norwegian front collapsed. As the German armies rolled through the Low Countries and northern France, both London and Paris desperately tried to work out a defensible front in northern France to stop the Germans before Paris. But this time there was to be no miracle of the Marne. Paris fell in mid-June. The large Allied forces, mostly British, cut off from the main French front by the rapidity of the German advance, were extricated from the port of Dunkerque only by the heroism of the British navy and civilian auxiliary rescuers and by the success of the Royal Air Force in keeping the *Luftwaffe* at bay during the rescue.

Nazi occupation had come directly to the French homeland, and the Germans were but twenty miles by channel from England. The total failure of the British and French defense, culminating in the fall of Paris, and the withdrawal of the French from the war shortly thereafter, had, with the complete closing of the Skagerrak, and even of access to the Swedish coast by the German march into Denmark and Norway, wholly blocked the West from the Baltic countries. Stalin, by this time, was well prepared, and very secure, in his next move there.

That move was long planned, though always earlier denied: the annexation of the three Baltic states, Lithuania, Latvia, and Estonia. The format of Soviet policy was the same in all three. Stalin made his move shortly after the Germans launched their major assault on France via the Low Countries in May, even before they had booked their first stunning military successes there. Well before the assault became the great *Sieg im Westen*, it was evident that neither Germany nor the Western Allies would be taking any immediate interest in the Baltic area, or in the doings of the Soviet Union in general. The Soviets' sudden barrage of complaints about the behavior of the three small countries thus went almost unremarked in the West. The Soviet Narkomindel trumped up complaints indicating various sorts of alleged local unfriendliness to the occupying Red Army garrisons. Molotov and others alleged that the small states themselves had secretly combined against the Soviets. He and Stalin then required that in each country governments friendly to the Soviet Union and approved by Stalin should be established. On June 15, the day after the Nazis occupied Paris, the Red Army marched into Lithuania; two days later it marched into Latvia and Estonia. The leaders in Kaunas, Riga, and Tallinn tried to save what could be saved, appointing Soviet-friendly personnel named by Stalin's agents to govern; they had no choice but to accept Stalin's subalterns from various People's Commissariats, V. G. Dekanozov, Andrei Vyshinskii, and Andrei Zhdanov, as the real local powers, supported by the now omnipresent Red Army.

In each capital a demonstration for a "people's government" was staged, joined in even by Red sailors and troops. Within a month, elections had been held for new parliaments. In each country only one party was allowed, a "people's party." All the candidates were approved by those chosen originally in collaboration with Stalin's underlings. Within a few days, to the surprise of some of the most ardent local leftists and communists, and even to some of their leaders, these new parliaments, "elected" by majorities reported as 99 percent or more, demanded that the three states be incorporated as new republics into the Soviet Union. Parliamentary delegates were sent to Moscow to ask for admission, which was then, with appropriate ceremony and formality, duly granted to the petitioners.

Stalin's format for legal appearances in this case was somewhat different from that chosen for Finland, where the People's Democratic Government had idled in wait to serve the anticipated Soviet military success. Had that success come, Finland, too, would undoubtedly have been drawn, by petition, into the "happy Soviet family." In the occupied Baltic states, the scheme Stalin directed was almost identical to that earlier followed in occupied eastern Poland.

Soviet subterfuges in the Baltic states were as subtly conducted as Stalin and Molotov could organize them. In Tallinn, Andrei Zhdanov simply said to his Estonian collaborators, "Avoid the impression of external interference, and create the appearance of a spontaneous movement of the people instead."[28] Since the Soviets had long practiced creating such appearances at home and had recently checked over and applied the techniques in occupied eastern Poland, the task was not difficult, even if the results in the Baltic states were spotty.

Also as in Poland, the Soviets immediately set about reducing the three Baltic states to economic dependency. Local currencies were pegged at ridiculously unfavorable levels to the Soviet ruble, thus artificially enhancing the value of the ruble. Bank accounts were frozen, so that citizens became immediately dependent on local authority for work or handouts. Properties such as farms, houses, and apartments were sequestered. Businesses were taken over by the state. In many instances the Soviets confiscated whole dwellings and their furnishings from the "bourgeoisie," who sought temporary refuge where they could in barns, or crowded in with relatives. The better abodes were given over to the newly arrived Red officials, and to Soviet carpetbaggers, local collaborators, and Red Army personnel, many of whom carried away what they wished in the way of household furnishings when they went to new stations— "gifts," they were called, and recapturable, because what bourgeois power had "illicitly" given could be retrieved by the exploited people. The latter group evidently included those who had dropped in from abroad uninvited.

The new arrivals, including some who came purposely to take advantage of the attractive merchandise and bargains, had no trouble buying and carrying away everything moveable that the desperate population would sell, at prices keyed to the vastly overinflated ruble. Huge amounts of such goods were carted off into the heart of the impoverished Soviet realm. Emigrés from the former Soviet Union today still tell stories of friends and acquaintances whose families returned from the "liberated" lands rich in "capitalist" sofas, dishes, clothing, bedding, rugs, and lighting fixtures.[29] This kind of wholesale looting was repeated again and again as the Soviet forces, in the course of the war, advanced into new and unexploited territories. At the British Legation in Kaunas, one diplomat (said in some circles to be pro-Soviet), who had a month before sent dispassionate dispatches describing the events of the Soviet takeover, soon lost his diplomatic composure. By the end of July 1940, he was describing the Soviets as "Asiatic hordes": they "threaten . . . civilization and bring misery in their wake."[30] From the legation in Tallinn, a British observer reported home after the rigged election and voting whereby Estonia requested to join the USSR, the performance "filled me with repugnance. . . . There is despair and terror among most of the population. . . . If I write with some bitterness it is because I regard Estonians as a fine race, and feel that the method of their virtual extinction might have been less ignoble."[31] It was a report that might have been filed, with local details changed to suit the terrain, from any of the Baltic capitals in the summer of 1940.

By the time of the German attack on the Soviet Union, one year later, hundreds of thousands of local citizens had been forcibly packed away, without their goods, to Siberia and the Soviet far north, joining the former leaders and chief officials of the three countries who had been sent off even before the official incorporation of their states into the Soviet Union. This was perhaps the first time in modern European history that one nation kidnapped and murdered the leaders of friendly foreign powers to whom it had given countless assurances of noninterference in their internal affairs, and with whom it had signed treaties of nonaggression. The same fate would surely have befallen the Polish government heads had they not escaped into Romania in September 1939, and the Finns, too, if their country had been taken according to plan.

What has been described of Soviet behavior in the Baltic states anticipates the same order of Soviet behavior as more and more European capitals fell within Stalin's grasp in the course of the war only just begun. From Soviet occupation, to planned coup, to de-

struction of the local leadership in every echelon of society, to a l
of Nazi-style "coordination" of all entities under the central gov
ment's authority, to calculated dispersal, as necessary, of native populations and forced colonization by means of masses of imported
Soviet agents—that was the basic program of Sovietization and its
perhaps deliberate economic proletarianization. All citizens were
made to serve one master, the state, dominated by the party and its
leader. The divided and conquered fought each other for the insufficient scraps from the master's larder. This unattractive but verifi-
able picture of Stalinist Russian actions was for years directly or
implicitly denied by some of the most influential leaders, and by
some of the greatest savants and most influential groups in the West.
And this denial, especially during World War II, carried out by the
manipulation and censoring of reportage and political opinion by
important Western leaders, was a major part of the background of
the diplomatic debacles leading to the sudden confrontations of the
emerging Cold War.

The Nazi offer to split eastern Europe had come to Stalin virtually
out of the blue in August 1939. One year later, Stalin had reannexed
nearly all the European territories that had once been part of tsarist
Russia, and some that had not. The old Russian empire was being
rebuilt as the Western democratic states lost the ability to defend
what remained of the orderly League of Nations–like world. Meanwhile, an obsessed Adolf Hitler had disregarded historical German
interests in the stability of east central Europe as a buffer against
the Russian colossus. He had his own plans for the reconstruction
of Europe, which, realized or unrealized, meant the destruction of
much or all of it.   *orthodox.*

Stalin had meddled, provoked, and annexed territory in Asia in the
1920's. Now a weakened European border offered similar chances.
In 1939, following the sweep of the Red Army through eastern Poland and the forced military alliances imposed on the Baltic states,
Stalin and Molotov, the latter citing Ivan the Terrible and Peter
the Great as their predecessors, initiated the plan to put Russia on
the Baltic.[32] Exhilarated by the success at already resetting a large
part of east central Europe's clocks to Moscow time, Molotov solilo-
quized about history, confidently claiming Ivan as the Kremlin's
mentor.[33]

But Stalin, unlike Hitler, was hoping to achieve his purposes without major conflict. The Finnish war had proved that his armies were

not yet ready for a thrust to the west, and though he would re-form and rearm them as quickly as possible, he would for the present, while the war heated up in the west, bide his time, waiting for the conditions to fix his hegemony on the whole continent from the Atlantic to the new Soviet borders.

Had Stalin not been so preoccupied with the helpless Baltic states in June 1940, when the German eastern border was totally exposed by Hitler's concentration in the west, he might then, even with a limping Red Army and an obsolescent Red Air Fleet, have risked an attack all along Hitler's disarmed frontier. Quite conceivably, he could have put his mobile Red cavalry troops in Königsberg, Danzig, and Breslau, perhaps even in Berlin, within a few weeks. He could have severed the Germans from their vital petroleum supplies by a quick turn south into scarcely formidable Romania. Panic and chaos, quickened by memories of the brutal Russian advance into East Prussia in 1914, would have swept over the Reich. The Germans would have had to pull out whole armies from the French front to drive them east. Poland would have been at least temporarily rescued, and most of France saved from the Germans. The Germans would scarcely have been able to mount a serious offensive in the east for months after they had stabilized a line of defense, perhaps as far west as the line of the Oder and the western Neisse rivers. At the same time, they would have had to contend with re-founded Western Allied armies on their western front. Another German disaster, a repetition of 1914 to 1918, could have followed.

But Stalin was too bent on his scheme for a different kind of advance westward, and perhaps still too loyal to Hitler, to seize the day that, once seized, could have crowned him and the Soviet Union with the glory and gratitude of the supporters of the Allied democracies all over the world. So, in spite of his immediate successes, Stalin had woefully miscalculated. He had expected a long war of attrition, as in 1914–18, between the West and Hitler, not the great, and speedy, German victories Hitler organized.[34] Suddenly, Stalin's grandiose plans were endangered. The German armies, which had blitzed across Poland, Scandinavia, France, and the Balkans, were freed of any Continental power that could try to stop them, save the Soviet Union. Stalin and Molotov had surely not forgotten Hitler's published ravings about Judeo-Bolshevism and the need to extirpate it from Europe. Perhaps, instead of Soviet Russia's picking up the

pieces and organizing them in its way after a European war of attrition, the rest of the world would ultimately reap whatever was left
to harvest from a German-Soviet war of attrition, a notion, even a
hope, not beyond the imaginings of some Western leaders.[35]

Stalin had on at least two occasions deviated from his contractual
obligations to the Germans set out in his pact with Hitler. In late
June 1940, again covered by the German occupation of France and
by Britain's wretched military state in the aftermath of Dunkerque,
he had sent his troops into northern Romania to take back the former tsarist territory of Bessarabia. In addition, he seized from the
Romanians a large part of the former Austro-Hungarian province of
Bukovina and some smaller territories. Stalin quite effectively drove
the Romanians into Hitler's arms with these moves, as his earlier
actions had sent the Finns searching for a powerful ally. And part of
Bukovina was not included in the Russian sphere of conquest in the
secret agreements with Hitler of the previous summer and fall.[36]

Moreover, in formally taking over Lithuania in 1940, Stalin failed
to deliver up to the Germans key border areas he had promised
them in the September 1939 agreement, areas that the Germans
now asked for. To be sure, in this case Stalin's motive has to have
been again the preservation of appearances for public relations ends.
He did not want to be seen "de-annexing" some "voluntary" Soviet
citizens of Lithuania, who had "elected" by a more than 99 percent
majority the parliament that would deliver them into the Soviet
Union. Stalin could hardly publicly hand over to the much despised
Hitler a large number of the volunteers, among them not a few Jewish citizens. Because Stalin could not appear to be cutting a territorial deal with Hitler, he had Molotov (whose wife was Jewish) privately beg and wheedle until he persuaded the Germans to sell him
secretly the western border areas of Lithuania for $7.5 million in
gold. Throughout the long negotiations over the selling price, the
Germans stuck to their guns (and paid for some of them), demanding
full payment long before June 1941: at last, the kind of deal that
former champagne salesman Ribbentrop knew how to make. Hitler,
in any event, intended all the time to return east shortly.[37]

Stalin was well aware that, to many in the West, the Soviet Union
was still a noble experiment, and he quite correctly continued to
value the importance of Western public opinion, even as Great Britain struggled to hang together. To the West, he argued that taking

Bessarabia and Bukovina was necessary in order to reunite the citizens there with their ethnic brothers in the Soviet Union, although for the majority in both provinces that was hardly the case. He had used the same excuse about eastern Poland. It was the kind of appeal to the fair-minded in the West that Hitler had also more than once capitalized upon. The British government, from the distance of London, found it diplomatic to ignore the "Asiatic hordes" that diplomats closer to Soviet forces complained of. In the beleaguered British capital, with Hitler organizing his invasion of England just across the Channel, it was not surprising that fear of the Nazis led many to judge the Soviet move against Romania and the establishment of Soviet power in the Baltic as defensive.[38]

Finally, in the hope of bettering relations with the Germans while at the same time advancing toward his pan-European goals, Stalin sent Molotov (without his wife) to Berlin in November 1940 to negotiate for Soviet control of the entrances to the Baltic and Black seas (as the tsars had once wanted), and for additional Soviet influence in Finland and the Balkans. In return, the Soviets pledged significantly more support for the German war effort, which was now concentrated on starving Britain by U-boat blockade and destroying its cities by bombing.

Hitler, however, had his own, very different, plans for the southeast of Europe. He recommended to Molotov that the Soviets distract themselves elsewhere with conquests of British satrapies in the Near East and India. Even Hitler seemed to recognize that there had to be a limit to Soviet expansion in Europe. Besides, he was offended by Molotov's expansionist pretentions. His limited patience with the "Judeo-Bolsheviks" had come to an end. Perhaps stimulated by a June visit to Napoleon's tomb and a megalomaniacal resolve taken there to better Napoleon's war record, perhaps by reflecting on Stalin's recent takeover of the Baltic states, perhaps also, as he said, perceiving that he himself had unchained the Soviet menace and fearing that Stalin's recent moves to the west were only the first of a series, Hitler had decided months before to have his reckoning with the Soviets. He would now open up that even vaster lebensraum in the east that he had long been promising the German people. Molotov went home from Berlin empty handed. On December 18, 1940, Hitler ordered the commencement of Operation Barbarossa, the code name for the plan to attack the Soviet Union.[39]

The Western powers could perhaps have acted together to make the most of a combined Nazi-Soviet debacle after Barbarossa began in June 1941, but neither London nor Washington took it upon itself to doubt that Stalin's earlier moves westward were defensive, as his actions seemed to suggest they were. British leaders themselves had regularly, even eagerly, viewed Stalin's expansionism from the fall of 1939 in that light.[40] Moreover, the British, and President Roosevelt, who desperately wanted to help them, were hamstrung by a powerful isolationist and pacifist American public opinion, which during the Finnish war had also become emotionally anti-Soviet. In Great Britain, too, the mood had changed: the Labour left, which took its usual foreign policy stance from an influential Communist member of Parliament, had, temporarily, turned away from Stalin.[41]

The Americans were, of course, still neutral. And the British were wholly off balance because of the proximity of the German danger and Britain's frailty as a military, as opposed to a naval and air power after the fall of France and the Low Countries. Churchill, now Prime Minister, though sharply anti-Bolshevik during the interwar years, was just one of those important Britons who had accepted Stalin's actions against Poland and in the Baltic as defensive. British politicians had been deliberately averting their eyes from Stalin's depredations east of the Bug since he began his invasion of Poland.[42] The British ambassador to the Soviet Union, Stafford Cripps (described by some of his Labour colleagues as an "innocent," and as having the political judgment of a "flea"), a diplomat who called the League of Nations an "international burglars' union," even went so far as to defend the Soviet moves westward in print.[43] Publicly he tried to deliver British recognition of the Soviet conquest of eastern Poland to Stalin as a bribe for his more favorable stance toward Great Britain. Churchill saw the Soviet imbroglio in Finland as making the Soviets less useful to Germany. "Russian naval power in the Baltic . . . could never be formidable. . . . It is Germany alone that is the danger there."[44] He was himself long preoccupied with the scheme of an assault on Norway and Sweden to keep Germany from getting the Swedish ores, though that idea was not indeed so very different from Hitler's moves against the Low Countries and Stalin's against the Baltic states.

Thus misled about Stalin's intentions, Churchill and Foreign Secretary Eden desperately sought a reconciliation with Stalin after the fall of France. The Labour Party and the trade unions, the former in the wartime national government, their members' hearts on the left where they still imagined Stalin was in spite of the Hitler-Stalin Pact, were all for the same reconciliation. True, they had condemned the Soviet invasion of Poland, and they were upset by the attack of the "workers' and peasants' state" on Finland. But they quickly forgot these deeds after France fell to the Germans, even when Stalin was busily blaming his invasion of the Baltic states on England and France's aggressive designs there.[45] None of these leaders, of course, nor anyone in these groups, knew the details of the Hitler-Stalin Pact. And had they had an inkling of Stalin's plans for the Continent, they would, in the circumstances, no doubt have regarded them as only slightly less than fanciful, given the flamboyantly manifested power of Nazi Germany astride nearest Europe. It is not too much to say that, together, British preoccupation with the closer German menace, Soviet collaborators and sympathizers entrenched in the inner circles of official and unofficial Britain, along with wrongheaded and wishful thinking in both Tory and Labour political circles, and insufficient British intelligence information about the Soviet Union's plans and capabilities, had simply wiped clean the slate of Soviet misdeeds. British sensibilities of a potential threat posed by a remote and underestimated Soviet army had been dulled.[46] Russia was, as it had so long been, "a faraway place of which we know little."

\ President Roosevelt, who was Britain's only remaining hope for major additional support in the war against Hitler, also held not unfavorable views of the Soviet Union. Since even the Hitler-Stalin Pact, the Baltic invasions, and the Finnish war could not eradicate his fixations, nor those of leading Britons, it was obvious that Stalin could, if need be, count on support from the West,[47] in dimensions that the Soviet leader probably then could hardly conceive. \

For the moment, however, Stalin was Hitler's apparently loyal victualer and supporter, though he continued to rearm the Soviet Union to the teeth to meet whatever opportunity he found to realize his plans—or to face any approaching danger. Yet by helping Hitler to take all Europe west of the Molotov-Ribbentrop line, he had brought about the very situation of risk to the still relatively ill-armed Soviet state that he had originally thought to avoid. Stalin's only allies, as usual, were, first, the many sentimental pro-Soviet influential Westerners, who were apparently able to stomach Stalin's purges at home and view indifferently the rape and looting of infant foreign states, and, second, the numerous important Western statesmen who were quite unable to imagine the possibility of Soviet expansion westward to the very areas where more proximate, deadly enemies now kept their total attention.

3

BEHIND RED ARMY LINES: POLAND

FOR POLAND, the largest state of east central Europe, the Nazi-Soviet Nonaggression Pact signed on August 23, 1939, meant total defeat and subjugation. At Brest-Litovsk, toward the end of September 1939, in what was then nearly the middle of Poland, the generals of the two invading armies went over the details of the pre-arranged line that would mark the two zones of conquest for Germany and Soviet Russia, subsequently to be rearranged one more time in Moscow. The military parade that followed (September 22) was recorded by Nazi cameras and celebrated in the German newsreel: German and Soviet generals cheek by jowl in military homage to each other's armies and victories.[1]

Even Hitler's published ravings had prepared few of the citizens of Poland for some of the awful realities of German occupation. Hitler immediately split the German area of conquest in two and annexed to the Third Reich large areas that bordered on Germany. Many ethnic Poles were immediately uprooted and forced into the remaining area, which was put under a Nazi governor, and called a "General-Gouvernement." As such it had an ambiguous status even in Nazi-dominated Europe: it was neither an annexed country nor an occupied country, but a *Nebenland*, an adjacent land. It soon became a land of horror.

Without delay, the Jews of the German-annexed areas were driven into the General-Gouvernement, where they were subjected to increasingly harsh discrimination, moving from the worst sorts of insulting behavior, random and sometimes locally systematic violence and massacre, to the wearing of the yellow star, and, within a year and a half, isolation in walled ghettos. All this was recorded by the cameras of the German propaganda ministry—even the most ghastly scenes of misery, starvation, and death.[2] Scholars and others have ever since mined this filmed record, and other records that subsequently fell into Allied hands, for the now well-examined history of the Nazi occupation.

But what could have prepared the Polish citizens of the eastern half of the country, plus the multitudes of western Polish refugees, many of them Jews, who fled eastward from the German armies in the first weeks of the German attack, only to be caught by the Soviets? Years before Winston Churchill, in 1946, made public his regret that an "iron curtain" had descended at the western perimeter of postwar Soviet occupation in central Europe, the Soviets had armed their borders with a virtually impenetrable curtain of defense against outsiders and outside ideas. Within it they had created a powerful propaganda apparatus controlling the dissemination of all information. If Moscow's propaganda of the times often lacked the sophistication and finesse of Goebbels's in the Third Reich, the vast bulk and remoteness of the Soviet Union, and the general lack of knowledge of the Russian language outside Russia, made its defenses against the ideas of the outside world more complete.[3] Moreover, thousands of Western and other do-gooders, and Communists of the Marxist-Leninist faith, had turned their own idealistic wishes and dreams into descriptions of Soviet life that omitted all the evils and showed only the few palpable virtues. Even pilgrimages to the promised land usually failed to shake their beliefs in the worthiness of the system. No matter that millions of people had already died from revolution, civil war, purges, and famines repeatedly induced by central intervention in the economy. No matter the almost permanent state of purge and the hysterical fear of foreign spies and agents, or a world of personal immorality in the highest places. No matter the systematic public intrusion in private lives and the catastrophic rural impoverishment. Mussolini's Italy was by contrast a land of freedom.

Little of this appalling situation was known in the West, partly because of the chorus of the foreign faithful who broadcast the party line. But Poles were generally more skeptical than most Westerners about the Soviet paradise. There was no local Communist party, partly because the Polish government had repressed its opposition, partly because Stalin had decapitated the Polish party that once existed by executing its exiled leaders. The elements of the party that did survive were rightly viewed as agents of Poland's traditional enemy, which coveted Poland's territory and had for centuries sought to control its soul. For more than two hundred years, Poland and Russia had been contesting the domination of the Slavic lands west and south of Great Russia, the latter, the historical settlement of the Russian people. The Poles had long connections with traditional Western Christian Europe and regarded their land and their culture as the glacis of the European West; but their centuries of struggle against Russia, during which there were bloody insurrections and wars conducted at levels of barbarism usually associated in Western imaginations with the terrible Turk, and years of Russian occupation, had brought home an intimate knowledge of Russian culture and behavior that was not vouchsafed the peoples of Western Europe.[4]

Too many times, the Russian tsars with their semi-Asiatic and Asiatic legions had marched as conquerors through the streets of francophile, latinized Warsaw. For the skeptical Poles, any change to the east, however awful, grand, and, at the same time, rotten with tragically misbegotten hope, like the Revolution, had to be viewed in a historical context they knew from experience: "Plus ça change, plus c'est la même chose!" And, in any event, the Soviets had sealed their border to them as to all outsiders. Only past experience, occasional repatriations of Poles east of the border, and direst imaginings might have suggested the awful truth the citizens of the eastern Polish lands would soon learn.[5]

What happened in eastern Poland in the fall of 1939 has not been easy to unearth. The overwhelming mass of information, the mass of films and photographs, the mass of books dealing with Poland in World War II tell only of the horrors of life within German-annexed and occupied Poland. Only in the last ten years have historians and others begun to examine the many available documents that will lead to a reconstruction of the events of 1939–41 in Soviet-occupied Poland. What we already know forebodes a tale of horror not far different from what we know about Poland under Hitler.[6]

When the Soviet troops, acting without a declaration of war, crossed the eastern Polish frontier on September 17, 1939, no one there quite knew what to do. Polish governmental authority had broken down in the disorganized flight of the central authorities from Warsaw and in the assault of the Germans on internal communications. The Polish forces, most of them facing the west and the invading Germans, were taken wholly off guard.[7] Because the Soviets had not declared war, some Polish citizens at first thought they must have come to help the beleaguered Polish armies standing off the Germans to the west. In the ethnic minority communities, which in the eastern territories constituted a majority, many naively hoped that Soviet authority would bring them the social justice promised in Marxist theory. Although these people—a few Lithuanians, and many White Russians, Ukrainians, and Jews—were Polish citizens, they had suffered from the nationalistic, polonizing policies of the short-lived interwar state, particularly from its assertion of the primacy of Roman Catholicism in a nation with large Protestant, Uniate, Orthodox, and Jewish minorities.

One of the themes most emphasized in Soviet propaganda was that of the Red Army as liberator of the people from the Polish *pan* (lord). This line appealed especially to the White Russians and Ukrainians, who were linguistically allied with people living in the westernmost republics of the USSR. Some of the Jews, who constituted about one-tenth of the population, were also sympathetic to this line because of the discrimination they had suffered under both private and governmental anti-Jewish sentiment.[8] Theoretical Marxism proclaimed that universal brotherhood would come from breaking the thrall of all religion. Being ignorant of the true situation to the east, where theoretical Marxism yielded to Stalin-imposed tyranny, many Polish citizens who knew discrimination at first hand welcomed the arriving Soviet soldiers as liberators, or, at least, as potential protectors from the Nazis.

The truth of the situation was soon evident—when even the not so prosperous people of eastern Poland were shocked to see the often shoeless, ragtag, Soviet conquerors and their bony horses. To the Soviet soldiers, Poland was a miracle of well-fed horses, cattle, and other domestic animals, of shops still full of food, clothing, and hardware items even after days of war, of properly uniformed and outfitted troops and police. Although older citizens now recall 1939 as one of the better prewar years for provisioning in the Soviet Union, the Red Army officers and men had, within a few weeks, bought for their valueless rubles almost everything to be bought in eastern Poland and had stolen whatever else was movable, even whole buildings—all to be dragged back to the workers' and peasants' paradise. Within a few weeks all was gone: shoes, dishes, pots, grains, fats, livestock, horses, saddles. Those middle-class and comfortable peasant White Russians, Ukrainians, urban and *shtetl* Jews of former Poland, who had greeted the Red Army as liberators, were, like the Poles, soon reduced to the penury of their least affluent neighbors. Polish officers, police, soldier-prisoners, even the wounded left behind, were both randomly and systematically massacred by the Red Army, the NKVD (People's Commissariat of Internal Affairs, recently known as the KGB), and their volunteer helpers. Other Poles who had been wounded in the war were thrown out of hospitals and sometimes even replaced by German wounded.[9] Incited by the Red Army and NKVD units, vengeful mobs attacked and killed the former civil authorities, who were then replaced by other civilians, many of them relatively well-educated Jews. Many of them helped the newly arrived and arriving commissars, until the Jews themselves were driven out and replaced by carpetbaggers of proved loyalty to the Soviet central administration and the NKVD. The long history of Jews as social outsiders no doubt helped them to adjust more quickly than others to a world of traditional values suddenly upended, especially to the widespread corruption and bribery endemic to the Soviet system. That many of the Jews, in reaction to the heavy religiosity and popular anti-Jewish sentiments in the Polish republic, had been drawn to the ideals of Marxism only made their welcome embrace of the Stalinist state, whose chief was systematically murdering his former Bolshevik comrades of Jewish background, yet more grotesque. It was a triumph of hope over tragic absurdity on "the dark side of the moon," as one contemporary titled his book on Soviet-occupied Poland.

The Soviets soon established the forms of controls that they would bring out on numerous occasions and in numerous places in the years to come—a year later in the three Baltic countries, Latvia, Lithuania, and Estonia, then in Bessarabia and Moldavia, and, after the war, once again in these same places and in the other territories occupied in the course of the Red Army's victory over Hitler. These events in eastern Poland are fascinating because they represent the first European example of what became regular methods for founding Soviet power in newly occupied territories.

Under the Soviet invaders in Poland, all publications, radio broad-casts, and cinema production were government controlled. Giant pictures of Stalin and the other Soviet chieftains appeared on walls. The streets were adorned with red banners carrying slogans extoll-ing the Bolshevik leader and his court, the Soviet system, the work-ers' and peasants' government. Within a few weeks, elections were set up. Voting was compulsory, and often rewarded by handouts of trifles and, by then scarce, food. In all districts there was one candi-date, or one list of candidates, on the ballot, nominated by those working with the Soviet authorities. Few voters knew that they were electing delegates who would "spontaneously" ask for incor-poration of their area of Poland into the USSR.[10]

Except for those many citizens actively collaborating with the Soviets, every one else quickly learned to line up, Soviet-style, for the barest of necessities. Collaborators got special rations. As in the Baltic states some months later, so-called "committees of public safety" confiscated, without trial and often without notice, dwell-ings, estates, lands, and other sorts of private property. Soviet pro-paganda films showed old "aristocrats" being dispossessed of their estates, which were to be turned over to the workers and peasants. Universities and schools were purged of "bourgeois" and Polish "ele-ments." The name "Poland" was forbidden, and references to places west of the demarcation line had to be referred to by the Poles as "Germany," so that, for example, if one was asked, "Where were you born?" the answer had to be, if appropriate, "Warsaw, *Germany*."[11]

By means of the Soviet *stroibat*, as much a punishment brigade as a construction battalion, thousands, even Polish Communists, were put to forced labor.[12] People in once style-conscious, francophile cit-ies like Lwów learned to adopt the plainest and severest dress in order to merge into the soon standard drab Sovietized mass. Attrac-tive advertising and shop signs were removed; nearly all the shops closed: there was little to buy in any case, especially in the official agencies of the state, which afterward soon became the only shops. Signs in Polish were replaced by signs in other languages, though at the time of the election, carefully selected Polish as well as Ukrainian and White Russian speakers and banners publicly wel-comed the new system in the Soviet-style mass meetings that were organized.[13] Soon a group of pro-Bolshevik Polish intellectuals began to extol in print the Soviet Union as the homeland of Poles whose state had ceased "historically" to exist. To be sure, Marx had always wanted an independent Poland, but times had changed. Stalin, one wrote, had envisioned this change as early as 1913.[14] In poverty-stricken, graying cities, fading slogans on decaying banners flapped overhead on streets where recently acquired subjects of the new master learned the mechanisms of survival that life in Soviet society required.

The disappearance of Polish as a public language came when the newly elected representatives were brought together to request incorporation, as the Western Ukraine and Western White Russia, into the Soviet constituent republics of the Ukraine and White Russia. Delegations of the newly important were subsequently transported to Kiev and to Minsk and to the Kremlin itself to request these incorporations, which were duly granted and massively celebrated. So it was true, many in Russia would surely have concluded, that all the horrors so far witnessed and sacrifices made in the years of revolutionary dismantling and reconstruction of society were necessary. Others, given the opportunity, had rushed to join the new society! Soviet press and film assured them it was so.

The removal of the Polish signs had a good deal of significance as a mark of change of control, for the secret agreements between Hitler and Stalin provided for transplanting the populations of newly divided eastern Europe to meet Hitler's racist, and Stalin's combination of security and racist, needs. Hitler wanted to move the Germans, those who for centuries had lived in agricultural colonies and even cities all over east central Europe and even in the Soviet Union, into the territories he had recently joined from his Polish conquest into the Nazi *Grossdeutsches Reich*. Having created some lebensraum, he wanted to people it. Stalin, for his part, wanted to depolonize the annexed territories in order to make it doubly certain that there would be no nest of Polish (or, *mutatis mutandis*, Ukrainian) nationalism and anti-Soviet agitation. This, too, was a technique that he had used before and would use again, on the theory that to divide and conquer and sow ethnic misunderstanding among neighbors weakened any possible resistance against the central authority. The changing of the signs cleared away evidence of individual enterprise and entrepreneurship, suggested the ubiquitousness of the new order, and encouraged russification: photographs and films of the period show that the new signs in the Western Ukraine, such few as there were to be, were written mainly in Russian, although before the coming of the Workers' and Peasants' Red

Army, there had been no noticeable Russian population in these Polish provinces.

Within a few months after the Soviet takeover, multitudes of Poles were suddenly aroused from their beds before dawn by Red Army and NKVD units, given a brief amount of time to pack suitcases, then driven to freight cars for shipment. Families were split up, and many would never be together again.[15] The trains moved for weeks across the vast Soviet Union to preselected points in the far corners of the east and north, where the deportees were then unceremoniously put out—among strangers, thousands of miles from ancestral homes. Often, fewer than half on the train survived the journey, the rest having died of starvation, dehydration, cold, and disease. At the points of deposit they were regularly left without shelter or food, in the harshest of Soviet climates of Siberia and Central Asia. Soviet guards there and elsewhere would say, "You'll get used to it, or you'll croak." The intended fate for these Poles was that they would slowly dissolve in the sea of nationalities that made up the Soviet Union, for Molotov had made it clear (as genuine tsars had made it clear in earlier centuries) that Poland had "disappeared forever."[16]

These systematic deportations continued at intervals—up until the surprise German attack on the Soviet Union in June 1941. Presumably the Soviets intended to keep on until the Poles had been reduced to an insignificant minority everywhere and the great Polish cities of the east, like Lwów and Wilno, had been largely depolonized. Reliable Sovietized populations came west to replace those who had vanished, along with the usual apparatchiki and carpetbaggers. The deportation of the Poles was a mass transportation of peoples east on a scale of cruelty theretofore unknown outside the USSR, except in western Poland, where much news of the like behavior of the Germans, directed toward both Poles and Jews, was filtering out to the exiled Polish government in London and to the anti-Nazi Western press through the more porous borders of the Third Reich.

The German attack eastward in June 1941, when it came, came so swiftly, the Soviet forces were so poorly organized and prepared, and the Soviet system of transportation was so chaotic that German troops took the cities of the "Western Ukraine" and "Western White Russia" before many Soviets and their collaborators could escape. Although Soviet intelligence of the actions of the Germans in the General-Gouvernement of Poland was good, and the fate of the Jews there was certainly well known in Moscow, nothing official had been done to alert the Jews of the western Soviet Union to move east before the advancing German armies.[17] Some, of course, had suffered so much during the 21-month government of the commissars in eastern Poland that they could not imagine anything worse. Others, better informed, and perhaps closer to the Soviet information centers and government, anticipated the lesser of two evils and tried to escape with the Soviet bureaucracy. At many points on the pre-1939 Soviet border, in the face of an onrushing tide of refugees, many of the Jews and others, especially those who did not have identity cards as citizens of the USSR and those who did not have the necessary travel documents, were turned back. In Lwów, and probably elsewhere, even before the Germans arrived, Ukrainian nationalists and Poles went on the rampage against Jews as collaborators, real or imagined, in the Soviet system. Many were killed on the spot. Even surviving Poles came out to greet the arriving Germans as liberators. The turmoil was but another proof of the disenchantment with the Soviet system after two years and of the terrible success of Stalin's deadly policy of deliberately turning group against group.[18]

In London the news of the German attack was greeted with restrained delight by members of the divided Polish government-in-exile. Almost everyone of importance—except, apparently, Stalin and some of his inner circle—had believed earlier intelligence reports that Hitler would attack the Soviet Union. Now that the attack had come, the hopeless situation of the Poles seemed to have opened up. British Prime Minister Churchill, in office since the spring of 1940, rushed pell-mell to Stalin's aid, offering unrestricted material help limited only by what could be delivered. He had already received Roosevelt's ill-considered approval, taken without consultation with his Secretary of State.[19] The invasion of the Soviet Union meant that Britain and the many exile governments resident in London were no longer isolated in their battle against Hitler. Now Hitler's ally in the attack on Poland, to whose defense the British had gone with their declaration of war in 1939, might be Britain's ally.

The Soviet Union was, of course, tightly secured by its iron curtain, but who, indeed, would have believed stories that told the truth about Soviet occupation, word from that "dark side of the moon"? Many members of the British and American governments and representatives of the Western press regularly refused during much of the war that followed to believe the stories, deriving from multiple Jewish, Polish, and other Continental sources, including German, of Hitler's torment and later mass murder of millions of Jews—all the Jewish population of the Continent that he could lay his hands on.[20] Most of that terrible work was done in death camps established in Poland. This disbelief persisted, though the British had special cause to detest the Germans and to believe all manner of evil attributed to them. But the Soviet Union was that faraway place of which even informed Britons knew little. It is therefore not wholly surprising that the British chose to ignore the mass of information that the Polish exile government in London collected about Soviet as well as German behavior in occupied Poland. Churchill, his mind focused on defeating Hitler, was probably inclined to put a better construction on Soviet behavior than his predecessor had been in the early days of the Soviet pact with Hitler, except in the case of the Finnish war.

It had to have been just that special feeling and two years of experience of Nazi ruthlessness, and persistence of the false analogy of World War I, plus an ignorance that was both real, and in part willing, of Europe east of the Rhine and of Soviet affairs and Soviet behavior, that then brought Winston Churchill and his Foreign Secretary, Anthony Eden, to what, we see in retrospect, came to be their unlimited and long enduring, as well as naively optimistic, commitment to aid that remote power whose chief was as evil as his nemesis in the Third Reich. The Poles, Britain's first wartime ally, were thus far the main foreign victims of Stalin, as they were of Hitler. Their London exile government had substantial inside information about the situation in eastern Poland that it was willing to share with Churchill. After June 1941, however, the Polish exile government came under increasing pressure from British government officials to patch things up with Stalin on his terms and to make common cause with him against Hitler. Much of the mass-circulation British press, perhaps under Communist influence or at least desirous of pleasing left-wing Labour leaders, took an anti-Polish, "antifascist" line similar to that devised in the Kremlin.[21]

In the long history of Poland's struggles for independence, its leaders have often been forced to choose between the lesser of two evils. In World War I, Poles fought on both sides, Austro-German and

Imperial Russian, each group of fighters, as they thought, standing for Poland's betterment—for its independence. Here, at the onset of World War II, General Władysław Sikorski, Poland's leader in exile, a man remarkably different in political stance from many of Poland's prewar leaders, seems to have had a propensity to lean toward the Soviets, especially under the relentlessness of Churchill's pressure. As the head of the government-in-exile of an occupied and dismembered nation, Sikorski had no real choice in the matter. Certainly he believed that he would receive significant British support in reconstructing his nation. But Churchill and his advisers, perhaps without quite thinking the matter through, were soon—much sooner than might be imagined, and for reasons that still defy wholly rational explanation—waffling before the Soviets with respect to the sanctity of the prewar Polish eastern border. Stalin and Molotov, even this early, were unabashedly up to making ugly threats to gain their ends.[22] Eden assured the Poles in the summer of 1941 that the Soviet-imposed border changes there were not recognized, yet on the same day he assured the House of Commons that Britain was giving the Poles no guarantees of its border in the east.

Quite obviously, Britain had finally gone to war with Germany in 1939 out of its traditional interest in not allowing any one power to dominate the Continent. The cause for war was not the Germans seizing non-German Bohemia and Moravia after promising no further annexations, nor was it Hitler's subsequent demands for the restoration of German-populated Danzig to Germany, or a reasonable demand for an extraterritorial connection between two parts of Germany awkwardly dissevered in balancing the national needs of the victor states, and their clients of 1918, at the expense of the losers. These were important Polish border issues, but they were scarcely of intrinsic interest in London or Paris. These German demands and unilateral acts of aggression did not bring the war.

The war came because Prime Minister Neville Chamberlain belatedly, but quite correctly, perceived what Churchill had concluded much earlier: that Hitler's demands were insatiable, that he was not just a revanchist German politician seeking the restoration of lands once held by a greater Germany, but was instead a cruel hegemonist, a nihilist who knew no bounds himself and therefore could set none. That the Soviet Union might itself have designs on Europe, and, indeed, just as grandiose, on the world beyond, was something the British leaders after Chamberlain did not, perhaps could not, choose to know. In the circumstances of fighting a major war against a powerful foe, they may not even have had the time to reflect on the possibility.[23]

In any case, Churchill's conditionless pledge of British aid to the Soviets, and British fears of a Soviet withdrawal from the war, blunted whatever might have come from any subsequent efforts to get Stalin to agree to restore the status quo ante bellum in Poland, or anywhere else. Later, Churchill and Eden did make occasional frantic efforts to restore the London exile government, or part of it, to Warsaw, but they never supported its efforts to regain its Soviet-annexed territories.[24]

President Roosevelt, frustrated by the reluctance of a sizable portion of the American people to get involved in Europe's disastrous affairs, was nonetheless giving Great Britain advice and important material help. The advice was that there should not be any postwar commitments regarding territories. He held to this position publicly, but not privately, even after the Americans had become a belligerent, thanks to the Japanese attack on Pearl Harbor and Germany's declaration of war in December 1941. He thereby withdrew American negotiating power from the scales at a time when it would have been the greatest—that is, when the Soviets, hard pressed by the initial German attack, most needed Western help. The United States had no commitment to the Poles, and by consistently deferring to British leadership on that issue, Roosevelt put himself in the position of abdicating control over diplomacy in eastern Europe to Churchill. But Churchill had effectively abdicated eastern Poland to Stalin, and Roosevelt was soon privately willing to do the same. Although Churchill had no "policy of postponement," he, like Roosevelt, had at the beginning of the German attack on the Soviet Union thrown away much of the leverage he might have had with Stalin. Soon he was hastily disencumbering himself of still more of it. Later, consistently, Roosevelt gave the London Poles ambiguous reassurances; in the long run he was indifferent to their interests, ultimately even hostile in his later richly developed faith in and misperception of Stalin. He was willing to the very end to play second fiddle to the British on the Polish theme.[25] Sikorski and his successors at the head of the Polish government-in-exile merited, by their significant investment and that of their countrymen in Allied victory, better, and more informed, allies.

Looking again for the sources of the behavior of the two major

English-speaking powers in this middle period of the Polish tragedy in World War II, it seems obvious that Churchill's determination to defeat Hitler and the Germans in this second world war led him to rely too much on his recollection of World War I diplomacy that had resulted in the drawing (by a British diplomat ignorant of the local circumstances) of the Curzon line as Poland's eastern frontier. That line, in one of its formulations, somewhat approximated the final demarcation line made between the German and Soviet armies in 1939, and though it was no more accurate as an ethnic dividing line than the 1939 demarcation line, Churchill, with no detailed or fresh knowledge of where historical Poland ended and historical Great Russia began and ended at any particular chronological point before 1914, probably had kept it in mind. Churchill had, after all, supported the war effort against Germany in 1914 in collaboration with tsarist Russia, and if Tsar Nicholas II had participated in the victory in 1918, Churchill would certainly have supported Russia in a demand for the restoration of its sovereignty over the mass of Poland, and probably for its expansion westward at the expense of the Poles then under Austrian and Prussian control. Such were the sometime wartime plans of the tsarist Russian government. And there is no reason to believe that Churchill, as a British statesman, in or out of government, would have opposed them.[26]

As for Roosevelt, his inadequate knowledge of European history was combined with the false analogies that so often derive from remembering only some of it. He recalled the early secret agreements of World War I that later made a mockery of Woodrow Wilson's "open covenants openly arrived at." But Wilson's slogan was, in any case, no more than that in an imperfect world. He would have changed the world's rules, but he had only the wish, and not the power, to do so. The fact was that people would continue and do continue to negotiate on issues on which they disagree from the strength of the bargaining positions they occupy. In such negotiations, public or private, they reasonably expect to get at least a partial reward for their compromises, and to pay some price for their winnings.

Roosevelt read out for his public's benefit the lessons of Versailles. He led them to believe that Wilson's hope would be achieved this time, that there would be no secret negotiations, and that all territorial decisions would be postponed until a peace conference, and that reasonable men could then arrive at mutually agreeable results.

As unaware, perhaps intentionally, of the extended Soviet goals as Churchill, he attributed to Stalin canons of rational, civilized behavior that none of his action had ever established as valid.

Both Roosevelt and Churchill ascribed to Stalin reasonable understanding of, and willingness to limit, Soviet self-interest. As pragmatic politicians, they fought the enemy they perceived as the greater threat, and certainly the closer threat, the enemy who was pursuing his avowed goals with terrible ruthlessness and efficiency. For the moment, there was little time to entertain the thought that the Bolsheviks meant to enact their ideology just as Adolf Hitler meant to enact his.

Roosevelt long held to his public faith in postponing decisions on the critical territorial issues until all the wartime crises had passed. It was only toward the very end of the war, when Stalin's behavior as an ally became so egregious, that Roosevelt began to show signs of impatience. Yet he never did, before his death in April 1945, recognize America's interest in the revival of the strength of a Europe of fatherlands united in opposition to traditional Russian expansionism and to corrupted as well as expansionist bolshevism. He had established his own diplomatic rule of faith, one shared to a measure by Churchill. Roosevelt's derived from an overweening arrogance (George F. Kennan described it years ago), epitomized in his pure and simple fantasy of a postwar world to be kept in order by the "Big Four," a selfless world court, policed by idealists like Joseph Stalin and Chinese dictator Chiang Kai-shek.[27] The faith lasted him until his death. If Churchill began as an appeaser of Stalin out of his historical misunderstandings and a fear that Great Britain could not triumph over Nazi Germany without Soviet help, Roosevelt was an appeaser of Stalin out of the same generational experience. Both Churchill and Roosevelt had therefore abandoned any attempt to use the majority of the political, military, and economic force at their disposal to try and establish a governmental status quo ante in postwar east central Europe. In effect, they quietly put aside the aims that would embody the ideals they had maintained in the Atlantic Charter.

It is true that the Western leaders did not have knowledge of the secret terms of the Hitler-Stalin Pact, or of Stalin's claims made in negotiations with Hitler (in 1940) for the expansion of Soviet influence far to the west in the Baltic and the Mediterranean. But Molotov's words with respect to the intended permanent annihilation of the Polish state were no secret, nor was the Soviet demand on Finland in late 1939 for its border territories, nor Stalin's demand, made to Eden in December 1941, for yet more of Finland and Romania after the war.[28] Moreover, British and American and other Allied diplomats were on hand in Helsinki and all the Baltic capitals, as well as in Moscow, to witness those earlier annexations and attempted annexations. Though some of them were clearly unable to view and report objectively, others did so, in sufficient detail to outline the pattern of Soviet behavior. Even knowledge of the forced transfer of the Polish population of eastern Poland to the Soviet east, and of Stalin's policy of depopulation there and elsewhere, though it was not directly relayed to the British and American diplomats, was available to them from the London Poles and other émigré sources. But they chose not to pursue these sources, and even chose to ignore and disbelieve what was pushed before them. Just as the continuing and then contemporary Nazi destruction of the Jews in the same geographical region failed to garner much of their attention, so did they not concern themselves with the prospect of a Stalinist advance—with their help—farther into east central Europe. And it was not really until the Soviets arrived to set up their occupation in the heart of Germany, in 1945, that the leaders of the Western powers, after Roosevelt and Churchill had gone, collected the presence of mind, and the determination, to set limits to Stalin's demands.

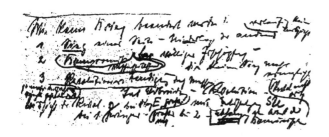

A portion of Wilhelm Pieck's notes from the German Communist Party "Information Meeting" in Moscow, February 21, 1941. Walter Ulbricht told of three possible outcomes of the war he had earlier heard reported in the Comintern Presidium. (Stalin was a member of this group, but was frequently represented by Dmitri Manuilskii, who often served as his stand-in in inter-party business. Stalin, in any case, had to approve everything that went on in the Presidium.) The key words follow number 3 (the third possible outcome, and clearly the one favored by the Kremlin, which was doing its utmost at the time to supply Germany and keep it in the war). "Revolutionäre Beendigung durch Massen je mehr Aussicht des Sieges schwindet—Int Verbrüderung—Revolution mit Unterstützung SU": Revolutionary end by the masses [all] the more [possible as] the prospect of victory dwindles—international fraternization—revolution with the support of the Soviet Union. See page 186, note 20.

J. V. Stalin at the signing of the Hitler-Stalin Pact, Moscow, August 23, 1939. See pages 28–29. (HA, William R. Philp Collection.)

Hotel Lux, Moscow, c. 1936. Members of the Comintern and other important exiled Communists lived here up to and during the war. (ZPA.)

Executive Committee of the Comintern, c. 1936. Georgii Dimitrov in center of front row; Wilhelm Pieck (in Stalin-type outfit), standing second from right. (ZPA.)

Polish (or Ukrainian) peasants in eastern Poland, late September or early October 1939, with Soviet-erected victory arch. Note manufactured symbols on the top, which, with the banners, were likely provided by the recently arrived, conquering Red Army. See page 39. (IS.)

German and Soviet troops parade together at Brest-Litovsk, central Poland, September 22, 1939. German and Soviet commanders are on the reviewing stand, right. A German soldier in an armored car salutes. A Soviet military truck is parked on the left. See pages 39 and 58. (IS.)

German troops leave eastern Poland through a Soviet-erected victory arch, probably end of September 1939. After taking much of the area assigned to the Soviets in the secret territorial agreement of August 23, 1939, the German troops turned their conquests over to the Red Army and departed to the west of the demarcation line. See page 39. (IS.)

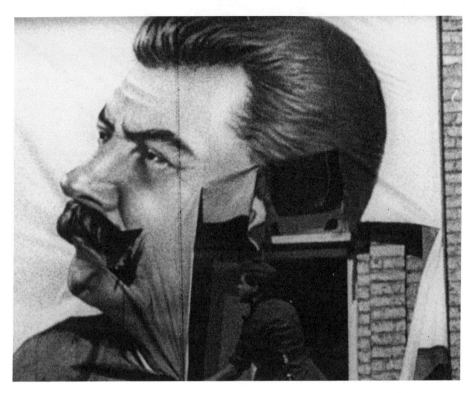

German, or Ukrainian auxiliary, soldier destroys picture of Stalin. Probably shot in Lwów, end of June 1941. See page 66. (*Deutsche Wochenschau/ Transit Film, Munich.*)

Ukrainian, or Polish, woman weeps over corpse, probably taken outside the Brygidka Prison, Lwów, just after the German troops and camermen arrived in the city in June 1941. The NKVD guards of the prison had massacred the prisoners, perhaps the vast majority of them political, before hastily decamping from the city before the onrushing Wehrmacht and its Ukrainian auxiliary allied troops. Such massacres occurred in most of the prisons of Soviet-occupied Poland at the time. See page 65. (*Deutsche Wochenschau*/Transit Film, Munich.)

Walter Ulbricht with Red Army propaganda group broadcasting to German troops on the front lines in the Soviet Union, 1942. Ulbricht is fourth from the left. (ZPA.)

Conference of the National-Komité "Freies Deutschland," in Moscow,
early 1944. Note Wilhelm Pieck, more the popular KPD figurehead leader,
correctly placed to suggest his leadership role, while Walter Ulbricht, even
then the more powerful of the two, takes a more modest place. (Ulbricht
with beard, facing camera, left center.) See page 82. (ZPA.)

Marshal G. K. Zhukov at a forward observation
post during the early days of the Battle of Berlin,
April 1945. See pages 115–16 and 218, note 18.
(Mosfilm, Berlin.)

Friedrichstrasse, central Berlin, two days after the German surrender in the city (May 2, 1945). On the right, the Friedrichstrasse railroad and overhead rail station. On the left, the Admiralpalast (today the Metropol theater). The Admiralpalast was one of the few theaters in central Berlin to survive the war. The first opera shown postwar was performed there in August 1945. The KPD used it for most of their initial large gatherings in 1945 and 1946. See page 114. (U.S. Army Signal Corps.)

Opposite page: Polish soldier with Polish flag on the Victory Column in the Berlin Tiergarten, c. May 2, 1945. See page 116. (PAP.)

Street scene with United States Army Jeep in central Berlin, May 4, 1945.
See page 114. (U.S. Army Signal Corps.)

Liberated prisoners of the concentration camp at Mauthausen, Austria, May 6, 1945, pull down the Nazi emblem. (Chronos Film, Berlin.)

The Allied delegation sent by General Eisenhower arrives at Soviet headquarters, Berlin, May 8, 1945. Note the absence of the French flag. See page
116. (U.S. Army Signal Corps.)

Air Marshal Sir Arthur Tedder and Marshal Zhukov, signers of the second
German surrender, at Karlshorst, around, or just after midnight, May 8–9,
1945. Note Zhukov's place behind the hastily gathered paraphernalia of
authority, ashtray and pen-and-ink holder. See page 115. (U.S. Army Signal
Corps.)

German Field Marshal Keitel salutes on entering the room where the second German surrender was enacted, May 9, 1945, in Karlshorst. See page 117. (U.S. Army Signal Corps.)

Beginning the all-night celebration *à la russe* after the surrender ceremony, early morning on May 9, 1945: left to right, Tedder, Zhukov, and American Army Air Force General Carl Spaatz. See page 117. (U.S. Army Signal Corps.)

Polish officers of the Soviet-organized Polish army and a Red Army officer, probably at a review on May 9, 1945, in Polish-occupied German Pomerania. (PAP.)

Victory Day (May 9, 1945) scene before the ruins of the Great Theater, Warsaw. (PAP.)

The Polish delegation arrives in Germany for the discussion of Poland's future borders at the Potsdam Conference, end of July 1945. Second from left, holding hat, Stanisław Mikołajczyk; Bolesław Bierut with hand on hat. See page 145. (PAP.)

German civilians being given bread by Red Army soldiers (probably staged) after the fall of Breslau, May 1945. See page 121. (PAP.)

DIE LEHRE
VON
KARL MARX
IST
ALLMÄCHTIG,
WEIL SIE
WAHR IST!

(LENIN)

A KPD cultural conference, probably in the Admiralpalast, February 1946. This shows how quickly the KPD was able to organize to influence all aspects of German life in the SBZ. Wilhelm Pieck is sixth from right in the front row, just to the left of his newly painted (January 1946) portrait. The slogan reads: "The teaching of Karl Marx is all-powerful because it is true!—Lenin." (ZPA.)

4

BACKDROP FOR THE DEVELOPING COLD WAR: WARTIME CONFLICT OVER POLAND

IN JULY 1941, after the German attack on the Soviet Union brought the strange alliance between the Allies and the Soviets, General Sikorski had to settle for an agreement with Stalin that was ambiguous with respect to the future of Poland. Churchill's concerns were still, as before, to defeat the Germans, but whereas Poland's western border had served him in his personal agitation for war in 1939 as an utterly rigid trip wire, he now seemed indifferent toward Poland's traditional role in the core of historical Europe. He also appears to have forgotten a strong, centralized Germany's even more critical role in that Europe.

Even the dimmest prospect of a victorious Soviet march westward into central Europe ought to have triggered an alarm in London and well beyond it, but if Churchill, and Whitehall, did have misgivings, the agreement of July 1941 put such misgivings aside. For the time being, differences and long enduring conflicts between the Western Allies and the Soviet Union were forgotten.

In the agreement with the Polish government-in-exile, the Soviets did recognize it as the representative of the Polish people, and did renounce the treaties made with the Germans with respect to the 1939 border changes. They also withdrew all references to ethnographical frontiers—as if such could really have been drawn instead of just concocted as in September 1939 in the lively Soviet propaganda mills. Although the London Poles still did not know the full extent of the Soviet murders and forced emigration of Polish citizens, it was agreed that Polish prisoners of war and Poles who had been forced into exile in the Soviet Union were to be given "amnesty"—implying they had committed some crime by defending, or residing in, a country Stalin had attacked. A Polish army was to be formed to fight on the Russian front, though essentially under the command of the London Poles. This was a concession that should have indicated to the Allies how weak a position the Soviet leaders saw themselves in at the time; it could well have been used to Allied diplomatic advantage, for it was quite evident that, with the German armies moving steadily toward Moscow, the Soviets needed all the help they could get from the West—and more. Indeed, their desperate imaginings probably pictured that aid far larger than the Western powers could, at the time, physically deliver.

The Polish insistence that the agreement of July meant the revocation of the territorial changes made earlier at their expense and without their consent was soon reinforced by the Atlantic Charter, issued on August 14, 1941. In it, Churchill and Roosevelt, whose country was still a big step from being a participant in the war, inveighed against territorial aggrandizement on behalf of all the democracies, for popular self-determination, and for open, liberal economic systems and international cooperation. Roosevelt deeply loved these declarations of principles. The Soviets, in September, issued what appeared to be an acceptance of the Charter, then almost immediately began to violate it—as did the British, and shortly thereafter, the Americans, by supporting Stalin when it came down to Soviet territorial aggrandizement.[1]

By December 1941, the Germans were only a few miles from Moscow. Nonetheless, Stalin, although in a desperate military position, was suddenly and disingenuously telling General Sikorski that he wanted a few changes in the 1939 eastern Soviet-Polish border. Ignoring the implications of Stalin's remark, Sikorski joined Stalin in issuing a statement seemingly concocted in the Comintern itself: "The German imperialism of Hitler is the worst enemy of mankind. No compromise with it is possible [in a Europe] . . . destroyed as it has been by the German barbarians."[2] A few days later, Stalin was telling Anthony Eden that he wanted the borders he got from his western conquest in Poland of 1939 (as well as the rest of his gains from the pact with Hitler); when these were set, he said, a postwar Poland could be territorially expanded in the west at the expense of the Germans. Once again, Churchill and Eden showed little interest in defending Poland's borders. Stalin's claims seem not to have raised any hackles. Yet neither the British leaders nor anyone else among the Western Allies seemed to doubt that the Atlantic Charter reflected the war aims and principles of all the "United Nations," as the allies now termed themselves, including the Soviet Union. Obviously the Germans had few advocates in London and Washington to take up their cause.

So the authors of the Atlantic Charter themselves helped to send it the way of Woodrow Wilson's Fourteen Points. Stalin had, at this point, initiated action involving German border changes to benefit himself as one prospective victor. He thought like an old-time pirate of garnering booty in war. For him, territorial swag, a spiritual scalp, or even the corpse of the vanquished, as shall be seen, were traditional rewards for winning. He was gifted at making up the excuses, fact or fancy, that he needed for any particular occasion. Like Frederick the Great, who is alleged to have said that he would find historians to make up his excuses, Stalin had whole echelons of historians directly or indirectly doing his job. He had no regard for the objective lessons societies have so painfully acquired in the course of history; by contrast, the anglophone powers, after their experience in World War I, shied away from such childlike diplomacy for their own behalf. They, in any event, had no territorial claims on the Continent.

It soon became altogether clear that the Soviet bureaucracy was not going to make any real effort to get the Polish exiles and prisoners organized and properly armed, especially difficult amid the chaos of war and the mass evacuations of government, factories, peoples, and livestock eastward. Still, the Polish command and newly arrived Polish diplomats from the exile government suddenly had some access to their far-strewn countrymen in the Soviet Union. But the provisions and arms necessary for the equipping of an army of the dimensions promised in the Stalin-Sikorski agreement did not appear, in spite of the urgent Soviet need for trained military manpower. Nor were thousands of Polish officers, known to have been captured by the Soviets, produced from the prison camps to staff the new Polish army.

The experiences of the Polish soldiers who could be located in the

Soviet Union, and their commander, General Władysław Anders, showed well enough what was to be expected from the Soviets. Anders, a prisoner since 1939, had been confined in the Lubianka prison in Moscow. The Poles recalled their brutal treatment, forced marches, massacres, wretched conditions of transport, disease, lack of food, and primitive camps. Some even then assessed the chaos and disorganization in the face of the Nazi advance inside the Soviet Union as portending its defeat, the latter a prospect bearing heavily on their own future there. All in all, the situation became such that the Polish commanders in London and the Soviet Union, acting in consultation with the British, decided to withdraw as many Poles as possible from the Soviet Union for further training in Iran and the Near East. That great trek south took place in the spring of 1942. Yet well over a million Poles still remained in the Soviet Union.[3]

Even in the second summer of the war in the east the Germans turned in great victories. But already the Soviet armies had proved that under the right conditions they could fight back effectively. Hitler's generalship eventually required the German eastern front to be stretched to the utmost, which of course also strained German lines of communication and supply. Once the Russians had built up and given their forces more modern equipment, including a vast supply of truck transport sent by the United States and Great Britain, they were able to face the Germans along broad fronts equally favorable to the operations of both sides. That happened by the summer of 1943. In the meantime, the Soviets began to take skillful advantage of the stretched German lines of communication, the brutal winter conditions, and Hitler's military incompetence, to push the Germans back, and, as in the case of the Battle of Stalingrad, to deal them harsh and costly defeats.

There is no doubt that Stalin's willingness to oblige the Western powers and the Poles in the summer of 1941 was directly related to how much help he wanted of them. But the blocking and defeat of the Wehrmacht, which had rolled across western Europe and France, aroused the national passions of Stalin and the technologically backward and remote Soviet peoples. The war was now a patriotic war of hatred against the western, Teutonic enemy. Suddenly the Red Army was holding and moving west. Stalin had mobilized the peasant hopes and wrath of millions of slaves of the new Russian empire to "annihilate the German aggressor."

What the British had effectively given Stalin diplomatically, what the Americans were giving him, at first only passively, was a free hand to arrange matters behind the Soviet front and to describe that arrangement as he chose. The Western Allied leaders were unaware of conditions behind Soviet lines, in part kept that way by Soviet censorship, and blocked by their preoccupations and preconceptions from being willing to learn, or from applying to policy design what the informed among their many counselors told them. It is said that Churchill even suspended British anti-Soviet intelligence for the duration of the war—at a time when the British ministries and other government agencies were riddled with Soviet spies. In such favorable circumstances, Stalin was effectively director of an institution, the "Big Three," where the other members were self-blindfolded. The British by early 1942 had privately allowed Stalin a free hand to arrange matters in the Baltic states, just as he had done in 1939 with Hitler's connivance, and to reclaim the parts of Romania that he had taken in 1940. He could therefore easily contemplate the reannexation of eastern Poland as well, though Poland was the one ally among his territorial acquisitions of 1939 and 1940 whose government had a wartime representation in London and Washington, and was, indeed, Britain's first ally, at a time when the Soviets were Hitler's.[4]

Churchill and Roosevelt had inattentively drifted into the position of being unable to deal with the settlement of the territorial and governmental issues of the war before its conclusion, leaving Stalin, who was free to disinform and obfuscate where he could control the output of information, the benefit of doubt in all encounters where he could sow confusion as to what was happening. Even that early, Western leaders seemed almost fearful of offending him and jointly prepared to appease him. Soviet and local censorship got in the way of would-be honest journalists, who were also put off by the forceful cajoling of American and British governments to go along with local authority in Moscow for the sake of harmony.

Some of the uncritical journalists were among the most famous voices of the time. Some reporters, even some of those from conservative journals, were zealous supporters of the Stalinist regime, if not Stalinist agents. (At least one correspondent of the *Times* of London and the *New York Times* stayed on after the war to become a full-fledged Stalinist propagandist, in a way duplicating the record of the long-term prewar *New York Times* correspondent there.) The main leader writer of the London *Times* systematically twisted poli-

tics, geography, and ethnography in his writings to suit a false picture of a benevolent Russian patrimony in eastern Europe, thereby
sustainedly bamboozling the conservative and influential readership that should have been most alert to Stalin's threat to traditional Europe. These journalists, and their editors, were the sole
interpreters and organizers of information for the English-reading
publics of what was happening on the eastern front, and in Moscow,
at a time when Muscovite and British wartime censorship and the
self-censorship of American journalists, plus the official might of
the American Office of War Information and an extreme amount of
goodwill toward the Soviet Union in some higher journalistic quarters, effectively blocked such critical or anti-Soviet information.
Writers and governments collectively encouraged the notion that
skepticism toward the USSR was the equivalent of denying support
to the domestic war effort.[5]

As a result of this kind of quasi censorship in the United States,
and active censorship in London, no major segment of Western opinion could develop in wartime to question attentively the all too evident willingness of Western leaders to accept Stalin's moves and to
support them, or at least explain them favorably, to their peoples.
From Hollywood to London, the media patriotically cranked out
pro-Soviet propaganda, "in support of the war effort." Soviet sympathizers, including some Communist agents, in the British and
American ministries and agencies and in Hollywood, helped shape
public opinion.[6] The British ambassador in Washington described an
important aspect of the contemporary American liberal stance as
"pro-Bolshevik," but he might just as easily have used the term also
to describe a vast amount of influential opinion much closer to
Whitehall.

To be sure, the Polish government-in-exile was itself not undi-
vided in its view of how to deal with the Soviets. It represented
many groups from prewar Polish society, where political discord was
abundant. General Sikorski was disposed to compromise with the
Soviets on the final line of the eastern border of a renascent Poland, partly because that position ensured him a better hearing with
the British government. But it was nonetheless quite apparent that
strong anti-Polish sentiment had developed among many members
of the British diplomatic service and in the British press—perhaps,
one can suggest, because the Poles had a discomfiting propensity to
flatten the illusions about the Soviets that the Westerners desper-

ately wished to hold.[7] In any event, Sikorski could not make enough concessions of the lands of the former Polish state to pacify Stalin.

Sikorski's original plan to block Stalin's move west was founded on the idea of a confederation of the western Slavic states, a middle European buttress against the Bolshevik state and the Germans. This was no more than the rebirth of a vision held by Polish Marshal Józef Piłsudski in the aftermath of World War I. In 1941, Stalin, in weakness, had cheered the notion, but by 1942 it was evident to the Poles, if not to the Westerners, that Stalin was not going to allow any potentially strong nation, or group of nations, to exist on his western borders, wherever he might fix them. The Czechs, who might have collaborated with the Polish exile government, moved steadily to a pro-Soviet position as early as 1942, and in 1943 made a private alliance with Stalin, thereby abandoning the idea of an east central European confederation they had begun to work on in 1940 after the Hitler-Stalin Pact. Churchill and Roosevelt failed to see the need for such a confederation and not only ignored Sikorski's warnings but also did nothing to deter the Czechs. Edvard Beneš, the exiled Czech president, who controlled the Czech National Council in London, raced inexplicably toward his fatal love affair with Stalin, and the subsequent loss of part of his own state and its independence.[8]

Stalin early on predictably began to move to disengage himself from formal diplomatic arrangements with the London Polish government. Even as Sikorski came to Moscow in late 1941, Stalin was secretly sponsoring a group of collaborators to represent a different Polish public opinion. At about the same time, he secretly dispatched a set of Communist agents to German-occupied Warsaw. They took their orders from the head of the Comintern, Georgii Dimitrov.[9] But in any case, Stalin soon had no need for the Anders army, for the Soviet Union could, by the end of 1942, bring up its own organized manpower. It seems unlikely in the extreme that Stalin would have used the Poles even if he had needed them, because he would not have trusted them. Reorganized, equipped, and trained by the West, they would have become a potential Polish fifth column inside the Soviet front lines, or, holding part of them, a danger to all the Soviet leader's schemes. Without the Poles on hand, Stalin had no military force to oppose his will in redisposing Poland's territories, or in organizing a new Polish state, or even in orchestrating its incorporation into the Soviet Union as another volunteer republic. The departure of the organized Polish units in 1942 simply removed an obstacle of potentially major importance to his plans to dispose of matters in the east as he wished. It is scarcely unlikely that he did his level best to create conditions that encouraged them to go.

At the turn of 1943, with the first stunning Red Army success in bottling up the German Sixth Army in Stalingrad, Stalin began to move directly to set aside the London Polish government-in-exile and to establish a Polish government that suited his plans. After the fall of eastern Poland to the Soviets in 1939, a small group of Polish pro-Soviet collaborators had been allowed to maintain a tiny remnant of Polish cultural life in Lwów. Though Stalin was hard at work depopulating the city and all eastern Poland of its Poles, this little group of intellectuals eventually began to support Polish plays, readings, and lectures in a city that was rapidly being stripped of its Polish character. Many of these people worked translating Soviet school texts into Polish. Under the editorship of a trusted Stalinist, Wanda Wasilewska, who was later married to Oleksandr Korneichuk, a member of the Ukrainian Soviet political hierarchy and a Soviet vice-commissar for foreign affairs, they had been permitted to publish a Polish literary-cultural monthly. This journal, *Nowe Widnokręgi* (New Horizons), printed in Moscow, became the political and literary journal for educated Poles in the Soviet Union. When the Germans attacked Lwów on their way east, many of the Soviet collaborators, including Wasilewska, escaped to the east along with the commissars. Some months later, far to the east of Lwów, the publication was expanded. Its contents serve as an important indicator of the development of Stalin's wartime Polish policy.

Wasilewska, who had become a Soviet citizen and a member of the Supreme Soviet in 1940, also wrote for *Izvestiia*, *Pravda*, and *Soviet Ukraine* both before and after 1941. After leaving Lwów, she became a "regimental commissar," later a colonel, in the Red Army. From her official Moscow apartment she later had easy access to the major Soviet governmental agencies. Through Korneichuk she may have had close connections with Stalin, who liked her writing; perhaps for that reason, she won a Stalin Prize for literature in 1943 (though the announcement of the prize, in the Soviet newsreel [*Soiuz Kinozhurnal*], did not mention her Polish origins).[10]

The eastern sources tell us that, in January 1943, Wasilewska and Alfred Lampe, another Red stalwart, sole surviving member of the prewar Polish Communist Party Central Committee, asked Stalin, who had liquidated Lampe's colleagues and still maintained diplomatic relations with the London Poles, to form a Center for Polish Affairs. It was to take over the tasks that the still officially accredited London-affiliated Polish embassy was designated to perform. It would not suggest undue skepticism to seek behind the move a hand more powerful than Wasilewska's.

The writers of *Nowe Widnokręgi* had for some time been printing complaints about the alleged misbehavior of the London Poles and their representatives in the USSR, and about their pretentions to the prewar borders. In a 1941 issue before the German attack, one writer in the journal declared that since there was no longer to be a Poland, Poles might find utmost joy in being citizens of the great Soviet Union, led by "great Stalin." During the summer of 1942, these Moscow writers suddenly accused General Anders, not long after he was released from the Lubianka, of being anti-Jewish, a complaint none of them had ever made about Hitler between 1939 and 1941. They also complained about unnamed reactionaries in the Polish government in London, and about the "pre-1939" view prevailing among them. In January 1943, *Nowe Widnokręgi* published a letter to the editor calling for the creation of a new Polish army in the east.[11]

This writing marked the beginning of Stalin's campaign to collect a larger group of Poles loyal to him to take over the remainder of Poland following the Red Army conquest he might now, after Stalingrad, more readily imagine. Korneichuk, the Soviet deputy foreign minister, used an article in *Pravda* to call for breaking the 1941 pact with the London Poles. The Soviet newsreel and other government organs of information announced the formation of a League of Polish Patriots (ZPP) in Moscow. Colonel Wasilewska, as she had become, at Stalin's behest served as its organizer, calling together old comrades and a variety of other expatriates, voluntary and involuntary, the latter (as it later gradually turned out) to serve as window dressing, from the far corners of Soviet exile. The group was to help liberate Poland, a cause Wasilewska had begun to espouse in 1941, after having remained silent on the subject from 1939 until the German attack on the Soviet Union.[12]

The League would soon become the official point of agglomeration of those Poles who could be relied upon to carry out Stalin's will, the beginning of the establishment of a new Polish government along Bolshevik lines. It would recall the Finnish "democratic" government that Stalin had set up for his purposes in that country in 1939, and it would be the immediate predecessor of its German equivalent, the National-Komité "Freies Deutschland," which would just as "spontaneously" emerge among German exiles and prisoners in the USSR a few months later.

The pattern of Soviet preparation for Europe's future was filling out. A non-Communist, friendly to the USSR, often a superannuated "social democrat," or a social democrat "we can work with," would head each "liberation committee." (Stalin reasoned that someone old would be easier to get along with, or, perhaps, to intimidate.) These committees were formats for, sometimes the very nuclei of, Stalin's later provisional governments.[13]

Out of the Kremlin closet came other long nurtured plans for Poland's future. First, a new journal joined *Nowe Widnokręgi*. It was the League's *Wolna Polska* (Free Poland), also edited by Wasilewska. The new journal had to have been long in the planning, for even the appearance of such an organ, in a land where the government had tight control of the main information enterprises, would have to have been carefully calculated. In the journal, the League of Polish Patriots announced that it was ready to renounce the Polish territories east of the Curzon line. Their slogans quoted the Soviet news agency, TASS: the Atlantic Charter cannot be held to stand in the way of the unification of the Ukrainian and White Russian peoples. A new Polish army, independent from the London government, was also announced, and was soon founded (April–May 1943) on Soviet soil to collaborate with the Red Army in the march to the west. Stalin now had exactly what he wanted: a group on which to build a tractable Polish government independent from London, with its own army, but of course under Red Army control.[14]

All Stalin needed now was some excuse to disestablish the authority of the London Poles and Sikorski. He still had diplomatic relations with them, but their representatives in the USSR had for some time been ignored, abused, and even imprisoned. Stalin's plan was typically simple: to have the Soviet diplomatic representatives in London, locally much feted by enthusiastic British patriots, start a campaign of complaints about the London Poles as being insufficiently "democratic," and unfriendly to the Soviet Union. The Moscow press began to thunder at the London Poles. Because Sikorski's government was adamantly opposed even to the small concessions that Sikorski himself might have agreed to on the issue of Poland's eastern frontiers, the Soviets were ideally placed to reassure the British that the London Poles were troublemakers.[15]

Stalin's excuse for the diplomatic break he sought was offered up, strangely enough, by the German propaganda minister, Dr. Goebbels. In April 1943, Goebbels broke the news that the Germans had discovered the stacked corpses of thousands of dead Polish officers, priests, and some civilians buried in sandy graves under recently planted pine trees at Katyn Forest, near Smolensk, in German-occupied Russia. The Germans had earlier collected at Katyn a team of internationally recognized forensics experts, including some from neutral nations. They had published a detailed investigative report, including the names of all the identifiable dead, and reported these along with the findings of the experts. They reported that all evidence confirmed that the execution-style deaths had occurred in the spring of 1940, when the area was under Soviet control. Many of the dead were, of course, Polish army officers—the Germans published their names and the details of their lives—who had managed to get away from the Germans only to fall into Soviet hands; others were civilians who had fought the German invaders. They were the thousands whom the Polish army recruiters in the USSR had been unable to find in 1941. Stalin's answer at that time to Sikorski's direct question about what had happened to them was that they had all escaped Soviet captivity into Japanese-occupied Manchuria.

The revelation of the Katyn Forest massacre was the first public indication broadcast to the West of the mass murders and similar horrors that the Soviet Union had effected during its occupation of eastern Poland from 1939 to 1941. We know now that the dead officers were only a tiny fraction of the Poles who died or were killed during the period of Soviet occupation. The Polish government-in-exile at that time knew something about the deportations and the deprivations and death in former eastern Poland, but not the whole dimensions, and they had difficulty getting the story of what they did know to the British political leaders.

In April 1943, the Poles in London could do little more than demand an urgent investigation of the Katyn matter. With a view to finding a reliable neutral opinion, they asked the International Red Cross to investigate. Though the area of Katyn Forest was under German occupation, the Soviets, according to international law, were still the landlords, and they denied the Red Cross all access.

Pro-Soviet public opinion was still so strong in Britain, as official policy demanded, that the Poles were seen to be impetuously provoking the ally, the Soviet Union. This was just one more proof that the Poles did not have the same desperate interest Churchill had in getting along with, that is, in fact, appeasing, Stalin. Stalin then denounced the London Poles as Nazi accomplices and forthwith "suspended" diplomatic relations with them. It was then simply a matter of time before the League of Polish Patriots, and ancillary groups, would furnish the nucleus of a new Polish government that would do Stalin's bidding.[16]

Advisers in the United States State Department and the British Foreign Office spotted the Soviet scheme and predicted its goals even then, but Roosevelt and Churchill chose to ignore their warnings, and, relying on wartime censorship and cooperative journalists, did their utmost to suppress all news about the Soviet Union's role in the Katyn massacre.[17] Churchill did, however, begin to see (as other diplomatic observers had seen long before) the possibility that Stalin was planning to set up his own Polish government. Churchill stood by Sikorski in spite of his anger with the London Poles over Katyn, but, privately, he began to pressure Sikorski to shuffle his cabinet to remove those whom Moscow was denouncing publicly as "fascists." So Stalin had not only created the nucleus of his own Polish government, he had also arranged to continue to interfere in the conduct of the one he had made out as his enemy. At least in this instance, the Americans stayed out of the picture, letting it remain a British show. And it was obvious from this time that Churchill, in his efforts to placate the Soviets, would ever more often run head on into the increasingly alarmed, and mulish, London Poles.[18] They perceived that the governmental "shuffle" Stalin was trying to arrange would certainly end with them out of office in Warsaw, and Stalin's friends in.

The matter of Poland was one of the main issues at the Teheran Conference of the Big Three held November 28–December 1, 1943. In direct, secret talks with Stalin, the British and the Americans agreed that an approximation of the Curzon line would constitute the eastern Polish frontier: it would be very close to the line agreed to by Hitler and Stalin. Anthony Eden even termed it the Molotov-Ribbentrop line, Stalin snapping back, "Call it what you like."[19] The Americans and British thereby totally conceded the Soviet position on the key border issue in return for what they then allowed themselves to think was Stalin's agreement to accept the return of the London Polish government, minus a few "fascists" (not a term anyone sought to define) to a liberated Warsaw. Roosevelt, clearly working at cross-purposes with Secretary of State Cordell Hull, did not want any of the information on the territorial cession or Katyn to get to the strongly Democratic, blue-collar, Polish-American voters. Although Roosevelt had never met Stalin, he had his own preconceived notion of him and wanted to construct an appealing image of the Soviet leader to suit the concessions he intended to give him in his role as ally and imagined partner in his new world government. Roosevelt fancied Stalin to be insecure, not well versed in international affairs, perhaps ill at ease with foreign statesmen. He had already resolved to concede him what he wanted in the nature of frontiers to alleviate his insecurity, and he particularly wanted to avoid giving him the impression that the Anglo-Americans were ganging up on him. The radical territorial and governmental changes Roosevelt was thinking of could be covered up by "plebiscites" and population transfers—like those the Soviets had conducted earlier in Poland and the Baltic states? The American president, in the case of Katyn and the territorial rearrangement of Poland and the destruction of the other east European states he intended, had absolute secrecy in mind to cover the whole business.

The British government had itself already forbidden all press references to the border issue. Roosevelt's public pose was that all territorial changes would await a peace conference. Following the governmental lead, the Western press assured readers that the Soviets had no plans for territorial expansion in Europe. Meanwhile, Stalin and Molotov busied themselves telling gullible Westerners and others that the Soviet Union would respect the rights of smaller nations.[20]

To sweeten the pill for the Poles at Teheran, the Big Three resolved to offer them major parts of Germany in compensation for eastern Poland. That had been Stalin's original proposal in 1941, and Churchill, Eden, and Roosevelt, apparently with little reflection, had accepted it. Churchill was soon to make it known, to be sure only privately, that the Atlantic Charter would not apply to Germany.[21] Nor had any of the Westerners then seemingly reflected on the forced transfers of population that would be involved: it was implicit that the indigenous remaining Polish population of the lands east of the Bug was to be forcibly moved west. It seems incredible at this point that neither Roosevelt nor Churchill seems to have been appalled by the prospect of the tragedy that would inevitably accompany such transfers, nor did they apparently feel much concerned about the probable reaction of their respective publics to this sort of secret conniving with Stalin—all too reminiscent of the forced depopulations that Stalin and Hitler had already so effectively mastered. Quite simply, what was left of the Polish people east of the Curzon line would be moved west (completing the work of depopulation Stalin began in the years 1939–41), to take over the shops and gardens, to sit down at the tables and occupy the beds vacated by the Germans who were to be evicted from eastern Germany.

Roosevelt, it seems, allowed himself to believe that the population transfer would be done voluntarily and humanely. Churchill might have remembered the forced exchanges of Greeks and Turks after World War I, but he was no more interested than Roosevelt in monitoring the transfers to make certain that they were peaceful. Roosevelt, indeed, was meeting privately with Stalin, dealing with him according to his fancy that he could handle him best of all, man to man, in this case behind Churchill's back and against the will of his Secretary of State. He put aside all that he knew of Stalin's crimes and warnings of Soviet expansionist intentions, suggesting that he and the Soviet dictator were one at heart. He flexed his private resolve and confidently assured Stalin that he, too, could be tough on the Germans.[22]

Thus coddled, and with the Polish border issue seemingly settled to his satisfaction, Stalin then suddenly volunteered a new proposal: he wanted the northeastern part of Germany and the hometown of, among countless others, many of Germany's most famous historical intellectuals, Königsberg. Although the grounds he supplied for this request were factually incorrect, no one asked about or checked the details of his claims.[23] Churchill's later rationalizations on behalf of Stalin's arguments harked back to his favorite historical theme, World War I.[24] Roosevelt may have been under the impression that the minor changes in the Curzon line that were to be arranged between the Poles and Stalin might still allow the Poles to retrieve the important city of Lwów and the surrounding area, but he did not press for any specific quid pro quo for his acceptance of Stalin's eastern Polish border. What the Westerners had done in secret with Stalin was to abandon Britain's first ally, the London Poles, and to seek, beyond public view, to compensate the Poles with what the West-

erners themselves did not own—all this in violation of the principles of national self-determination so ringingly announced in the
Atlantic Charter.

The London Poles were not themselves wholly innocent in this
demographic mayhem. Even before 1939, Polish nationalists had
been methodically beating the drums to expand Poland westward at
Germany's expense. Sikorski early in the war foresaw that the Poles
might have to compromise their aims on the eastern frontier and get
compensation in some way in the west. He, apparently encouraged
by the French, was one of the first to suggest changes in the prewar
German-Polish borders. His diplomats had early begun to push the
notion of Poland's expansion westward at the expense of the Germans, though not fixing it as a quid pro quo for possible losses in
the east. They began their assault to the west by arguing that Poland
must acquire German East Prussia, which had ancient connections
with the former Kingdom of Poland (as did, for that matter, lands
from Latvia to Saxony to the Black Sea).[25]

In the long run, however, the Poles had very little to say about
what was decided. Few of them were ever to get back to Warsaw, and
most of those who did, after the war, soon fled, once again in fear
for their lives, to London. Stalin, having succeeded in his plan to
get an Allied agreement on changing Poland's borders to meet his
wishes and on satisfying the principle of population change, went
on to arrange matters exactly as he chose behind the screen of the
advancing Red Army front. His agents for this work were his Moscow Poles, suitably rewarded for their faith and collaboration.

Stalin wasted no time in taking his prize. Beginning in January
1944, only a month after the conference at Teheran, Soviet troops
began crossing the old Polish border westward. The Soviet media
celebrated the reconquest of the cities there as they had celebrated
the recapture of the cities of the prewar Soviet Union, with an-
nouncements and fanfare, and the proclamation of their return to
the *rodina*, the Soviet homeland. There was little doubt about the
future of these Polish centers. Nothing was said about postponing
the people-moving decisions, and the matter in fact never came up
in Western minds until the end of the hostilities, when many of the
dismal victims of Stalin's work appeared before Western eyes. So
far as Stalin was concerned, everything with respect to Soviet borders was already completely settled. Only Roosevelt and Churchill
would somehow persist in believing it was not.

Then, in July 1944, Stalin brought out one more big surprise. In Chełm, the first town west of the Curzon line, he suddenly introduced his Polish candidates of the League of Polish Patriots mixed with some underground Communists from German-occupied Poland as the Polish Committee of National Liberation (PKWN). This was the scheme he had been working on since the Teheran Conference, except that instead of putting his picked Poles into power behind the usual façade of a provisional "democratic" government, he set them up as a National Committee. The name—Molotov's suggestion though perhaps originally Stalin's—was meant to recall that of General de Gaulle's London-based Committee of National Liberation. The members were selected by the NKVD. Their appearance in the first liberated corner of the Poland Stalin recognized as Polish was meant to be taken as a spontaneous expression of the Polish national will. In fact, Stalin, as we have since learned, invented this government-to-be, gave it its name and role, helped pick the members (and told some of them their party affiliations), personally allotted their resources down to the last lend-lease Studebaker, put them in place, told them what they had to do, and drew the borders of the nation they would rule. To those members of more independent spirit among them who wanted to wait for the slow movers toward revolutionary social change in wartime, Stalin made the course clear: *perestroitsia ilii ustupit'* (change things or scram).[26]

In exchange for the enormous gains that Poland was to be given at the expense of the Germans, this Polish cadre could allow itself to give up all claims to the eastern half of their country. Stalin made this renunciation a precondition of their status, effectively the new government of Poland. The territorial booty to be taken from the Germans was to be not only compensation for the loss to the east but also implicitly a modest revenge for what they had suffered at the hands of Germany.[27]

Thus Stalin, without a peace conference, had in place a government in all but the name, of his own selection, on Polish soil. He would make it a government in name as soon as possible, moving stage by stage while the West stood by in diplomatic silence and kept up their constant secret prodding of the London Poles to cooperate with him. Churchill still imagined that by bending to Stalin he might get the exile government back to Warsaw. As news came from Moscow of the future Lublin group's new status, he assured the cabinet that its members were neither Quisling nor Communist.

Yet Quisling was the very term he would apply to them, along with one or two others even more insulting, just a few months later in one of his rants directed at the London Poles. At just about the same time, he vowed to the Polish premier, Stanisław Mikołajczyk (who had replaced General Sikorski after his untimely death in July 1943), that, "for him personally the Polish question was a question of principle. . . . If the Soviet government were to prove unreasonable and impossible, he . . . would back the Poles wholeheartedly. . . . Poland was Great Britain's original ally. . . . If the Soviets wanted to legalize international 'rape,' he would be in the vanguard of those who would be ready to resist oppression"[28]

The implicit doubts behind the bravado notwithstanding, Churchill was probably working from the hopes inspired by 1944 British policy documents forecasting British-Soviet relations in the postwar world. They were drafted in the Foreign Office and presented to the cabinet by Foreign Secretary Eden. The authors of these papers, among them not a few distinguished academics, overlooked manifest current and past evidence of Soviet duplicities and internal Foreign Office and Moscow chancery minuting and reports critical of Soviet behavior to arrive at some perhaps predictable conclusions. They supported the notion that Stalin would be tractable in dealing with postwar European matters, at least for a few years. Once these position papers were drafted, they evidently fixed general British Foreign Office thinking along paths not dissimilar to Churchill's and Eden's original, and obviously continuing, efforts to appease Stalin. Only considerable further, and disastrous, experience, could now change the course long set (first by inaction, later by choice) in London. For the balance of force on the European continent had radically shifted since 1941 and 1942 to the Soviet side.[29]

Most of the hand-picked members of the PKWN (usually termed the Lublin committee for the city in which it sat), had lived both under the Soviet occupation of Poland and in the Soviet Union; they knew Stalin's treatment of Poland and his own citizens at first hand. When they arrived in Lublin, they had an army and a press, as well as a news and propaganda service that had been set up for them and their new fighting force in the Soviet Union. They also started yet another newspaper, *Rzeczpospolita* (The Republic), which soon became a daily. Lublin, the second important city occupied and indisputably assigned by the Soviets to the new Poland, remained their headquarters from their arrival there in July 1944, until after the fall of Warsaw. In line with Stalin's standard techniques of dissimulation, the most radical social schemes of these Polish Communists and their allies were hidden under a façade of "antifascist" democratization. It was, as we shall see, virtually identical to the façade erected hundreds of miles to the west in Germany in 1945–46.

But the Lublin committee and the Soviet armies in liberated Poland were faced with a critical problem: the existence of a large underground Polish Home Army, the Armia Krajowa, supplied and supported from London, which had been fighting the Germans for years and expected to take control of the country on behalf of the government-in-exile. This army had the backing of the overwhelming majority of the population, the mass of which was rapidly coming to detest the Red Army wherever they met it, if only because of its thefts, looting, and disciplined and undisciplined brutality. It was the sort of behavior that had characterized the Soviets abroad between 1939 and 1941, and that was typical of the Red Army wherever it went.[30] The Lublin group had to rely on the Red Army for its authority, however, and this need inevitably brought it to the point of using it and its own Soviet-controlled Polish Army to demobilize, arrest, and destroy units of the Home Army. In some areas this campaign brought about, at this time as well as later, a virtual war of annihilation behind Soviet lines in the Polish countryside.

It was the Home Army that brought Stalin his second great Polish embarrassment after the revelation of the massacre at Katyn by Goebbels. By August 1, 1944, the Red Army had swept to within a few miles of Warsaw, its tanks allegedly moving forward at over 40 miles a day. Soviet radio encouraged the Poles to rise up against the Germans. Acting after these events, and on orders from London, where the government-in-exile, well aware of what Stalin was doing in eastern Poland, hoped to seize and hold power in the Polish capital before the Soviets arrived, a long-planned uprising broke out against the Germans. At first, the Lublin group's press widely disseminated the news of the uprising and its successes; even units of the Communist-controlled underground—a very much smaller group than the London-directed army—patriotically joined the Warsaw uprising of the Home Army. In the first days of the battle, *Rzeczpospolita* stressed the quick advance of the Red Army toward Warsaw. "Warsaw is bleeding," it reported, but the Polish Army and the Red Army are on their way to the rescue. "From a million Polish hearts, from thousands of soldiers' hearts one cry bursts out toward

Warsaw: Warsaw, hold out in the struggle. We hasten with help!" A day later *Rzeczpospolita* reported that it was "at one with the underground Polish army."[31]

Just that very day the chiefs of the Lublin committee had arrived in Moscow to consult with Stalin and to meet with a delegation of London Poles, led by Premier Mikołajczyk. The purpose—and they had been encouraged in this by Churchill and Roosevelt—was somehow to arrange a compromise with the Lublin committee on a postwar government for Poland. Two days later, *Rzeczpospolita* reported that the German defenses before Warsaw had stiffened. The Red Army would not be able to take the city with a direct assault. Furthermore, the Soviet military chiefs wanted to spare the city from destruction. *Rzeczpospolita* also suddenly began calling the uprising a tragedy, and one that could only be blamed on the London government. It quoted from TASS, saying that the Soviet Union denied that the Red Army had encouraged the uprising and that only the emigrés in the West were responsible.[32]

Stalin's policy on this apparently unforeseen uprising now emerged: the uprising would finish as a disaster, in which not only the largest group of the Home Army but also units of the armed forces of Moscow's own left-wing supporters in Warsaw would be destroyed, and along with them much of the influence of the London Poles in the nation. *Rzeczpospolita* signaled the event in the words of the commander of the Soviet-founded Polish army, Michael Rola-Żymierski: the decisive battles for Warsaw would be fought before the year was out. (In early August, Stalin had told Mikołajczyk in Moscow that it would be only two weeks.) Ironically, in the west of Europe, Paris had just been liberated by the Free French and the Americans, who had made an enormous effort to take the city undestroyed. Warsaw, at the same time, was being systematically turned into rubble by the Germans as the Soviet armies studiously devoted their attentions elsewhere. Stalin also said he did not want to make a frontal assault on the city for fear it would be destroyed.[33]

From the very moment of arrival of the Lublin committee leaders in Moscow, they had begun criticizing the uprising, defending Soviet behavior in not advancing toward Warsaw and blaming the impending military failure on London. The Lublin leaders got their instructions, even their terminology, directly from Stalin: Rola got his information from the chief of the Red Army on the central Polish front, General Rokossowski. He also got his orders from Stalin.

Rzeczpospolita began to report that the uprising was an "insane and criminal step" that had been undertaken in order to establish the authority of the London émigrés and to thwart the Lublin committee. (This was, of course, not far from the truth.) *Izvestiia* said the Polish patriots acted from "egotistical interests." The leaders of the uprising and the London Poles were "traitors." Although *Rzeczpospolita* went on to suggest that help was to be offered to Warsaw—it actually held out until early October—the suggestions were vague and unspecific.[34] The editors in Lublin, perhaps not privy to Stalin's real intentions, continued to express hope that the city would be rescued by the "glorious Red Army" and that Stalin's Poles would be Poland's liberators.

Once again, with Warsaw in chaos, the issue of Poland's borders became paramount. In 1942, Churchill, and at Teheran, Churchill and Roosevelt, had virtually conceded Stalin the part of Poland east of the Curzon line (wherever that was agreed to lie—on which side of the line, for example, was Lwów?); the London Poles were then to receive territorial compensation at the expense of the Germans. By the early winter of 1944, Churchill and Roosevelt, who still only declared that he would resolve all matters at a peace conference, were ready to concede the Poles all of East Prussia, the League of Nations' territory of the Danzig Free State, and the rest of eastern Germany, including Pomerania, the Eastern Mark Brandenburg, and a substantial portion of northern and eastern Silesia, up to the Oder River 50 miles from Berlin.

Then, in the summer of 1944, Stalin's Polish correspondents from the German-occupied areas then in the Soviet capital, and those others from Moscow who would soon make up the PKWN-Lublin committee, had all found out that Stalin himself wanted the Königsberg area of East Prussia, on which they had set their hearts, and which, it may be inferred, he had earlier promised them.[35] They wanted compensation. They could only win the support of their countrymen, they said, and pacify those Poles reluctant to part with Wilno, Lwów, and the East by giving them compensation in the form of an even more enormous bite of Germany. In a secret agreement in July, Stalin then unilaterally turned over to them the vast bulk of the rest of Silesia all the way to the Lusatian Neisse River, plus a major German port west of the Oder, Stettin.[36] There was no doubt that the Germans there (like Poles to the east of what Stalin described as the Curzon line) were also going to be dispossessed of their homelands. Churchill and Roosevelt had long since agreed to that principle in conceding East Prussia and the other territories much earlier, and by ratifying even vaster changes at Teheran. But now, Stalin unilaterally doubled the numbers of Germans to be driven out. He and the PKWN prepared to keep the whole matter secret until the deed was done.[37]

Roosevelt, unaware of this radical emendation of the already radical surgery agreed to at Teheran, was still trying to convince Mikołajczyk, who, as premier of the London government, was compelled to represent the most democratic face of the London Poles in hope of achieving some sort of reconciliation with the Lublin committee, that the United States would hold out for the return of Lwów. In this Roosevelt had only frail support from the British.[38] They, too, were apparently unaware of Stalin's new border manipulation.

Meanwhile, the Lublin committee, which, though not a government, was acting like one and had publicly been granted diplomatic status as Poland's representative by Stalin, was moving secretly to finish the deal with Stalin about the Curzon line. For this they now would be even better compensated with the considerably larger sections of Germany. In early September, during the darkest days of the Warsaw uprising, the leaders of the White Russian, Ukrainian, and Lithuanian Soviet "governments" went to Lublin.[39] The committee then contracted with them for a mutual exchange of "minority" populations. Stalin's Lublin committee was negotiating the final deal to turn over the eastern half of their country while their capital-to-be, its patriots, their colleagues of the People's Army (Armia Ludowa), and thousands of innocents died. Many, many thousands of others, and not only Poles, would die in the population shuffle to come.

Stalin's policy of depolonizing eastern Poland was to be completely carried out in the middle of the war. He had now arranged all new borders for the future Poland, and was organizing the population transfers that would make the new borders quite final long before the Western Allies had concurred. As with the establishment of the Lublin committee, which would finally declare itself, on January 1, 1945, the Temporary National Government, he had by a final fait accompli gained all his purposes in Poland.

In the fall of 1944, Churchill met with Stalin in Moscow, as Mikołajczyk had done earlier. Part of Churchill's purpose there was a determined quest for some sort of avenue of return for the London Poles. The Lublin Poles, whom even Anthony Eden pegged as "creepy," were, of course, masters of the Stalinist school of disinformation. They let Western reporters know that their choice for premier of a new Poland was Mikołajczyk, and that the last thing on their minds was socialization and nationalization. Their story, not at the time untrue with respect to the premiership, was earnestly reported in the West. The first step toward agricultural collectivization, the breakup of the landowners' estates and other properties above a bare minimum of acreage, began simultaneously in the fall of 1944.[40]

Churchill returned from Moscow to London after the collapse of the Warsaw uprising. He perhaps had some sort of idea of what Stalin had done about increasing unilaterally the German territorial reward to the Lublin committee, seemed publicly to have supported it, then later speciously denied that he did.[41] Averill Harriman, the American ambassador in Moscow, was also aware from the Soviet press of Stalin's singular machinations with respect to the Polish borders. He informed his superiors in Washington that a fait accompli appeared to be in the making.[42]

One can but wonder whether Churchill and Roosevelt had by this time not lost track of the basic issues of a policy toward Poland. Certainly they were substantially in the dark about where matters had settled. Earlier that fall, at the Quebec Conference in September, Churchill and Roosevelt had together contracted in the obviously unworkable Morgenthau Plan to prepare the total dismantling of Germany—its "pastoralization." But the Morgenthau Plan conceded the Poles only East Prussia and a small part of Upper Silesia—far less than Churchill had been pushing, and Roosevelt secretly accepting, for almost a year, and but a fragment of what Stalin had just two months earlier given his Lublin Poles, and what Churchill may have accepted, then denied in October.[43]

What could Churchill and Roosevelt have been thinking of at Quebec? What could Churchill have been thinking about in Moscow, where he and Stalin allowed the discussion to pass in silence over recently destroyed Warsaw, Stalin's refusal to supply it systematically from positions a few miles away during the uprising, or to ease the burden of the British and others, who lost many planes and fliers in the long-range, vain effort to do so? Astonishingly, Churchill seemed pleased with "Uncle Joe," and the two of them together set about dividing up paper spheres of influence in east central Europe and the Balkans in the infamous "percentages" agreement. Perhaps Churchill was now so used to parceling out vast amounts of other people's territory that he never gave such deeds a thought. In any case, the percentages agreement, like the Morgenthau Plan, was never ratified. The former was opposed by American Ambassador Harriman, never directly accepted by Roosevelt (perhaps acting disingenuously), and later ignored and violated in spirit and fact by the Soviets. Yet Churchill's effort is another revelation of his dogged impetuousness, the kind of move that had got him into Stalin's Procrustean bed of territorial change from the outset, and into the kind of trouble he did not seem to know he was in. Perhaps the Western leaders felt that matters only discussed with Stalin were not settled, while the latter assumed just the opposite: once raised or discussed, and unopposed, for him meant settled—so his thinking went, Ambassador Harriman in Moscow later concluded. Roosevelt, Stalin surely had decided, could have his peace conference later to ratify what had already been done.

Events were, in any case, outrunning negotiation and the time that could be allotted to it. With the normal daily preoccupations of wartime, with such distended lines of communication and want of time, the wholesale lack of goodwill and candor on one side, all decisions should, ideally, have been postponed until the calmer atmosphere of a postwar peace conference, as Roosevelt publicly argued. But in the hell of wartime animus toward the hated enemies, ideals clearly never ruled.

And where was moral sense—except in the public platform of the Atlantic Charter and Allied propaganda? Neither Roosevelt nor Churchill ever shied from the idea of a "transfer" of population. Churchill was "not alarmed by these large transferences." Yet the prospect of the same "transferences" appalled the London Poles—those who were supposedly to benefit from them.[44] Both Churchill and Roosevelt had swallowed the Soviet promises to promote the "transferences" humanely, the two Westerners manifestly enshrining their conscience-activated faith as reality.

When the Big Three finally met once again at Yalta, in the Crimea, February 4–11, 1945, the Red Army was close to crossing the Oder River on the way to Berlin. One Soviet commander at the time thought it possible to push on to take the German capital. Behind the Soviet forward lines lay isolated German citadels and vast pockets of German troops and civilians. Major parts of the German east had already fallen, and were being looted and pillaged in the style of the Mongol invasions. Even towns and areas earlier determined by Stalin, or by all the Big Three, to be booty for the Soviet Union and its Polish clients, were being systematically burned, gutted, pillaged, and looted, and subjected to the numberless caprices of the Red Army, whose commanders perhaps knew nothing of Stalin's new borders, and took no trouble, or more likely, were given no opportunity to learn what they were. These months saw an orgy of mindless destruction all over eastern and central Europe, papered over by its remoteness from Western eyes, by the curtain of Soviet disinformation and stonewalling, and by the tractability and voluntary want of curiosity on the part of many Western correspondents behind Soviet lines.

At Yalta, Stalin for the first time suddenly came forth before Roosevelt and Churchill with his newly drawn map. It showed his claim on behalf of the Lublin Poles of the Lusatian, or western, Neisse River as the southern extension of the Oder River line, Poland's new western border. Here he was fulfilling his secret promises of July 1944 to his Lublin clients. The Soviets had already made propaganda mention of the idea by publishing in *Pravda* these territorial demands as those from one of the Lublin spokesmen.[45] The Soviets also permitted it to be made known through the Western press that the Lublin committee (now called the Temporary Provisional Government of Poland) would be taking over administration in the German territories east of that "border" after the Soviet advance farther to the west. They did not, however, reveal that the Poles east of the Curzon line were already, in the middle of winter, being dispossessed and transported west, that they were being pushed in masses—driven by the will of Stalin's Ukrainian satrap, Nikita S. Khrushchev, to complete the job by the impossible date of January 1945—into a hungry Poland disorganized and torn apart by battle and occupation. Warsaw and Cracow had only been liberated in January; Poznań was liberated in late February 1945. The expellees had no fixed destinations and could only move in a vaguely westward direction. And at the same time, the Ukrainians west of the new border were being uprooted in yet more bloody fashion for return to a Soviet homeland they had never known.[46]

Stalin was then continually pressuring the Lublin committee to force through the comprehensive land reform that would parcel out the greater and lesser estates to some of the agricultural population; the same reform was to be carried out in the lands west of the Vistula on the heels of the Red Army moving west, in the spring. No one knows why Stalin pushed the agricultural reform in this period of total confusion, or why he decided that the Poles of the east should be moved out of their organized and potentially productive agricultural areas before the areas had been sown, planted, and harvested, and battle dust had settled. Presumably the idea was to win over the peasants to the new administrations. Stalin made the same hasty moves in eastern Poland in 1939–41, and he pushed quick "land reform" in similar confused circumstances in Soviet-occupied Germany immediately after the war. Clearly, the Provisional Government, after January 1945 in Warsaw, had only vague plans for resettling the easterners to the west and moving out the Germans there. The whole process was going to take a good deal longer than any of them had imagined, and though they had no experience in such matters, they hoped to prevent any Red Army and NKVD brutality to their own citizens, if not to their remaining Ukrainian minority, those Stalin wanted moved east.

The whole situation worsened; everywhere was chaos, everywhere hunger. In the early summer of 1945, a Russian officer driving through what had once been German Silesia noted the empty farmsteads, the unsown fields, the fruit rotting on the trees, a rich land that had only birds for its tenants. In the fall of the same year the British ambassador, making a tour, reported large-scale disorder: Poles, robbed of all their possessions before they had passed the new Soviet borders to the west, dumped without warning in a landscape in which the Red Army had run off with the harvest, the horses, cattle, farm implements, and seed, and had dismantled and shipped the factories eastward. The new Polish government could do little but issue panicky commands to bring in the largely nonexistent harvest. Stalin declined to help with food from the Soviet Union. Probably he had none to give. The hasty "transferences" over vast areas contributed disastrously to the dangerously low food supplies of Poland and the Soviet Union, not to mention the health and safety of the people directly affected, during the inevitable famines of the first postwar winter.[47]

So the Polish borders were already almost an accomplished fact when Stalin took out his new map at Yalta. The State Department

had urged that the Soviets be confronted on Stalin's proposed Western Neisse extension of the Oder River border, but Roosevelt once
again ignored his advisers. The British, in any case, were strangely
determined to adhere to the Oder line even if, as the State Department suggested, withdrawal from support of the Teheran concessions could be used as a powerful pawn to push the Soviets to take
back its unilateral Neisse extension, supported by neither Western
power.[48]

At the same time, the Soviet border work was quickly welcomed
by Charles de Gaulle and the Free French. They, who had apparently
learned nothing from the history of Alsace-Lorraine and the efforts
of the French after World War I to attach parts of western Germany
permanently to France, seemed to expect the precedent of Soviet and
Polish land acquisition in the east would justify their proposed acquisition of German territory in the west.[49] Roosevelt obviously still
preferred at Yalta to ignore the evident truth about Stalin's high-
handed behavior, presumably in the hope that the Soviet goodwill
he still counted on would someday manifest itself. Churchill only
circumlocutorily allowed his disgruntlement on this issue to show
by telling how he thought the Polish goose was being too heavily
stuffed with German food.[50]

By this time the facts ought to have caught up with them, and
perhaps in Churchill's case some of them had. The Poles would
never get Lwów, as Roosevelt still fancied. He and Churchill saw a
Polish government they had not approved stuffing itself more than
they had ever approved. The government was an accomplished fact;
they did not know how much the stuffing was also. This was the
government whose members Churchill, behind their backs, had
taken to calling "those horrible Lublin Poles," and "filthy, loath-
some, bestial Quisling[s]." (Though Eden settled for the adjective
"creepy," he applied that term only after long reflection, so perhaps
there was something in Churchill's less public description.)

Churchill and Roosevelt therefore, responding to Stalin's bold border move, stonewalled at Yalta, not actually approving what Stalin
had done territorially, suddenly reserving their final decision on all
borders for a peace conference to come. Roosevelt maundered about
some sort of compromise that would give the Poles Lwów, and Stalin
allowed him, without providing further factual enlightenment, to go
on.[51] Stalin certainly knew, as he listened patiently, that Lwów was

once again being depolonized at his command as fast as transport—provided in large measure by the Americans' lend-lease Dodges, Studebakers, and Fords, transferred from Soviet forces engaged in the actual war effort—could be found.

Stalin's strategem had worked, owing in part to the extraordinary trust that his two allies still seemed to have in him. In not directly confronting Stalin at Yalta on the issue of the extended Polish borders he alone had arranged, Roosevelt and Churchill could still continue to hope that the Lublin Provisional Government would soon be reorganized with the addition of some of the London Poles; that Mikołajczyk would lead the new government, and that free elections would be organized by the Warsaw regime in the near future. Roosevelt had already given away another of his biggest bargaining chips in telling Stalin that American troops would remain in Europe for only two years after the war. In so doing, he forfeited even this chance of putting up a bluff.

In fact, the forfeited bluff of force majeure was all that would have moved Stalin, beyond the simple sentiments and odd loyalties that occasionally infected even his cold heart. There were truly some of the latter, like his russophilia, that inclined this Georgian to outbursts of pan-Slavonic loyalty. That perhaps explains his strange devotion to getting the Poles a sufficiency of compensation from the Germans for the lands he took from them in the former Polish east. But force was what he really understood and lived by. He put his deep understanding of human nature to his Polish clients, as usual, bluntly: With the Red Army behind you, "you now have such power that if you say two times two is sixteen [even] your opponents will confirm it."[52]

There is yet one small bit of the story to be told to finish off the illustration of Stalin's policy of settling all matters to his own satisfaction, whenever he could, with a fait accompli. As noted, Stalin had promised the Poles in July 1944—indeed, probably well before then—the German harbor city of Stettin as part of their takings. This offer was probably made to compensate them for the loss of the harbor they coveted at Königsberg. But Stettin lay west of the Oder and could in no way be considered part of the territory that Churchill and Roosevelt had earlier included in their concession at Teheran of the Oder River line as the western border of Poland, whatever river was to be regarded as its southerly continuation. It was news to Roosevelt and Churchill at Yalta that they were also ceding Stettin.[53]

There was confusion about that city in the Soviet camp also. When Moscow-trained German cadres affiliated with the National Committee "Free Germany" arrived in early May 1945 in the vans of the Red Army to start the Soviet reorganization of Germany, one group set up their first headquarters in a suburb of heavily damaged Stettin. As part of their work they quickly established a German local authority in the city, with the permission of the Red Army, of course. They obviously intended Stettin to be their northern political headquarters in Germany. The Lublin Poles, now in Warsaw, thought it was theirs by the terms of the secret agreements of the previous July: the Red Army would take it and give it to them, their propaganda had long maintained.[54] On this assumption, a Polish local administration had arrived even earlier and had taken over the city for Poland.

Stalin must have failed to tell his German clients and even his highest agents, who passed the line along to the Germans on the spot, of his promise to the Poles. The local Red Army commander had no idea which of the two claimants was the right one. The Poles, too, were unsure: they received information from the Provisional Government to withdraw, but then they returned, and then they left again. Finally, the Provisional Government authorities (Stalin himself was, well before, the summer of 1945, calling them *the* Government) were joined by token representatives from London, but not quite as agreed upon at Yalta. Around that time the Warsaw government persuaded Stalin, who evidently had been neglecting the matter for some time, to confirm via the Soviet occupation army in Berlin that Stettin would go to the Poles. One Polish author said, without offering any proof, that the Western Allies, whose first echelons arrived in their sectors of Berlin on July 4, denied the Polish proprietorship. But the Soviets ignored them and went ahead issuing their land deeds here, as elsewhere, untroubled. They were in charge. Stalin's German friends were ultimately driven out of a large area west of the Oder, including Stettin, but it required units of the Soviet-controlled Polish army to do the job.[55]

Finally, on July 17, Stalin announced the transfer of Stettin to Poland, therewith confirming the Red Army's move. He would later agree with the Poles to move the border even farther to the West. It was the day of the beginning of the Potsdam Conference. President Harry S Truman, who had assumed office upon Roosevelt's death on April 12, and Churchill were both right on hand in Berlin. They had waited there on Stalin for the beginning of the great postwar conference of the Big Three. They were not consulted. Stettin went unmentioned in the final communiqué from Potsdam on the Polish border, evidently because Stalin did not want it brought up. Nor would he have wanted discussion of the circumstances of its going to Poland at the conference. It therefore came to the Poles as Stalin's ultimate gift.[56]

Early in July, the Western powers at last recognized the Stalin-anointed Provisional Government as the Polish government after Mikołajczyk and a few other London Poles, denounced by the Polish government there, joined it in Warsaw. With this action, the West had completely disowned Britain's first ally, which sat in London, abandoned, reviled by the Soviet press as "pro-Fascist provocateurs," up to "criminal activity," "a gang of pro-Hitlerite agents . . . united in bestial hatred for the U.S.S.R. and the desire to save Hitlerite Germany." This was the same hyperbole that Soviet propagandists always used—against the Finns in 1939, and against the Germans almost all through the war—and would use again as new targets emerged.[57]

At the conference of the Big Three, held in the Berlin suburb of Potsdam, the Westerners reluctantly conceded Poland's administration in all the German territories that they in part, and Stalin acting alone, had given his protégés. The Americans and British had conceded him everything he had taken, the Polish government he organized and the territories he chose, in return for another promise, this time one of future free elections. They never occurred. Meanwhile, for the edification of his Western colleagues, and that of Mikołajczyk, when he finally joined his new colleagues in Warsaw, Stalin put on public trial in Moscow, convicted, and sent off to Siberia the main leaders of London's Home Army in Poland. That army, for years, even as Stalin collaborated with Hitler in the destruction of Europe, had fought for Mikołajczyk and, to be sure, for Churchill, Roosevelt, and later for Stalin, too, against the Germans.[58]

5

BEHIND RED ARMY LINES: GERMANY

SO FAR, we have been following the trail of Stalin's foreign works beginning in 1938, with his prewar encouragement to international conflict in order to dispatch the Red Army west across Europe. The war came to him in a form he did not expect, but the wartime allies who swiftly fell in with his unpublished wishes, and willingly helped him at painful cost to themselves, saved him from even greater disaster. After extravagantly purchased wartime successes, the Red Army began to march west.

Stalin had long been developing his plans for Germany, the keystone of a future bolshevized Europe. German Communist party leaders in Moscow exile had been coordinating their planning on this subject with him at least since 1939. The different local conditions taken into account, the scheme was essentially the same as the one Stalin had in mind for postwar Poland, but he would have to effect it in completely different, largely unpredictable circumstances. And therein lay the trap Soviet power would finally encounter. In 1945, Stalin, flush with success and crowned with laurels from home and abroad, plus a few from his own garden, was yet typically cautious. His purposes in Germany required his agents to carry Soviet influence far to the west of the Red Army occupation lines in central Europe that had been worked out with his Western allies. If his agents carried out their work too boldly, a clash sooner or later between the Soviet Union and the Western Allies was all but certain. That clash would occur when the Western leaders and their advisers realized what most of them had been denying systematically or unsystematically for years—that Stalin was effectively a Trotskyite, running grand-scale schemes having worldwide dimensions from the more than somewhat bizarre ambiance of the Kremlin.[1]

Here we shall tell additional, some egregiously petty, instances of Soviet conduct unbecoming an ally. Many of these were crafted with all possible deliberation in the Kremlin; others appear to have been little more than local eruptions, some unintended, and some certainly uncontrollable, not surprising given the propensity to violence of Stalin's general system of tyranny. They indicate the odd quirks in Stalin's thinking and the strange nature of mechanisms of control he had in mind. These cases offer us now, as additional evidence, what they were beginning to suggest to close observers even then: a view of Soviet leadership and its foreign purposes completely different from that purveyed propagandistically at the time in East and West.

The following account, also founded on documentation from the former East Bloc, builds chronologically on what has come before. The focus of this history of the coming of the Cold War moves westward geographically to carry the story forward as the Red Army and NKVD, the prime mobilizers of Stalin's efficient local support, moved. The facts set forth radically erode the always insubstantial base for the efforts by many earlier writers on the Cold War to cling to rationalizations of Stalin's foreign policy purposes and to fix much of or all the blame for the breakdown of inter-Allied unity on the West and its leaders. The history of this phase of the coming of the Cold War is visibly a play of good and evil, a type of scenario that experience and common sense would under normal circumstances reject. But this history was set in a milieu determined by two of the past's most accomplished practitioners of the dark arts.

The Germany that came under occupation in 1945, though once rich and highly developed, was an utterly defeated land, joined as well in millions of European and North American minds and hearts to immediate memories of bestialities on a scale never before so widely discovered—and almost immediately revealed to shocked Western publics in photograph and film. Nonetheless, it is scarcely to be doubted that, were the evidence now available massed to reflect all the areas of Red Army and NKVD occupation, the following descriptions of Soviet behavior (frequently justified in the German case by apologists as deriving from an excusable need for revenge) might readily be generalized to cover the other Red Army–occupied nations. In any case, they should in large measure help establish why the Soviets and their erstwhile allies were quickly at odds after they met on the field of victory. They should also help make clear how ill-suited Stalin's crude agencies were for the incredibly difficult tasks he had assigned them.

To be sure, in 1945, recent events during the German occupation to the east had no doubt increased, if only by setting their ghastly examples, the Soviet propensity to enormities of all kinds, especially in the defeated nation. Memories of those discoveries also increased the propensities of the Western Allies, who were finally going to view the Soviets man to man, to suppress their immediate revulsion at what they soon came to learn. Only in the relatively short run could these Westerners squelch their long cultivated sense of fair (that unique English word) and just conduct. So with the coming together of the victorious armies in the center of Germany in the spring and early summer of 1945 a new and, of course, different Western appraisal of Soviet conduct at every level was soon to take shape.

At this point, the strangest, yet perhaps most indicative, instance of Stalin's personal behavior so far known must be set down. It epitomizes the state of mind and spirit it reveals—which the mass of Westerners and their leaders had still to encounter consciously, and certainly not confrontationally—peculiar, perhaps inexplicable, except as Stalinist Soviet Russian.

Sad to say, given the long persisting lack of Soviet collaboration in describing the events of the Soviet past, or in opening to a wider readership the sources that might do so, the best efforts at historical explanation may sometimes still lead us only to bafflement and to the kind of unsatisfying personal and socio-ethnic explanation just supplied. All that, combined with the peculiar malevolence, increasing paranoia, and concomitant unpredictability of Stalin himself, make this part of the past still only unsatisfyingly explicable. Historians are very much obliged professionally to try to do better by way of producing their facts and accountings. But the carefully maintained shadows over there were well designed to keep us, even

in times of glasnost', far from the necessary historical verisimili-
tude. Glasnost' may come or go, but beyond the Iron Curtain, which
only a few years ago literally and figuratively still stretched across
the very heart of Europe, encouragement in the search for the complete truth remains, so far, in some milieus, anything but steady.

On May 2, 1945, the Germans in Berlin surrendered. The Führer-
bunker fell into Soviet hands. Specially assigned Soviet units then
began to search its ruins for the corpse of Hitler, of whose death, we
now know, they had been told, but whose final accounting they did
not, of course, necessarily believe. As is now well known, Adolf Hitler and his new bride, the former Eva Braun, had committed suicide
at just about the same time on April 30, as the first Soviet units
penetrated the Reichstag, the building of the former German parliament, about 500 meters from Hitler's Chancellery and the bunker
itself. It was to the Reichstag that Stalin had misdirected his forces
in the mistaken notion that it was the center of Hitler's government.

Hitler poisoned himself. He had for years been guaranteeing to
one and all that he would shoot himself if the going got tough. Post-
humously he confused everyone, just as he had in life. He had promised one thing and done the other; in his worried and prematurely
decrepit state of April 1945, he may have feared botching a suicide
by revolver. He wanted to be sure he died. He expected, should he
be taken alive by the Russians, Pugachev's fate, exhibited in a cage
on Red Square; perhaps, he worried, he would end up in a Soviet
zoo. So he had inserted a cyanide capsule between his teeth, then
clamped his jaws.

Eva Braun likewise bit down on a cyanide capsule and died in-
stantly, as Heinrich Himmler and Hermann Goering were later to
do. The two corpses of Adolf and Eva Hitler had then been burned,
though the job was not completely finished, if only for want of
sufficient gasoline, or because the would-be cremators took early
flight because the shells outside the bunker were falling thick and
heavy. The Red Army was no more than a few blocks away at the
time of the unusual cremation. A similarly incomplete job of burial
followed.

When the Soviets arrived at the bunker two days later, after the
Berlin garrison had capitulated, they immediately found the bodies
of Goebbels, his wife, and their six children. The children had been
poisoned in their sleep at their parents' orders. Joseph and Magda
Goebbels had both taken cyanide. Again, the parents' bodies had

been only partly burned, and hastily and incompletely buried. By the next day, despite the plea of one Soviet cameraman who wanted to record the scene for the "documentary" victory film *Berlin* (then being shot), the bodies of the Goebbels family had been moved to Ploetzensee prison. But Hitler's body could not be found; indeed, the Soviets later reported that they found a double of Adolf, quite dead; it could not be the real Adolf Hitler because it had on darned socks. It must have been a Soviet preconception that the head of state, even in the dismal conditions of the bunker, would not allow himself to wear darned socks. Two days later, after considerable searching, they found the right body.[2] (Unfortunately, the feet of the corpse were burned away, so they could not subject this notion of what official elegance demanded to the ultimate test.)

The only news that the world had had of the death of the Führer was an announcement on Nazi Berlin radio that he had fallen fighting at the head of his troops. The truth of his death—suicide in a bunker some distance from the field of battle, where thousands of Germans were still fighting on several fronts, most of them still unremittingly combating Soviet armies—would certainly have come as a shock. At least some of these last-ditch fighters might have believed the story of his suicide if told by those at the scene, and accompanied by pictures of the corpse.[3] Perhaps some would have been brought to lay down their arms. But instead of broadcasting the discovery, or waiting only to make certain when the positive identification of the corpse was made by Hitler's captured dentist and his assistants, the Soviets chose to keep the whole matter secret.

The command to do so came from the highest authority, from "great Stalin" himself, now taking on the added role of body snatcher. On festive occasions in late May and June with the other United Nations commanders, as they celebrated the great victory, both Soviet marshals, Georgii Zhukov and Vasilii Sokolovskii, denied to their Berlin guests, Marshal Bernard Montgomery and Generals Jean DeLattre de Tassigny, Dwight D. Eisenhower, and others, any knowledge of what they certainly had heard about Hitler's body. In fact, both Russian marshals specifically denied that any corpse had been positively identified as Hitler's. Earlier in May, Zhukov had given some American diplomats to understand that Hitler was dead, that the body had been found and identified, but in June he took back his earlier story. Andrei Vyshinskii, the criminal prosecutor of the terrible purge trials of the late 1930's, who popped up all through the war when Stalin needed a ruthless on-the-spot agent, stood at Zhukov's side as he did so. Sokolovskii, too, who had himself arranged for the positive dental identification of Hitler's corpse on May 8, now denied that the body had been found. Vyshinskii's presence is significant, particularly since Stalin had made it clear that he had no trust in the political sense (that is, reliability) of military men, even of famous marshals.[4]

Meanwhile the Soviet-controlled press and TASS were broadcasting all sorts of rumors of Hitler's escape from Berlin. Stories in *Pravda* and other Soviet journals put the dead Führer on a submarine, or, in one case, on a red yacht heading for Spain or Argentina. In another well-planted story he was somewhere in, or off the coast of, the British zone of occupation. Some of the stories said that Hitler's face had been altered in a last-minute operation and that dead doubles had been planted here and there to confuse the conquerors.[5]

All this mystery and rumor, emanating as it obviously did from Soviet sources, some of them official, must have had some purpose, though not necessarily a rational one. The only explanation that makes any sense at all is that the stories of an escape by Hitler were meant to suggest that the Western Allies had been, or were being, lax, or clumsy and careless, in letting Hitler get away. Perhaps the stories were to supply excuses for Allied or Soviet action against Franco, or another of Stalin's many declared and undeclared enemies. Such purposes fitted later Soviet lines of propaganda systematically developed as the Cold War stiffened. These early reports were what we now call disinformation, and it was deliberately spread during the sweetest days of common celebration and victory, and, one has to infer, at the command of the highest Soviet authority. Moreover, this campaign of confusion was being carried on with the help of two Soviet military celebrities, Zhukov and Sokolovskii, at the very time when they were being lionized in the West and awarded the highest Western military honors for their part in the common struggle against Nazism. Like the stories of Hitler's escape to the West, the reversal of stories by Zhukov and the story told by Sokolovskii had to have been ordered at the supreme governmental level. In fact, Stalin himself gave the same false account to Harry Hopkins when this personal envoy of President Truman visited the Kremlin in May.[6]

At the very moment of combined victory, Stalin had secreted the ultimate proof, the supreme victory symbol, the corpse of the man who had been the instigator of a world war that lasted six years and cost millions of lives. And for fifteen years to follow, the Soviets kept the theft secret. When the first hints of the story were allowed out in Moscow in 1961, the Western press, preoccupied with contemporary demons (Mao, Khrushchev, Castro), and Hitler scholars, still not paying great attention to Russian sources, took little notice. Most everyone, except the odd journalist looking for a Sunday-supplement story, was certain that Hitler had died in the bunker and that the body had never been found. Moreover, proofs of Soviet wartime and postwar hypocrisy were by then already legion. The historical importance of the body snatch of May 1945 had been lost sight of, passions of war had cooled, Adolf Hitler and even his philosophy of hate, not to mention his Third Reich, had ceased to loom important in a post–atomic bomb world where confrontations with the Soviet empire were virtually constant. In 1965, when much more of the strange story was told, it was just one more tale of Soviet wartime duplicity, and the figurative unveiling of a corpse long dead raised no Western hackles. Indeed, few people even believed the body snatch story then, though some began to do so a few years later. The story first revealed in the 1960's was so outrageous, and, at the time, as it was to turn out, the partial details of the last moments of the Führer's life then told by the Soviets so much at odds with what was known in the West, that it took contemporaries some time to understand what to make of it.[7]

Yet this bizarre episode helps us understand the state of tension that prevailed in Soviet-occupied Europe in the late spring and early summer of 1945. The tenor of Sovietization was rapidly heightening; it was becoming an ideologized, deliberate territorial grab behind sheets of lies, purposefully sown confusion and misinformation, the entire environment supercharged by more than a touch of carefully concealed madness at the directorial level. True, the most extreme forms of hyperstimulated wartime states of mind still permeated every capital. Every week, sometimes every day, new German death camps or Japanese atrocities were revealed. Yet, except in central Moscow, no one, perhaps in all history, ever concocted a scheme anything even remotely like filching the corpse of a former dictator in order to provoke international political consequences.

Of course, Stalin's diplomacy of those days must be seen against its background of contemporary personal diplomacy. The Western leaders, Roosevelt in particular, had also blown themselves up with self-importance from their new-found power: earnestly reorganizing Europe and much of the rest of the world, many times moralistically planning and replanning monumental programs of European settlement, in part out of a need to respond to the endlessly novel challenges from their Soviet ally and those deriving from the confusion of the war situation in its final days. Then, suddenly, Roosevelt was dead, and a new and inexperienced President Harry S Truman entered the White House. He came there almost totally without experience in international politics, and with no inkling of his predecessor's secret diplomacy. The complexity of the postwar situation he and the other Western leaders faced would be vastly increased in August 1945 by the collapse of Japanese power and the sudden movement of Soviet power into large parts of east Asia, just as that power was already supreme over all of east central and much of central Europe.

The Western leaders' states of mind, after desperate attempts at collaboration with the unfathomable Stalin in such rapidly changing circumstances, and in parts of the world virtually unknown to them, were themselves scarcely predictable. Recall the mystification-induced behavior of Western leaders in attempting to account for and respond to Hitler's trickery in prewar times. Was he to be taken as serious, or just as mad? In 1945, there still persisted among the Westerners a willingness to suspend criticism of all opponents of Hitler, for the common recognition of the horrors he had worked in the name of the German nation had bound together the most disparate lands. The Soviets, therefore, really had to undo masses of honest goodwill directed their way before the Westerners could come close to the state of mind necessary to call a halt to Stalin's adventurism.

As for him, the excesses of World War I, and civil war and exile, imposed upon his early religious training and sinister conspiratorial background were influences he could scarcely hope (were he even conscious of the need) to put aside latterly. And these experiences were combined in him with a later long history of "liquidating" individuals, whole masses, and whole "classes." Such a past can only have pushed that Torquemada-like soul further and further toward a ruthlessness conjoined with well-merited fears of a deserved potential retribution. Since no one was safe from him or his henchmen where Moscow's steadily expanding power touched, Stalin certainly knew that, were circumstances to change, what he had visited on others might be visited on him. Sequestered behind high walls, both physical and spiritual, as he was, his lively fears had to play a frequent role in fomenting his obviously dire imaginings. Gudonov per Pushkin à la Musorgskii.

To encourage his opinions and carry out his decisions, Stalin had collected around him a cast of subalterns as a nighttime cabinet. After the manner of Hitler's midday prandial soliloquies, Stalin held forth at his *soupers* and other evening séances, forums for the expression of some of his most strange as well as dreadful intentions. Along with Stalin, these Kremlin cronies, through flattery, suggestion, and influence, set the structure of the crooked Soviet system.[8] If, from the outside, Soviet direction appeared secure and assured at this time, it was only because Stalin had yet to meet any serious opposition to his foreign plans, and because the double shield of propaganda and silence could cover mistakes and clumsy ruthlessness. We recall how long the appearance of an intelligent purposefulness stuck during the war, and has stuck in histories since, to Hitler's direction of the Third Reich. The theft of the Führer's body bespeaks plainly that all was not just right in the center of Moscow either, and that things could not be at all right wherever the march of the Red Army extended Stalin's power.

Hitler's strange end was no Götterdämmerung, though Berlin and its recent Führer were largely devoured by flames. No grand finale marked the juncture of the two crackpot, destructive tyrannies, one succeeding the other in the ruins of central Europe. Still, Stalin's theft of Hitler's body marks, absurdly and then secretly, the spiritual bringing down of the Iron Curtain in the heart of Europe. It catches the true measure of Soviet wartime goodwill, because that goodwill had been, was indeed being, parceled out according to the needs of a deranged dictator. It epitomizes the inescapably devious and calculating nature of Soviet wartime and postwar behavior toward its wartime allies.

The campaign for political control where the Soviet armies advanced in Europe was everywhere accompanied by a coordinated program of arranging the distortion of information. We have earlier noted, as an example, how the Bolshevik-controlled press in Poland manipulated, for Stalin's purposes, the Warsaw uprising. That same campaign was simultaneously carried on in the Soviet homeland. Everywhere among the Allied nations, there was celebration of the great victory, but the reporting of the victory in the Soviet Union reveals a far different state of mind from the omnipresent public testimony to the unified grand alliance, and the hopes for its future, that prevailed in the West.

In May 1945, *Pravda* and other Soviet journals duly printed the series of speeches and reports of the Soviet leaders on the end of the war. But the speeches of Stalin, Molotov, and Zhukov on the victory over the Germans did not mention the military and material contributions of the West to that victory.[9] Most of the Soviet peoples were likewise slighted. Stalin praised the "great Russian people"; he always referred to them alone, even at wartime conferences.[10] At the great Day of Victory parade in Moscow on June 24, 1945, only Marshal Zhukov, and he only briefly, mentioned the Western powers or their considerable military and material help in the Soviet success. The same Marshal Zhukov had just returned from Germany, where Western military leaders had feted him as a partner in victory.

The Moscow Victory Day ceremony was itself remarkable in its heavy emphasis on traditional forms of imperial behavior. On that dreary, rainy, Moscow summer day, representative after representative military unit of the Red Army, Air, and Sea fleets came up to the reviewing stand where Stalin and other party figures stood on top of Lenin's tomb, and in gestures reminiscent of the Roman legions threw down before them the massed conquered swastika banners.[11] It was a scene that no Westerner might imagine, in the slightest, before Buckingham Palace, or on the grand space before the United States Capitol. Perhaps it might have been staged more elegantly, in Napoleonic style, before General de Gaulle, if he had been capable of allowing himself the illusion that France itself had won a victory. It speaks much for him that he evidently was not. It also speaks much about the immediate postwar attitude of the Soviets toward their Western allies, and toward their Polish ally in victory, that they were not invited to share the place of homage.

What such acts, like Stalin's theft of the Führer's body and his soon-to-follow, demonic quest for the central place in the annals of wartime glory, establish is that he would, indeed could, where he held the power, brook no inter-Allied limits to his purposes. In Moscow he was omnipotent. From there, even during the war, he had done his utmost to dispatch what he could of a Western presence, and even its image. After the war he hastened to banish any remaining traces of the West. In Moscow he could remake history in both word and picture. He could, and would, rebuild village streets into

settings for an imperial capital. He could, in an instant, banish conquering Soviet heroes to local versions of Coventry, as he soon did
with Zhukov, and crown himself with their laurels.

By the late spring of 1945, Stalin had ruthlessly carried out his
aim of installing a Soviet-dominated government and establishing
Soviet control in war-ravaged Poland, the western half he had not
reannexed to the Soviet Union. He had reannexed the Baltic nations,
and was just then fitting the Red Army–occupied Balkan states into
the Soviet harness. In Germany, where he envisioned even weightier
projects of building and increasing his empire, he would move at
once toward that same end. But there he found a solid threat to his
plans. Not only the powerful Western armies were on hand, but so
were countless Western civilians, part of the bureaucratic apparatus
sternly commanded by Western leaders to remake a peaceful society
of the nation that had terrorized Europe.

Stalin did not want for local, and able, collaborators in Germany.
Many days before the grand parade on Red Square, on the day before
the Reichstag fell and Hitler committed suicide, Walter Ulbricht,
the real leader of the group of survivors of the Muscovite leadership
of the prewar German Communist Party, landed with a dozen or so
of his party cadre at an airport behind Soviet lines not far from Berlin.[12] This was the central, Moscow-trained leadership destined by
Stalin to organize Germany from Berlin on the Soviet model. To
him, Germany was, in the Marxist-Leninist tradition, the key to
Europe.

Similar echelons from the well-schooled German Communist
cadre from Moscow were flown into conquered Saxony, and, a few
days later, into Pomerania; mention of the latter group has already
been made in connection with the postwar contest with the Poles
over Stettin. Many of the members of these groups were members
of National Committee "Free Germany" who had completed the
Soviet-organized "Antifa" (antifascist) schools. Their program for
the new Germany was to work with the Red Army in bringing
Soviet-style antifascist democracy to the ruined country.[13] But perhaps only Stalin, Molotov, Zhdanov, Ulbricht, and Wilhelm Pieck—
the latter two later premier and president, respectively, of Sovietized
East Germany—plus a few others, knew for certain that the program
they intended to carry out was to be extended to the whole of Germany and not just to the part that was occupied by the Red Army.
Milovan Djilas has said that Stalin once told him that a state that

takes territory imposes on it its social system, an alleged historical law he evidently found revealed somewhere in the Bolshevik canon. In the case of Germany, as many Soviets and East Germans have since testified, Stalin meant to impose his system far beyond that territory. His pre-1941, ideology-infused dreams of the westward expansion of Soviet power were going to be carried out, insofar as he could manage it.[14]

It is nonetheless clear that Stalin, however he may actually have acted, preferred to achieve his purposes by working cautiously, avoiding serious confrontation with the West; to do this, he would use all the tricks he could muster. But the Soviet record we have already examined should have suggested that his tricks would be far from suitable in postwar circumstances. Even his eerily complicated efforts to manipulate history and information suggest that he would eventually be caught up in webs of his own making.

Moreover, the Red Army's standard behavior was scarcely an instrument suited to the restraints of diplomatic finesse. In wartime, behind the Red Army lines as in Poland and Czechoslovakia, the schemes had often succeeded, often almost undetected or, if detected, not believed or explained away. Too many writers on the Cold War have ignored the real state of Stalin's adventurous spirit, preferred to see as defensive (and sometimes even as proper) the general cast of Soviet behavior to the east of Germany. Most have also failed to investigate his plans for his zone of Germany and for the lands to the west of the original lines of demarcation set for the Soviet Zone of Occupation in Germany. They have, therefore, inevitably failed to record the consequences of those plans, and of his early failure to gain his key purposes in Germany, in the history of the Cold War.

In the early summer of 1945, the Soviets controlled all ingress eastward from the Red Army front, a line that ran from the Baltic near Lübeck to Trieste on the Adriatic. Luckily for them, even scrupulous Western observers and journalists who were allowed to observe the Soviets behind that line were still infused with the spirit of cooperation in Allied victory and with what was assumed to be the common task of constructing a better world after six years of terrible war. To be sure, the Westerners saw very little on the east side of the line, and their reports on what they did see had to pass through Soviet censorship. The Soviets still had such a passion for secrecy that they draped tarpaulins over the horse-drawn wagons and the tanks that they brought in to take over as the Americans and British pulled out of their forward positions in the Soviet Zone of Occupation.[15] For years, the Soviets limited travel in their zone, and censorship continued. Under these conditions, it was not going to be easy to substantiate honest observers' skepticism about the Soviet commitment to truth; under the occasional but continuing emotional and alcoholic binges of friendship, skepticism only developed slowly.

By contrast with the many lands well behind Soviet lines, in Berlin and Vienna, each under four-power occupation from the summer of 1945, encounters with the Soviets were open. Some things could not be hidden. East and West met on more or less equal terms. These cities, therefore, quickly became the public laboratories of postwar collaboration, and the reflectors of Soviet behavior. We know considerably more about Germany because its former Soviet Zone Communists over many years proudly published so much of the early history of the "republic" they designed in Moscow and then created from central offices in the eastern sector of Berlin. Their newly opened archival sources make clear how closely Moscow controlled their enterprise: that is to say, Moscow gave them direct orders through the Red Army, as Stalin gave the Poles direct orders through his picked leaders in the PKWN. The German Communist party leaders had agreed in advance to do as they were told. (Wilhelm Pieck had, after all, publicly lauded Stalin as "the father of the Soviet people and of progressive mankind.")[16] The campaign that culminated in their open assumption of power in the eastern half of the former Reich capital, and in the Soviet Zone of Germany, ultimately became the central point of public attention in this central, postwar Western Allied–Soviet meeting. Berlin, starting in 1945, was to become the dramatic focus, and the main symbol, of the Cold War.

The publics in the outside world, and particularly those of the Western Allies, knew very little of what was going on in Soviet-occupied Germany and elsewhere in east central Europe during the early days. On May 4, 1945, two days after the surrender of Berlin, then about 100 miles from the nearest American front, a small American army group was apparently allowed into the city on a photographic and sightseeing mission. On May 8, an entire contingent from the Allied command flew into Tempelhof airport, bringing

German Field Marshal Keitel and other former luminaries of the Nazi armed forces, for a restaging of the unconditional surrender on all European fronts. The original had been signed with Soviet participation on May 7 at General Eisenhower's headquarters at Reims in France. Stalin, upon hearing of the simple surrender ceremony, which reflected none of the pomp of empire or drama of humiliating a foe, seems to have been annoyed that it had not been staged to mirror Soviet grandeur and justice, and to focus central attention on the Soviet victory. He therefore commanded a repeat performance on his own terrain, where he could set the theatrical props for his own history.[17]

The contrast between the unconditional surrender in Reims and the restaging for the cameras in the Berlin suburb of Karlshorst is clear from existing film evidence. At the first, Eisenhower, the Western Allied Supreme Commander, did not appear, but instead turned the scene (fortunately caught by the army's cameras), set in a simple schoolroom, over to his deputies. His Soviet liaison officer sat at the head table. There were no masses of marshals and generals to witness the handing over of the symbolic sword of the vanquished. Eisenhower then read elsewhere a brief statement for the news cameras announcing the surrender to all allies. All were thanked, the Soviet forces quite notably, for their contributions to the victory.

At Karlshorst, Marshal Zhukov was placed at center stage, flanked by the Allied generals cooperatively flown in from the West and here arrayed as international supernumeraries. The room was packed with Soviet generals. A massive phalanx of Soviet cameramen, plus the few Western pool reporters who could be accommodated into the official delegation aircraft, worked every possible reportorial and dramatic angle. In the Soviet film versions of the event, which evidently reflect some historical reality, Zhukov was kept in center screen to emphasize the Red Army's major importance, this point likewise iterated and reiterated by the narrator. The omnipresent voice of the vozhd', Andrei Vyshinskii, inevitably bobbed around Zhukov's right elbow and ear, constant with advice, as if Stalin did not trust his famous military commander to handle the drama of a staged surrender; or perhaps Vyshinskii had in his pocket the storyboard of the film that Stalin, whose interventions in all aspects of the Soviet film world, as elsewhere in Soviet life, were frequent, wanted made.

After a heated East-West squabble over place that lasted well into the night, Eisenhower's deputy, British Air Marshal Arthur Tedder, ranking among the Western delegates (who seem to have had no way of asking for advice on the matter at issue from headquarters far away) resigned himself to signing the "surrender" document on behalf of all the Western powers. The squabble and the lack of Western preparation for the Soviet's pettifoggery here anticipated the conflicts to come and recalled such past inter-Allied wartime diplomatic exchange. It was an almost too obvious display of the East-West dichotomy that Stalin already had in mind. On the one side were the victorious Soviet armies; on the other, seated together as one scarcely significant group, were the Western Allies. This split is particularly emphasized in the Moscow-edited film, most certainly the official Soviet version, that was released in June. Already the Soviets were scorning that wartime parlance about "allies"—the terminology Eisenhower used at Reims—while, at the same time, new American President Truman was speaking earnestly, via the newsreel cameras, to his people of the victory of "the United Nations." The Poles were, of course, not invited by the Soviet hosts to the Karlshorst formalities, though they had fought with the Red Army in the battle for Berlin and had symbolically hoisted the Polish colors on the famous Column of Victory in the Berlin Tiergarten. Indeed, Eisenhower himself had to organize the invitation to the French to Karlshorst, and he had also made certain they were seated at Reims. But the Red Army at Karlshorst initially failed to post the French flag among the props; reminded of the oversight, the Soviet seamstresses repaired the situation by hastily sewing up a Dutch flag.[18]

The carefully contrived filmed account of the Karlshorst ceremony made no reference to the earlier surrender at Reims, which had gone unmentioned in the Soviet-controlled press and about which the Soviet public knew nothing. It was to be a Soviet victory only. The film, *Berlin*, was an important part of the Soviet celebrations. It made the great drama available to the millions miles from the drama in Karlshorst. It obviously holds many plot aspects similar to the victory parade documentary filmed on Red Square. Both productions were in keeping with the line taken everywhere in the Soviet media.

Stalin had already privately identified the new enemy in the battle for Germany, for all of it. The battle between what he called socialism and capitalism had, for him, already been reborn. Stalin believed that the British had already stiffened their opposition to him. (He always saw the British, and Churchill, as more dangerous than Roosevelt and the Americans, perhaps because he remembered that Roosevelt had told him the Americans would soon be going home.) In any case, the conflict he was recreating was to take in all Europe, not just Germany, and even places beyond. In addition, Stalin was then already possessed with preparing the way for the assertion that the Soviets had won the war single-handedly, and that he, as the "great Stalin," had been the supreme tactical, as well as strategic, wartime commander. His unseemly grasping for all the laurels obviously reflected one more dimension of his mental disequilibrium. He had already had his tailor make up a generalissimo's uniform for the new honor he had conferred on himself. It would require that all serious rivals in honor—potential enemies—be banished. So popular Soviet hero Zhukov was soon to be sent away to a command in the provinces.

Indeed, per Soviet insinuation, already in preparation as the war ended, the Westerners had negotiated with the Nazis to turn them eastward against Soviet armies. In historical reality, just after the signing at Karlshorst, and long before the postwar historical fabrications had begun to appear, the Soviet command hosted an all-night celebration for all guests present, with multitudes of toasts. Oddly, even Keitel and the other players for the vanquished, though banished to separate chambers for the losers after playing their parts in the grand dramatic climax, were treated to rich food and plenty to drink. Meanwhile, at the main affair, Vyshinskii, taking the woman's role, danced the *gopak* with Zhukov. Sad to say, this colorful episode—part and parcel of that apparently eternal Soviet Russian swing between insanity and jollity—was never caught by the otherwise ubiquitous cameras of either side. The alcohol worked its way with all, and especially with the exhausted cameramen.[19]

Out beyond the all-night binge in Karlshorst, Germany was in a state of disorganization, chaos, and fear. German civilians and armies were rushing to surrender to the West. Their state of terror at the prospect of falling into Soviet hands is graphically recorded. So-called displaced persons (DP's, as they were then named), including hundreds of thousands of drafted and slave workers whom the Nazis had brought to Germany as labor, were moving toward distant homes in organized and disorganized groups. Most of them scavenged from the land what they needed, or thought they needed, for the trek home and for the possessions to support new lives once they arrived there. Obviously the armies of the Allies, which had so recently witnessed the German concentration camps and the wartime conduct of the German armies, were in no mood to supervise too carefully the behavior of the former downtrodden toward the former master race.

In addition, there was perhaps an equivalent number of refugees from Soviet-conquered Europe on the road or in temporary camps: Estonians, Latvians, Lithuanians, Ukrainians, Poles, Hungarians, Slovaks, and others who, in one way or another, had either fought against, or retreated from the Soviets, in willing or unwilling collaboration with the armed forces of the Third Reich. And there were others who did not want to go back even though they had booked no specific crime against the Soviet Union and its newly established friends in government in the occupied regions. Then there were the Germans, themselves in flight from the eastern areas where the Red Army had first struck, others in flight toward the center from the west. And there were literally millions more Germans whom the Soviets, Poles, Czechs, Hungarians, and others, who had repossessed their nations from Nazi collaborators or Nazi occupiers, were forcing out in the midst of all the postwar chaos. In this way, these governments pursued their nationalist plans of ending the large German colonies that had existed for centuries in their countries. Behind these schemes ultimately lay the idea of punishing the guilty en masse while pulling into the new "socialist" centers of bureaucratic reorganization the forsaken lands and other property to redistribute to those who would be properly grateful. For the handouts, the Stalinist "socialists" at the center, like the Polish agricultural reformers pushed by Stalin, could hope to harvest significant peasant support in their quest to establish political control legitimately. Other Germans were being pushed west as states on the Soviet border carried out Stalin's and their governments' plans to change the ethnic borders of Europe in order to accommodate the westerly expansion of the Soviet Union.

Only those Germans, Poles, Czechs, and countless others who witnessed scenes of the great treks of 1945, or those who have seen the film and photographic and written reports of those days, can comprehend the horrors—to whose ghastly dimensions tales of the looting, pillage, and rapine of the Red Army soldiers must be added.

This behavior occurred not only in Germany but also in Austria (officially considered a Nazi-occupied state), Yugoslavia, Czechoslovakia, and Poland, and in the German territories that the Soviets had already officially transferred to Polish administration—where, as elsewhere in Germany, the pillage was called "reparations."[20] Some scenes would be comical were they not set against so tragic a backdrop. Visualize the Soviet troops covering their booty with oriental rugs for the long trip home, the fabled encounters of these backwoods warriors with the wonders of modern Western plumbing, the former slave workers returning east with everything that wagons, baby carriages, and suitcases could carry. One particular scene of a caravan of Russians, or Ukrainians, in covered wagons pulling along behind them three captive camels (looted from a German zoo?) is unforgettable, like so many other images of that world turned upside down. Many were recorded by American army cameramen.[21]

Against this background, but quietly, well beyond our eye of the camera, Ulbricht and the others had earlier set about the tasks for which they had long prepared. Even in the concentration camps, many German Communist prisoners had organized themselves, so that when they were released by the Red and other Allied armies, those who could quickly regain their health, and could move back into society, provided a ready nucleus of determined recruits for an antifascist campaign. Many, though not all, proved willing to take orders from Ulbricht and his accomplices.

Here, then, the important place of defeated Germany and the role of the *Gruppe* Ulbricht, completely at the disposal of the Red Army, come forth as critical in the history of the Cold War. Ulbricht and his Moscow-trained organizers were well equipped with Red Army Willys Jeeps (American-supplied for the winning of the war, and in no way meant for the use of the German Communist Party) and Red Army–"liberated" civilian vehicles, and they were permitted free passage through a tightly controlled environment by PURKKA, the political administration of the Red Army. In the Communist fashion, most of these organizers knew only the immediate goal at hand; only the top leadership knew the larger plans.

Before the flames of battle had died in devastated Berlin, Ulbricht and Pieck were visiting old Communist comrades and even Social Democrats from the pre-1933 days. They brought with them specially picked Red Army political officers with whom they and the old comrades ostensibly consulted to pick mayors, members of town councils, and other civilian administrators. All came from groups they identified as "antifascists." Although political parties and other organizations, including trade unions, were strictly forbidden, and no meetings were allowed, Ulbricht and company went about this consultative work without any interference from the military law of the Soviet occupation forces. All this activity had been worked out by Ulbricht and his group of Moscow-based exiles in numberless meetings: the aim, to establish a Communist-directed Bloc for Fighting Democracy, which would assume political control of the Soviet Zone of Germany. The plans had been put together in February and yet more finely designed in April and May 1945, and completed in discussions in Moscow in June. In this task they had collaborated with the International Division of the Soviet Communist Party and with the Kremlin itself.[22] The essence of that program was another fait accompli—to create the agencies for Communist control before other forces inevitably opposed to their yet unadvertised goals could arise.

The Red Army Political Administration and the German Communists were operating in close cooperation to serve common purposes.[23] There was plenty of cooperative enthusiasm among the masses of German leftists and other anti-Nazis, in spite of the obvious brutality of the liberator's army, for getting to work with a will to cashier the Nazi scoundrels once and for all, and to rebuild an antifascist society in which such groups could never again achieve power. And, as an important touch, just a few days before the start of the final assault on the remaining Nazi pockets of resistance, in late April, the Soviet propaganda organs had abruptly reversed the vituperative campaign of hate that had been directed against the Germans since 1941.

It had been at first a campaign of slogans—not a response to actual crimes the Germans committed on Soviet soil, for many of those could not have been known to the Kremlin for some time.[24] Throughout the war, until early 1945, the standard slogan was, "The Soviet people will neither forgive, nor forget."[25] Then, quite suddenly, on April 19, 1945, Il'ia Erenberg, one of the most vitriolic of anti-German practitioners in the Soviet media, was scathingly censured in *Pravda* for his vicious tirades. *Pravda* followed up this criticism in its issue of May 8 in an article saying that it was not the German people with whom the Soviets were at war, but only the Nazi leadership.[26] By May 9, Stalin had also wholly reversed himself,

without consulting his Western allies, on the postwar dismemberment of Germany, though this was a punishment he had pushed for,
and all had agreed to, at Yalta.[27]

So, almost overnight, the four-year propaganda campaign of hate
and calls for revenge stopped. The long-planned campaign for winning the souls of the Germans could now begin. Stalin is said to have
told the army commanders that the German people must be fed before the final battles for what remained of Germany started. He may
have done that only to keep the Soviet Zone of Occupation from
becoming an even vaster cemetery, about which word would surely
escape to the sentimental in the West, but it sounds like a part of
his new friendship campaign. Yet the sudden friendly turnaround in
Kremlin directives did not help the working-class women of the Soviet Zone of Occupation; they might wrap themselves in a red flag
out of sentiment or fear yet nonetheless fall victim, as did many
women of all social levels, to the sexual demands of the Red Army
"liberators." Obviously, larger Soviet goals and local Red Army behavior could not be completely coordinated.[28]

As early as May 9, Stalin had Anastas Mikoian as his economic
consultant in Berlin and Dresden. Mikoian's task was said to be
to survey the health conditions of the Germans and to organize
the economic means for their survival. Quite astonishingly, when
Pravda on May 19 published parts of Mikoian's report on Germany,
he recommended the establishment of a free-trade economy as the
best means for promoting Germany's quick recovery. Even British
intelligence summary writers remarked on the "extremely moderate" program of the German Communist Party, which, following
Moscow's directives, soon came out for "the unhampered development of trade and commerce on the basis of private property." Was
Stalin going to such lengths to cover his real goals, working for a
good press in the West by summoning up the terminology of the
moribund Atlantic Charter? Or was it, as George F. Kennan, then in
Moscow, suspected, an appeal for the support of the solid German
burgher? Probably it was both, for it repeated the line that Stalin,
through Georgii Dimitrov, had been preaching to his Moscow-loyal
Polish Communists during the war. In any event, Mikoian's publi-
cized recommendations had very little to do with the program the
Soviets actually carried out.[29]

The Red Army under Zhukov had begun to appoint German civilian political authorities before Ulbricht's Muscovite command ar-

rived, and it was well organized for the political tasks before it. Zhu-kov later remembered those as being, first of all, the establishment of a newspaper, and second, putting the comrades in the key roles. This was Zhukov's direct formulation of Comrade Ulbricht's more theoretical program: "It's quite simple, it must look democratic, but everything must be in our hands"—by which he meant, in the long run, in his hands.[30]

The Red Army moved with exemplary speed in setting up the lo-cal units that were needed as the basis for the Soviet-oriented civil-ian government. The first project, the radio station, was on the air in Berlin on May 13; the first newspaper, *Tägliche Rundschau*, ap-peared on May 15; a second newspaper, *Berliner Zeitung*, began pub-lishing on May 21. On May 17, a local central government was an-nounced for Berlin; Ulbricht was behind that decision. On May 20, a police force was reestablished under the command of an NK "FD" military officer, Colonel Paul Markgraf, a former Nazi who had been retrained by the Soviets. On May 19, the Red Army commander for the city, Col.-General Nicolai Berzarin, spoke at the solemn instal-lation of a new city mayor and council (*Magistrat*). The German appointees were the new mayor, Dr. Arthur Werner, and the new vice-mayor, the Muscovite party functionary Karl Maron. Maron had himself nominated the aged, unpolitical Werner. In his speech, Berzarin told those assembled that it had never entered the minds of the Soviet people to take the territories of others. In other circum-stances, and given other information of which few in his audience were probably certain as early as May, this remark would surely have induced gales of laughter.[31]

A few days later, Berzarin ordered a special showing of Soviet films for the benefit of an invited audience of German artists and intellectuals and some Soviet officers trained in film propaganda. Projectors, reels, the newest cinematographic celebrations of the So-viet past, and Soviet film classics were part of the Red Army's bag-gage wherever it went. This was the start of a campaign that ulti-mately was to pay off in winning a great many from the cultural uppercrust to active work in Soviet-organized creative and propa-ganda institutions.[32]

Although the Moscow-loyal Communists were, relatively speak-ing, a small group in 1945, they were put in charge of all the new institutions except for the "nonpartisan" local governments, where, in Berlin as elsewhere, they took only certain important agencies that were vital for social and opinion control, such as the police, internal affairs, and education. Maron's role as adviser to the suitably aged Dr. Werner is an example. The tactic was to set up a façade of power-sharing among all "antifascist" groups while downplaying all expression of social revolution. With their Social Democratic allies, with whom they were then as friendly as traditional party hostilities, dating from pre-1933 days, allowed, the Communists easily controlled a majority of the council in Berlin and elsewhere.[33]

Thus, within two weeks of the German formal capitulation, in a close approximation of the Moscow-laid plans for the Bloc for Fighting Democracy, the Soviets and the Moscow-based German Communists had set in motion the initial programs for the postwar control of their zone of Germany and all of Berlin behind the so-called Antifa front. The initial successes of Ulbricht and his people were not only abetted because of their close connection with the Red Army. Ulbricht and his group were exceedingly single-minded and industrious. And they were assisted by a strong force of pre-*Gleichschaltung* leftists, persons whose socialist leanings predated the Nazi seizure, in 1933, of all the forces of internal control in Germany and the dissolution of all political and labor organizations except those of the National Socialists. Many of these members or sympathizers of the Communist and Social Democratic parties had escaped detection and now emerged; many, as noted, had spent years in prisons and concentration camps and were ready for an antifascist cleanup.

There were, inevitably, some unauthorized retributional campaigns to purge German society of the Nazi oppressors. Antifa as a program had long been broadcast over the Soviet radio to encourage anti-Nazi revolutionary action, and its ideas were now spread broadly over the Soviet-controlled German radio, with the obvious support of the new authorities.[34] Motives for going after the local Nazis and their profiteering collaborators of the Third Reich were strong.

Old rivalries between the Marxist German Communist Party and the Marxist Social Democratic Party were put aside, at least for the time being, to deal with the now-defeated Nazis. It was time to pay them off for the disaster they had brought to Germany and Europe. The feelings were not confined to Germany. People all over post-Hitler Europe seemed to have a will conditioned by the terrible events of recent times to put aside past antagonisms by ending the

history of intra–working class struggles, and to establish a new economic and social basis for a better society. The triumph of Labour
over victorious and popular Churchill and his Conservatives in the
elections of July 1945 in Britain showed this dramatically. On the
Continent, the ideological force for reform was Marxist, reflecting
both local socialist traditions and the popular Soviet victory over
Hitler.

Local Antifa committees arose spontaneously, not only in the
Soviet-occupied area but also in the Western zones and in the large
areas captured by the American and British armies, those German
lands scheduled to come under Soviet control as soon as the three-
power agreement fixing the division of Germany was implemented.
Outside the Soviet area of occupation, political activity, indeed all
group activity of every political persuasion, was still tightly regulated without exception. Hence there even Antifa was an underground activity. But where the Red Army was in control, Antifa
groups were initially tolerated and even encouraged as local "committees of public safety" (*Volkskomitees*). They acted to purge libraries (pyres of books were now again a common scene in the German landscape), school faculties, factory management, among other
Nazi-infested institutions. Taking over the organizational personnel
files made this work rather simple.[35] Revenge was sweet.

But Ulbricht, who knew the long-range strategy, soon moved
quickly to purge the self-appointed purgers. It would not do for their
"infantile leftism," originally encouraged, to frighten the bulk of the
population and enhance fears of future Sovietization. As early as
May 9, the day Mikoian and Vyshinskii were in town, Ulbricht had
subdued the Antifas in his area of control around Berlin. He issued
stern orders for party discipline among members who were too zealous in their purges, or who ignored the Bloc "antifascist" democratic
message in their impatience to purge not just the Nazis but all the
bourgeoisie, now that the long awaited revolutionary guarantee in
the form of the Red Army was really on hand. Such persons, the
zealots, had been out of touch too long, he said, and needed party
schooling.[36]

Tightening the central cadre control of potential enemies and opposing and anarchic spirits in the still illegal German Communist
Party was one thing Ulbricht could do in the Soviet Zone. Securing
the loyalty of other working-class sectors of the German population,
especially those, the most numerous, loyal to the Social Democratic

tradition, was another important part of the program. To this end, long before there was any official licensing of political parties or groups in the Soviet area of occupation, Ulbricht and his colleagues were busy bringing together pre-Nazi union chiefs, getting voluntary worker organizations under way, and rekindling the fires of the once-powerful independent German labor union movement. This, too, was done with the collaboration and consent of the Soviet authorities.[37]

With the situation in Soviet-occupied Germany well surveyed, the Communists now organized, and the trade unions organizing sub rosa, Ulbricht and three others from the groups of Germans earlier sent from Moscow returned there in early June. There they held meetings with Stalin and with Georgii Dimitrov, former head of the Communist Internationale, now chief of the International Division of the Central Committee of the Soviet Communist Party. Dimitrov had worked closely with the Germans before their departure from Moscow, and had earlier been consulted when he and Molotov had begun to patch together the Polish cadre, now at the core of the new Polish government that sat, triumphant over its London rivals, in what remained of Warsaw.

The purpose of the meeting was to hear Stalin's ideas and make corresponding plans to launch his new political system for Germany. Its aims went well beyond urging spontaneous mass Antifa on the nascent worker groups and Soviet-decreed local authorities in the Soviet Zone.[38] Within a month, in early July, the Americans and British were to exchange the rather large segments of the Soviet Zone they occupied for their previously agreed sectors of Berlin, parts of which they would share, with Stalin's tolerance, but not with his territorial contribution, with the French. The main Allied leaders, Generals Eisenhower and Montgomery, were already in Berlin making plans with Zhukov for the occupation. And at just about the very same time, Ulbricht and his group were in Moscow secretly working on quite different plans. Clearly, Stalin wanted his system organized and ready to take over as soon as the territorial transfer occurred, and that meant in place in the Western Allied sectors of Berlin, too. If Zhukov knew of the planning going on in the Kremlin and in Dimitrov's international office in Moscow, and that seems more than doubtful, he never said a word of it to his eminent guests.

Less than a week after the Moscow planning meeting, and the liaison visit of Eisenhower and Montgomery, the Soviet authorities suddenly and surprisingly announced unilaterally, without consultation with their Western allies, the resumption of political activity for their zone and Berlin. These were orders handed down by Stalin. All the hand-picked "nonpartisan" local governments would be part of a new political order. "Antifascist" parties, potentially of national scope, could be founded. The Communist Party, with a manifesto written in Moscow in collaboration with Dimitrov, was the first party to be licensed; the Social Democrats were the next. Backstage, under Ulbricht's encouraging eye, the Communist and Social Democratic party leaders were eagerly attempting to bridge over their traditional antagonisms by establishing special cooperative working groups, and they spoke hopefully of the prospect of reestablishing the long demolished unity of the German Marxist front. It was Stalin however, who had ordered the separate parties. Certainly, establishing a single workers' party immediately, as had been proposed earlier in Moscow and considered later in Berlin, would not only alert the Westerners to his plans but also provoke the founding of a Moscow-hostile German Social Democratic Party somewhere beyond the Soviet zone of control.[39]

Still, the two Marxist parties in Berlin, if they could be brought to work together, would carry a heavy weight in the Bloc. Given the ascendant, popular leftist state of mind, they could effectively influence the new social and political order in Germany. Stalin even had in mind that they would definitely continue to collaborate. Indeed, less than a year later they "spontaneously" merged, in an operation that Stalin himself oversaw, into one party.

Because the Soviet forces from the beginning of the occupation ran the censorship and all presses and controlled all printing materials in Berlin, the Communists quickly had their own newspaper on the stands. Production was organized in Moscow. The paper was edited, although few were aware of the connections then, by one of the Moscow group, Paul Wandel, a Soviet citizen. The Social Democrats had to wait for their newspaper until July, some time after the Americans and British had come to Berlin; it, too, was published in the Soviet sector of the city. Also in July, two middle-class "antifascist" parties were launched in the eastern sector and licensed by the Soviet authorities, again with Stalin's blessing, in Berlin.[40] This group of parties, and the specific organizations that were attached to them, were not significantly different from the partisan and representational organizations founded earlier in the other

Soviet-occupied states of east central Europe. Those groups also, as we have seen, not surprisingly furnished the political leadership installed by the Soviets.

The overall goal of the Soviet political work in Germany is evident. And here again the Soviets stole a march on the Westerners: they clearly expected as part of their scheme to organize political life from the former capital of the Reich, the center of German political activity since 1871. There organized, the parties they put up were to operate also, under Moscow control, in the Western sectors. It was easy for the Communists to assert party discipline from Berlin, running their agents even in the difficult circumstances of those days in the Western-occupied zones of Germany. But the Soviets, relying on Berlin's leading role as the former and prospective German capital,[41] expected to get the jump on the West in party life all over Germany. Once they had molded all the parties into an Anti-Fascist Bloc, using the Communists and their influence in the Social Democratic Party, they would have a potentially strong agency for asserting political influence in the network of corresponding parties in all the zones. Presumably everyone, or, at least, Stalin, who gave the original orders, imagined that all parties could be disciplined as completely as their own.

The Western Allies were very skeptical about an early renewal of German political life. They regarded all Germans as probably infected by the Nazi bacillus and in need of severe and sustained political reeducation. But the Westerners had not created any specially trained and dedicated German party cadres like Ulbricht's to undertake reeducation and eventual political leadership. Though they had named some German local authorities and assistants to help the military governors, they had no definite plan to license German political activity in their zones. The Soviet move to do so in their zone, even when only half of its assigned territory was under Red Army control, was an effort to seize popularity and at the same time to get one step ahead of the Westerners in constructing a new Germany. There is no doubt that the unilateral decision to allow political parties in their zone was popular among the Germans, an eager mass of whom, including not a few former Nazi sympathizers more than zealous to prove that the past was behind them, wanted to join up to serve in the new era that Ulbricht's *Moskali* promised. Few, if any, were eventually turned away: those who were incompetent, or were obvious political adventurers and insincere hangers-on, could always be reschooled or eliminated, as need be. Sudden disappearances, which later turned out to be more or less permanent removals to Siberia, or to local mass graveyards, became frequent in political life under the Soviet Military Administration in Germany (SMAD) for years to come. Nor did the Soviets confine their Moscow-style justice, which often was little more than kidnapping and exile, or murder, to its own zone and sector. Alive or dead (like Hitler), those from West or East who fell into Soviet hands were rarely heard from for years, sometimes never.

If the Bloc was viewed by the Kremlin as being all-German in importance, so, too, were the new Soviet-licensed trade unions that came out of the early liaison with workers and their former leaders. They served as an instrument for Soviet influence more indirect than the parties and the Red Army, and they gave Ulbricht and his group yet another popular organization for the repression of excessive spontaneity and ill-timed revolutionary action among the working classes, and for subordinating them to the party and Bloc chiefs in the zone. Not the least, they were another Soviet zonal organization to link up with comrades and to control trade unions in the rest of Germany.

Quite simply, behind the attractive slogans, "antifascist" and "democratic" (the words "socialism," not to mention "communism," were kept well in the background), the Soviet authorities were out to try to assert their authority over all Germany, working slowly, and by infiltration and persuasion.[42] The Soviets also expected to exploit the four-power Allied Control Council for Germany. They saw that it was contractually responsible, per inter-Allied agreement, for Germany as a whole. Once the Western partners had taken up their places, it was to sit in Berlin, and be the representative body of all the occupying powers, to have authority over every sector of the city and every zone of the former nation—except, according to Soviet thinking, which prevailed, for those parts behind the Oder–western Neisse line. The Soviets had of course already unilaterally expropriated those lands and assigned them to themselves and their Polish clients. Under the Control Council, each power would have a veto in what had earlier been designed by the wartime diplomats as a temporary central Allied government for all occupied Germany. The conception behind the Control Council suggested that, at least back then, all the Allies had imagined postwar German political and economic life as being reestablished collaboratively and slowly, under strict control of all the occupying powers so as to ensure its thorough democratic nature. By the time the Council first met, the Soviets were well ahead of the Westerners in planning and forming that political and economic life.

Walter Ulbricht, who had survived the Moscow school of hard knocks and the *Ezhovshchina,* one of the cruelist Stalinist purges of the 1930's, meant to allow the Social Democrats their illusions of future party and parliamentary democracy and unionism, and also to allow the "bourgeoisie" their hopes for some moderate influence in politics toward the preservation of private property, even in a land under the occupation of the Red Army. In June, even before all the parties had been founded, Marshal Zhukov had brought together all the potential Bloc party leaders to express bland hopes for the new "antifascist, democratic" political system. His associates from Pieck, Ulbricht, and company, were meanwhile getting their secret hopes for Germany's Soviet future organized at the meeting with Stalin in Moscow. Therefore, when the first four parties were actually brought together as an antifascist bloc in July, the Communists and their collaboration-minded allies in the Social Democratic Party were already quietly staking out their roles. The Social Democrats, however, were unaware not only of the tenor of Stalin's discussions with the Communist leaders but, indeed, also of the fact that such discussions had been held.

The Yalta agreements had stipulated that the borders of the four occupation zones were to be made formal, and that the Control Council would have its first meeting, when the respective Western armies took over their sectors of Berlin and moved and removed there and elsewhere to the prescribed edges of their zones of occupation. As early as the middle of April, the Americans and British were far east of their designated zones of occupation, having established a military line in central Germany where they would wait for the onrushing Red Army. They had done this in order to ensure effective liaison and the security of both sides when they finally met. The Westerners were established in Czechoslovakia—they could well have penetrated to Prague and beyond, had the Russians not insisted on taking that city themselves—and they were deep in Austria and in occupation of major centers of what was to be the Soviet Zone, including Leipzig, Halle, Chemnitz, Schwerin, and Wismar.[43]

Although the corridors by which the British and American armies were to reach their sectors of Berlin had been previously designated, the Red Army chiefs were very stubborn in the negotiations over the actual movement of the troops (the French were only allowed into their sector much later), but the movement of the Western armies finally commenced; even then, the Soviets did just about everything they could do to obstruct the Allied occupation of the assigned city sectors. Some American units had to camp along the road, which was itself temporarily blocked by the Soviets. Perhaps this difficulty only shows Soviet disorganization, one Soviet hand frequently being unaware of the other's task.

But what the Westerners found in the city can scarcely be attributed to blundering. They found the Red Army and its civilian employees from the German population, and the local "governments" and their paid bureaucrats, in firm occupation of the local administrative centers of the districts, including those assigned to the Westerners.[44] They only then discovered that both district and central political life were already well organized and that the Soviets were in possession of all the apparatus of civil government in all sectors.

The Soviet-organized propaganda apparatus was also already well oiled. All these agencies took their international news from TASS, the single official Soviet agency. Its masters had overlooked no propaganda forum. They had booked the film theaters with quickly dubbed, classic Soviet films, and with newer productions like *Berlin*. *Berlin* was already showing on the Kurfürstendamm on July 19 (in the heart of the British sector), and it opened at 30 or 40 other Berlin theaters just a few days later. Lucky Berliners could also see the Soviet film of victory day in Moscow, with the tossing of the Nazi banners at Stalin's feet, in their choice of 30 different cinemas. Soiuzintorg, the Soviet trading agency, had already signed exclusive multiyear distribution contracts with cinema managers in all sectors of Berlin.[45] By not broadcasting the imminent arrival of the Western armies to their sectors, the Soviets had magnificently upped the level of their already considerable force of blackmail in the business dealings they forced with the house managers.

These machinations, scarcely unique, of reinforcing fear simply by withholding information suggest how important it was for Soviet purposes that their press, radio, and film distribution system in Germany held access to all important information about the major events that were affecting its audiences. And once again we witness how important was the Stalinists' ability to exploit confusion as well as to sow it.

For this, the Russians and German Communists also used the Soviet-controlled radio, which could easily be heard in many of the areas occupied by the Western Allied forces. Out in western Germany, for example, even British intelligence observers for weeks gave credence to the Berlin radio reports of a higher standard of available food and the prominently announced higher levels of basic rations for Germans in the Soviet Zone. Such gullibility establishes both that the Westerners faithfully believed the Soviets at the outset, and that the Soviets had already effectively blocked most communication between their zone and those in the west. These reports worried the British, because some of their German charges in the west grumbled about the relative severity of the treatment they were suffering. As soon as the Westerners arrived in Berlin, they realized how misled they had been. Babies were dying regularly because of the complete lack of milk; the former well-to-do and workers alike were selling whatever goods they had; and some women were selling themselves for food.

To be sure, TASS had then not yet taken up an overtly anti-Western propaganda line. That only appeared in mid-August, after the end of the war in the Pacific. For the present, the Soviets were still in some sense allies of the Western powers, and would be in fact as soon as the anticipated Soviet attack on the Japanese empire began. The campaign to defame the Western states and their economic and governmental systems, though it had already been launched with considerable subtlety in Soviet and satellite journalism, therefore remained superficially unremarkable in the early summer of 1945.[46]

The crucial public issues of the summer of 1945 in Germany were food and housing. These matters of basic survival were enormously aggravated by the influx of millions of Germans who were being driven out of heavily agricultural Soviet- and Polish-occupied eastern Germany, as well as out of the Sudeten borderlands repossessed by the Czechs. The German population west of the Oder-Neisse line, especially the young, the old, and the females, these heads of households because of the wartime deaths and prison camps full of German males, was expanding on a much smaller territorial base in a time of utter social chaos.

Except for Walter Ulbricht and a few others, no one in Germany knew how much of the nation was to be lopped off to create its Moscow-planned eastern border. And it is unlikely that Ulbricht knew the full extent of the pending changes when he left for Berlin.

It appears that during the first month of the Red Army occupation, he was unaware of the creation of the western Neisse border that cut almost all of Silesia away from Germany. He, and Dimitrov as well, also did not know that Stettin, on the west bank of the Oder, was to go to Poland, for, as we know, the Germans in Moscow, with the support of Dimitrov, who was one of Stalin's closest advisers, sent a group to Stettin to organize party work and government there.[47]

The Western Allies, who thought they had a say over all of occupied Germany in its prewar (1937) borders, most assuredly did not know that Stalin's territorial plans were fixed, but they did know that he was, with his early people-moving, already violating the sense of the Yalta agreements. As we have seen in the case of Stettin and Lwów, the comforting illusion held by the Western leaders until they met actual Soviet determination head on at the Potsdam Conference in July, was that a final resolution had been reserved at Yalta for a postwar conference that would deal with the "humane" transfer of populations and the final fixing of borders between Poland and Germany, and between Poland and the Soviet Union.[48]

Hard information on the population transfers was simply not publicly available in Germany, except from personal observation, for all frontiers were tightly controlled. The Polish descriptions of those events were more propagandistic than systematic, hyped up in the shrillest revanchist language to give an emotional sop to Poles at home facing the loss of the Polish east. Nor were they distributed beyond Poland's borders. The difficulties of the Polish language, moreover, blocked reception of the reporting by the Germans affected, and even by Western reporters. The latter could not, in any case, move freely across the Soviet-manned frontiers and zonal borders to collect the information they needed for their reporting. Meanwhile, the Soviet-sponsored media were almost totally silent, except for broadcasting a speech by Ulbricht, which few probably heard, late in June telling that the eastern territories were lost but saying nothing of the human dimension. The few newspapers and radio broadcasters in that part of Germany abutting the new Polish borders made no references to the moving of people during the summer of 1945, though it was the most massive combined deportation ever carried out in Europe west of the Soviet frontier. By orders from Communist Party headquarters in Berlin, the hapless, footsore refugees were detoured around the cities. People traveling or living on

the major thoroughfares or anywhere where the refugees passed saw
the refugee columns, but they never read of them, or officially heard
of them. No one knew how many refugees would come, where they
would go, or how long they would stay.

Hence neither the Western Allies nor the captive Germans had
any complete idea of the dimensions, and especially of the prospective dimensions of the human flood that was crisscrossing the nation bearing it more deprivation and even pestilence. These luckless
civilians would ultimately require the care and support of the war-
enfeebled west of Europe. The French and British governments, already struggling to feed and care for their own peoples, masses of
German prisoners, and the millions of displaced persons who were
fighting return to Soviet-occupied Europe, were unhappily obligated
to support their zones of occupied Germany. That meant also, as
they soon discovered, the millions of refugees, most of them coming
in from the former German east. And though the Soviets were directly and indirectly responsible for the expulsions and for some of
the conditions that had brought about the deluge of refugees, they
obviously intended to let others deal with the consequences. Simply
by their inaction they had shifted much of that responsibility to the
Western powers.

Soviet maps that were published compounded the misinformation
and illusion. They illustrate another measure of how the Soviets
purposely misled the people. Maps in Soviet-controlled newspapers
in Germany showed only two occupation areas within the borders of
1937, not de facto 1945, Germany: a Soviet Zone, including the territories that, as those in the Kremlin and higher-ups closer to hand
knew, were already being forcibly depopulated and, as far as Moscow
and Warsaw were concerned, incorporated in Poland and the Soviet
Union; and a "Western" Zone, in which the British, French, and
American zones were lumped together as one. The intention was
clearly to put the Western powers together in thought as one "capitalist" bloc, although they had been propagandistically celebrated as
individual allies all during the war. Pieck dutifully described to his
party faithful the postwar zonal situation in Germany in exactly
those terms in late June.[49] The obvious division in the dramatic
replay of the German surrender at Karlshorst had the same intention—to divide the world, per Marxist heritage, into us and them.

The Soviet maps showing Germany in its prewar borders quite
certainly were also meant to keep alive for German opinion the il-

lusion that those would be the postwar borders as well. Stalin had no intention of restoring the old Germany, so this was another deliberate dictatorial suppression of the facts. He had turned a great mass of Germany over to the Poles, and he was in the process of taking in a large morsel himself, but he had to try to woo the Germans while separating them from a large part of their ancestral lands. By giving as little information as possible, rumor and time could work their way. It was months before even Soviet films produced for the home market mentioned the expulsions, or the Russian annexation of Königsberg and part of East Prussia, or the redrafting of the western borders of the Soviet Union with Poland. The Soviet peoples apparently knew nothing for months of their territorial expansion at the expense of the Germans and particularly the Finns, or of the amended postwar borders with the Poles. (Finland had, indeed, lost even more land to the Soviets than they lost in 1940.)[50]

This information blackout appears in odd contrast to the loud domestic trumpeting of Soviet territorial expansion that accompanied the "liberations" of 1939 and 1940. There was no need, this time, for self-righteous sloganizing about the monstrous nature of the enemy and the defensive nature of the war. On the contrary, Stalin had good reason to redeem the wartime promises given him at Teheran and Yalta, and to take what he wanted in addition, without calling attention to himself as the author of some inevitably gruesome results. Perhaps he had decided that nothing should be described officially until all was legally signed, sealed, and delivered in the postwar peace treaty, where he could draw the Westerners into some of the problems of responsibility. Or perhaps his Western allies were not then to have their attention called to the fact (of which they were aware) that he was, on his own, settling matters to his satisfaction, and often at their expense. In any event, his play was calculated to keep the German audience he now so ardently courted in the dark for as long as possible about this part of the war's disastrous cost. And it also reflected more than a bit of that obsession with secrecy that dominated the Stalinist, and even post-Stalinist, systems in the USSR.

When the Soviet-controlled press, with no advance notice, at last announced the establishment of the four sectors in Berlin, it did so only on the actual arrival there in early July of the advance units of the British and American armies. It would have been difficult to postpone the story, vitally important to all Berliners, much longer.

But, even with that announcement, the Soviets never mentioned the quid pro quo evacuation by the Western Allies of thousands of square miles of Germany: Mecklenburg, Thuringia, Saxony, and the Mark Brandenburg. The Red Army, the press reported, had conquered Berlin. Now the city was to be divided, according to the agreement, into sectors—generous Soviet gifts of territory to the West, the reader seemed meant to assume. It was but another aspect of the Soviet scheme, centrally designed for domestic as well as foreign purposes, to rule the Western powers out of the credit for the victory over Nazi Germany.[51]

It was a consistent plan: no information, or misinformation, or disinformation, all to the end of creating a dark pall behind which Stalin could work out his purposes for Germany, and for all of Europe, in the late spring and early summer of 1945. The idea was to keep matters as flexible as possible, and to keep the Western Allies distracted, while keeping political partisans of non-Communist persuasion uninformed and off guard, allowing Stalin to make the maximum possible in claims and advances and to take full advantage of the chaos he had helped to create.

But he had made another serious error. Fearful as ever of straying beyond any place where he held control, he had once again required that the Western leaders come to him for the upcoming third wartime conference of the Big Three. They would meet at Potsdam, not far from the gutted heart of the former German state, and only a stone's throw from the sectors of Berlin so recently taken over by the two Western armies. Against the bleak backdrop of war's destruction and the chaos and terror that existed wherever the Red Army and NKVD ruled, the Western leaders could not miss the cries of outrage and frustration from the armies and administrators whom they had sent into the city just a few weeks before and who were now desperately striving to make some kind of order for their prescribed reigns in Western sectors of the Soviet-organized and looted former Reich capital. The sounds and movement of the Soviet occupation seemed an ominous sign of trouble to come. The shock of the Berlin milieu of July 1945 was a foretaste of the shock that the encounter with Stalin at Potsdam was soon to provide their leaders.

6

STALIN IN THE HEART OF EUROPE:
THE STALEMATE AT THE CECILIENHOF

MEANWHILE, with as much efficiency as their style of work could bring to bear, but with masses of idle Red Army hands available, the Soviets were carrying out the first part of their economic program in Germany. It was most assuredly not the "free-trade" economy that Anastas Mikoian had earlier suggested: they were carting away everything productive, and some things simply valuable, that was movable, even completely scavenging the sectors of Berlin that were assigned to the Western powers. The Red Army seemed bent on carrying off as much as possible before the Western armies were on hand and a reparations agreement was signed with the Western Allies; perhaps the Soviets thought the Westerners would not notice the material deficit when they arrived. This wholesale looting may not have been ordered from on high, however. Since Stalin was so ungenerous with information, and given the rampant lack of coordination and consequent disorganization, it may be that only Moscow and, significantly later, the highest command levels knew that the western sectors of the city would have to be surrendered. It is possible, also, though unlikely, that the sack of the Western sectors was a mistake arising from the postwar chaos and confusion. But whether it was simply the pillage of the victorious, vengeful army or something more deliberate that went too far—and even central Soviet authority, with the possible exception of the NKVD, had a long history of failing to carry out plans systematically—the Soviets made no offer to restore what they had removed.[1]

The German invasion and retreat had brought about incredible damage in the Soviet Union. Most people had forgotten by late in the war that a great part of the damage had actually been incited by Stalin under his 1941 "scorched earth" policy. During the war, that policy was affirmatively celebrated by Soviet propagandists and rapturously sung by excitable Western journalists as testimony to the steel will of the Soviet peoples.[2]

What the Soviets now did to help recompense themselves for the damages was to confiscate "fascist" enterprises and goods wherever they could lay hands on them. To a lesser extent, such seizures were also made by the Western Allies, though for a different announced purpose—that is, to break up cartels, trusts, and monopolies. This program all over occupied Germany collected its steam from the then prevalent, Marxist-fired obsession, official in the East and also widespread in the West, with big business and armaments makers as having been the secret instigators of war. For their confiscatory work the Soviets at the time therefore amassed more than a measure of respect and applause on the traditional American, Western, and Central European left. They appeared to be implementing a socially meritorious program, likewise anti-Nazi (and antifascist, insofar as the two words then had separate meanings in the West), directed toward the breakup of big business and the so-called arms cartels. For influential leftish popular economists, literati and litterateurs then as so often in this century garnered the most influential, and often the largest share of words in Western press productions. They held concomitant political influence. Visions of the sinister opponent of Lanny Budd, Sir Basil Zaharoff, and the other "merchants of death" possessed many an authoritative head. Names like Krupp and I. G. Farben were subsumed under the then common idée fixe, that such business undertakings were the direct institutional progenitors of the Nazi movement and board of directors—committed suppliers of funds to Hitler.[3] Indeed, one can almost see I. G. Farben in the mental pictures of some anglophone and other Western writers and would-be reformers as the big boss of that enterprise.

The Soviet search for reparations was hasty and sometimes unsystematic. They raced ahead of the Western Allies to proclaim seized properties and businesses forfeit as having belonged to the German government or Nazis, war criminals, or sometimes even "monopolist" enterprises. Any seizure qualified as reparations; and the qualifications for forfeiture were vague: "monopolist," undefined, was the approximate terminological equivalent (and not alone in the Soviet Zone) of "fascist." The result was the unconcealed sack and looting of the Soviet Zone of Occupation and Western sectors of Berlin propagandistically covered over under the rubric "reparations."[4]

Like every work of longtime social and political importance in the Soviet Zone, except for those the Soviet Military Administration chose to advertise, these strikingly visible undertakings went unreported in the Soviet-controlled press and radio except as shadowed in generalized attacks on "plutocrats, industrialists, bankers ("who organize war and robbery"), monopolists, Junkers," and the like. Behind every move, except, perhaps, the random thefts and robberies carried out by the undisciplined Red Army soldiers, lay the plan of a sweeping economic and social revolution that would first take in industry and then agricultural land. The extension of the line of confiscation to domestic agriculture, almost identical to one pushed a year before in Poland, began without any public notice except for the announcement of the necessity of seizing the property of large agricultural owners, Junkers, Nazis, war criminals, and other corrupt landholders. Publicly, all that was said was that there would be economic, social, and political moderation. And these changes, even the planning of the revolution in landownership, were all well under way long before the conference at Potsdam, and in a time of absolute chaos. The conference had in fact been chiefly organized to deal with just these economic, social, and political matters all over Germany.

Yet these Soviet programs ultimately backfired, locally, and also nationally and internationally, because they were too swift and too sweeping. The seizures of property along with plundering and *démontage*, and overtly socializing economic moves such as the sudden abolition of private banking, hindered rather than served Stalin's purposes. Certainly they did nothing to help relations with the often flabbergasted Westerners who had to deal with the consequences, and they also inevitably alienated the Germans who were struck by them. And even their opinions, with the Western leaders coming to town, came to be important.

The Potsdam Conference, which lasted from July 17 to August 2,

1945, brought the three Allied heads of state together for the first time in victory to settle matters hanging over from the war in Europe, and to plan for the war still continuing in the Pacific. Most of the conferees flew in; Stalin came on by train, no doubt hounded by a well-merited fear of flying. But in the later film version of those days, *Padenie Berlina* (The Fall of Berlin), made by one of Stalin's pet directors, Stalin, resplendently clad in the white-tunicked uniform of a generalissimo, is shown flying in over the gutted Reichstag and landing to the cheers of masses of Red Army soldiers, DP's, and released Nazi prisoners. (Even years later the Stalin chosen, but improper, symbolic target could not be put aside.)

Potsdam was a Soviet show, in their zone. The Allied leaders were invited by the Soviets to sit at a round table in the lovely Cecilienhof, a pleasant, once royal Prussian, palace in the English style set in a large park with a sweeping view of the Havel River and lakes and the forests and palaces of Berlin. A member of the American delegation, Admiral William D. Leahy, remembered that in the room where the conferees met, "a huge recessed window gave a beautiful view of the landscaped gardens."[5] That broad panorama of river and forest was, after 1961 and for almost thirty years thereafter, obscured by the grotesque Berlin Wall standing some 100 meters away.

For all the charm of the grounds, the setting had been turned into a Soviet-sanitized hothouse, clearly marked in the entry courtyard by a large red star of newly planted begonias. From these precincts, Germans had been forcibly excluded. The heavily guarded estate, just inside the Soviet zonal borders, was well away from gutted Berlin and much destroyed royal Potsdam. The conferees were perhaps supposed not to notice the ugly reality of the terrible local destruction, rapine, and starvation, pervaded by what Charles Bohlen called the "ambient odor of death."[6] The symbolism of the meeting at the capital of the defeated Reich was of course meant to be portentous. But the effect of the scene on Harry S Truman, and no doubt on the others, was more than that. Truman wrote of it: a horrible place, "ruined, dirty, smelly," inhabited by a "forlorn, bedraggled people."[7]

Twice before, Stalin had got his way in the choice of location for Big Three conferences. Potsdam was his milieu, as Yalta and the Soviet Embassy in Teheran had been in earlier years. In his own security zone, he probably felt safer, and he also could, if he chose, monitor the intimate discussions of his Western rivals in their own quarters. That both Roosevelt, for whom travel was always difficult, and Churchill, who was older than Stalin, had, on both earlier occasions, agreed to make long journeys to meet Stalin in his own environs and to discuss matters within Soviet-controlled premises says something about the whole odd relationship between the trusting Western Allies and the paranoid Soviet dictator.

This time, however, with the Western leaders on hand just a stone's throw away from Berlin, the conferees, although housed and fed in the best style in the carefully prepared and insulated surroundings, were nonetheless to live and work in an environment where the daily realities of practical dealings with the Soviets, at a level lower than that of the earth-shaking manipulations and festivities at the "summit," inevitably lurked in the near background of their decision making. Their choices and decisions at the conference came to be made partially in the light of the experience, vicarious and real, of that background. Even in the rarified atmosphere of the Cecilienhof, those on hand could not miss hearing tales of the unpleasant, sometimes ugly, encounters across the river at the level of daily life with the Red Army.[8] In this Soviet setting, where the newspapers and radio were all in Soviet hands, and where the local as well as general state of affairs in central Germany was to a measure the product of by now characteristic Soviet occupational behavior, there was bound to be conflict.

The chief preoccupation of the Potsdam Conference was supposed to be the organization of postwar Europe and Germany; there was also to be some secret military planning for the promised Soviet attack on Japan. But the main political and economic subjects for discussion were Poland and Germany. There were enormous questions to be considered about Germany's borders, the economy, government, and reparations, including the final amount, and the method, not yet fixed, of assessing the value of the entities making up the amount to be paid. A reasonable person would have stood in awe of even these latter tasks, which manifestly required a will to work together built on an ardent wish to compromise on salient issues of disagreement.

But was it possible to sustain the spirit of international cooperation when the will to cooperate, perhaps the very knowledge of how to do so, was so evidently lacking on one side? Could the illusion that Berlin, and all Germany, were occupied in common possibly be maintained? The Westerners thought so. American and British policy planners continued to pursue as their central goal the establishment of a peaceful Europe by means of East-West cooperation toward the construction of a democratic Germany, or a group of small democratic German states. From long democratic experience, they knew that in such negotiations each side had to be willing to collaborate. They thought they had earlier arranged such collaboration with the Soviets. In Berlin, at Potsdam, they met postwar realities head on. They met Stalin, now victorious, and a generalissimo, and illusion soon vanished.

Since May, President Truman had been trying to see the best in the Soviets, in spite of early doubts deriving from what he believed to be their abuse of agreements made with his predecessor, President Roosevelt. At Potsdam, where Truman encountered the Soviets himself for the first time, his earlier doubts were substantially confirmed. Indeed, there may be much to be said for diplomacy at the summit, if, as in this case, the participants are shrewd and well prepared. Neither Truman, nor, before the conference was over, the new British leaders, Prime Minister Clement R. Attlee and Foreign Secretary Ernest Bevin, seem to have been cursed with a will to self-deception.[9]

It was quite evident to the Westerners that the Soviets were already conducting totally independent economic, population, and political policies in their zone of what, according to earlier inter-Allied agreements, was understood to be an economically and politically unified Germany. Before long, but gradually and reluctantly, they also realized the Soviets undeniably had their own wholly different scheme for Germany's future. Toward that end, Stalin had, as noted, earlier proclaimed a retreat from the Yalta-agreed plan to divide postwar Germany into small states. By suddenly moving to hold Germany together, with the exception of the vast parts he had already annexed for himself and his friends in the east, Stalin was trying to court the German public; he also meant to maintain the prospects for Soviet influence and, in the long run, control in Germany all the way west to the Rhine.[10]

One crucial element in this long-range scheme had to be the Germans themselves. Many had already been terrified during the first days of the occupation by first- and second-hand encounters with the Soviets' misbehavior. Though the worst Soviet excesses had largely stopped and some order had been restored by the time the Western forces took up their places in Berlin in early July, there were still daily personal assaults and irregular interventions in the precarious postwar social, economic, and legal order, already battered by systematic interventions requiring that almost everything be founded anew. A state with years of experience in handling its own citizens as swine could scarcely be expected to treat a defeated enemy's civilians differently, even under ideal conditions. And Soviet propaganda and German wartime behavior in the east had created the basis for anything but ideal conditions.

In those days, many Germans, and the Western Allies on the spot, found it difficult to reconcile high-minded Soviet propaganda slogans with the arbitrariness of Red Army behavior. The brutal and petty acts of the Red Army soldiers, which continued substantially unabated for months, plus the random confiscations, directed against the defeated civilians and their possessions, even in the Western sectors of Berlin, alienated the very German public opinion Stalin had recently shown himself so eager to cultivate. Frightening rumors, which later turned out to be true, of Soviet-instigated mass imprisonments and mass executions also surfaced and circulated.

Against this background of systematic and haphazard terror, the Soviet authorities were relentlessly pursuing de facto their semi-secret social and political revolution in Germany. Unannounced, it was being directed from the Kremlin through émigré theoreticians, propagandists, the Red Army, and Stalinist apparatchiki, not all of whom it seemed, had the same marching orders. Given Stalin's personal concern to control even the smallest details wherever his power extended, this was a crew collectively not fitted to any task except that of upsetting what remained of the devastated social order.

To be sure, some of the dedicated, middle-aged (and older) German Communist refugees, who had long languished in the Hotel Lux and elsewhere in Muscovite rooms, plotting and planning out of the fantasies of distant exile, were tactically astute. Knowing the nature of the frightened German petite bourgeoisie they would have to deal with in creating a Communist-controlled postwar Germany, they understood that they would have to proceed circumspectly. Before they could get matters in their control, they would have to satisfy the urgent demands of Germans at the local level. But they never did get matters completely in their hands, as did their counterparts elsewhere. Risks that never came into play in the forced Sovietization already under way, for example, in Poland under Red Army occupation, were abundant in Germany. Notably, the task had to be done in the presence of others who were far from sharing its concealed goals. The all-important difference in central Europe was the Western Allies, who proved to be the ultimate disruptive element for Soviet planning. They were on hand as a major armed force in the center of Germany and its former capital (as they were also in Austria, and soon in its former capital), as they were not in the Red Army-occupied states in the east.

Inevitably, the discontents of the civilians along with those of Allied forces in Berlin were, in the ways that reports and rumors travel, also carried up to the conference table.[11] One British intelligence observer, evidently somewhat astonished at the reception the Westerners got when they arrived, wrote: in Berlin "the Germans seem unreservedly glad to see us. . . . After years of the heaviest bombing the city was put to the sack, a sack which lasted two months"—all this in the face of Soviet placards proclaiming that the Red Army is incapable of racial hatred. One woman, he noted, said, "The only time Goebbels didn't lie was when he told us about the Russian character."[12] If few Western observers were prepared to extend much sympathy to the Germans, they were at the same time not spiritually prepared to overlook random theft, kidnapping, murder, rape, starving children, and dying infants.[13]

The two new Western leaders who came to this last conference of the major Allied powers, Harry Truman and Clement Attlee, supplied important changes of personality. Attlee as the new British Prime Minister took over the British seat midway during the conference after the Labour victory in the general election in July. Churchill's departure left Stalin as the only one of the original Big Three.

Stalin had arrived in Berlin for the conference a day late, presumably because of illness. This delay, and a later indisposition, along with the British change of leadership, compressed substantially the time that the Western leaders could spare far away from urgent domestic business of state. Truman was impatient with the whole diplomatic process, and having a long sea and air journey on each end of his stay, he wanted to make decisions as quickly as possible.[14] The newly elected British Labour leaders had a social revolution of their own to effect at home, and an electoral mandate to do it, and were no doubt eager to get on with making their theories and plans into reality. The Westerners therefore pushed to set a limit to the proceedings. In so doing, they worked to their own disadvantages. By

fixing a time limit, they put themselves under pressure to make concessions and compromises they might otherwise not have made.
With the discontinuities of personnel and experience, and with the
wide-ranging discussions over what suddenly emerged in fabulous
new Soviet claims, and with the inevitable delays and complications
of translations, it was difficult to hold to the subject matter.

In spite of original expectations that Germany's future would be
the center of discussion, the heads of state and their representatives
at the Cecilienhof were soon preoccupied with both German and
still unresolved Polish matters that were hanging over as yesterday's
much marked-up agenda from earlier conferences. Discussions also,
thanks to Stalin, ranged over Soviet demands for control of the Dar-
danelles (recalling Molotov's demands of 1940 in Berlin); pressure to
do something about Francisco Franco (probably in retaliation for Soviet interference in the Spanish Civil War, he had sent a division to
fight on the German eastern front); Soviet requests for mandates in
African territories, and even the conduct of elections in such disparate nations as Romania and Italy.[15] The appropriation of lands east
of the Oder–western Neisse by the Soviets and the formidable economic and population disaster the Westerners confronted in Germany, which was in significant measure a consequence of that appropriation, inextricably bound Germany and Poland together in the
discussions.

The renewed wrangling over Poland, its borders, reparations, and
government, was not altogether unexpected. Poland had been one of
the main topics at all the previous conferences. The Second World
War had begun with the assault on Poland's borders; the first conflicts of the nascent Cold War arose out of the failure over the entire
course of wartime diplomacy to deal satisfactorily with the governmental and geographical issues resulting from the earlier division
and political settlement of east central Europe, Poland at its center,
between Hitler and Stalin. Long before the conference at Potsdam,
Churchill, who by the spring of 1945 was expressing outrage at what
he had learned of Soviet behavior, had pegged the issue of Poland's
frontiers in the west as the touchstone of the conference's success
or failure.[16]

Stalin had already resolved the Polish governmental issue, and he
was now bent on resolving Polish border issues, by himself. He had
even succeeded in getting the Westerners to accept a Polish government consisting of his crew of former political unknowns of the

PKWN-Lublin group. (Clement Attlee, recalling the appearance of the PKWN group at Potsdam, wrote of them, "I had never seen such a collection of shifty looking individuals in all my life"; Churchill had earlier termed them, "filthy, loathesome, Quisling[-Pole]s," and Eden had called them "creepy.") Stanisław Mikołajczyk was also in attendance, but not as premier of the new government. He had soon found himself after arriving in Warsaw forced to take a lesser portfolio than the premiership that had earlier been systematically noised to him, and, for widespread confusion, to the Western press.

One undiplomatic scene presumably contributed to Stalin's boldness in changing his Polish colleagues' earlier personnel program: Churchill had appallingly browbeaten Mikołajczyk in Stalin's presence in the Kremlin the previous October. Presumably this episode and his further successes in putting his own captive Polish band in place in Warsaw virtually unchallenged led Stalin to believe that the Westerners were still pushovers. Churchill, for example, who several times at Potsdam sounded enthusiastic about Stalin, even congratulated Stalin on his success in settling the matter of the Polish government. Stalin had also, of course, settled the issue of Poland's western frontiers to suit himself, "without so much as a 'by your leave,'" as Harry Truman noted.[17]

Churchill's apparent ambivalence, veering from skepticism to enthusiasm, was not helped by Anthony Eden's continuing good faith in what the future would bring. Eden had persuaded himself before Potsdam that things were going well in both Poland and Germany.[18] Perhaps he had not read the intelligence summaries reporting Soviet behavior and Stalin's carping, anti-Western propaganda lines. At the same time Stalin, behind his screen of insinuations, lies, disinformation, and the Red Army, and taking advantage of the spirit of cooperation still prevalent among Western leaders, was determinedly pushing his influence westward as best he could.

These Polish successes probably encouraged Stalin's aim in Germany: to fix his control over all of it. So, keeping to his secret agenda, the Soviets, just before the Potsdam Conference, had quietly advanced their deliberately unarticulated, but all-important, political plans to expand their control to the Rhine. They secretly founded central government portfolios—in effect, began to build a government—in Berlin.[19] Trusted German comrades, led by those trained in Moscow, took the key roles in these specialized ministries. No one bothered to consult the diplomatic or military representatives of the other Allied powers, even then locally on hand to help in governing Germany, with respect to collaboration in this undertaking—just as no one had consulted them on establishing local governments (even in the Western sectors of Berlin), or on the establishment of the all-German political parties. The Westerners, in the meantime, had been making plans to propose at Potsdam the establishment of local German political entities on a four-zonal basis.

The Soviet plan for the expansion of its realm of control in Germany, a combined operation, was being put to work on two levels, the first, that of *die grosse Politik*, Stalin working at the conference table; the second, that of the local faits accomplis. The latter were directed by the Red Army Political Administration and its German helpers. They were relentlessly enacting, day by day, as unobtrusively as possible, programs for getting and holding economic and political power all over Germany. At the same time, they were proceeding in much the same way in the Balkans and in Austria; they had already unilaterally established central governments in Bulgaria, Hungary, and Austria and were pushing the Western Allies to accept them.[20]

The existence of the Soviet-inspired governmental portfolios for Germany went publicly unmentioned all through the conference, in spite of the fact that the offices were organized and functioning. Then, toward the very end of the plenary sessions, Stalin suddenly proposed that a German central government be established. He made this proposal in the middle of a discussion about the German economy, without any reference to the existing Allied Control Council for postwar governance of Germany (then just beginning to meet), and, indeed, without any plausible reference to the day's agenda, or to the list of discussion items the Soviets had presented when the conference began. Stalin slipped in his proposal very casually in reference to a vague document that had been presented the previous day; a few minutes later he repeated the proposal.[21] It was as if he had been waiting for a favorable moment to bring out this formidable novelty.

But Stalin had not reckoned on Western skepticism. His ministries were in existence, but his undoubted plan of making them part of a larger government of all of postwar Germany was never realized. Earlier, the suspicious Western leaders had indeed refused to sanction Stalin's anointed Austrian government without closer investigation. Even then, they held firmly in mind the examples of his Balkan governments, which they had so far refused to recognize despite Stalin's appeals, and the new one in Poland, for which only Churchill among them maintained enthusiasm. Therefore, when Stalin brought up this amazing proposal for a central German government, the Westerners were quite prepared. The proposal was tactfully put over by new British Foreign Secretary Ernest Bevin and Truman to consideration by the Allied Control Council itself. There they held half the votes and a veto. Stalin saw one basis of his private German program, plainly a key move in his would-be political *Drang nach Westen*, fail Western ratification.[22]

Quashing Stalin's disingenuous proposal, the Western leaders proceeded on their original assumption that a four-power Control Council would work out all the specific problems of internal German economic and political administration. This would obviously be a slow undertaking. To carry out the tasks of governing, they planned to employ Germans as consultants and representatives, presumably as nonpartisan technical help.[23] This was, of course, quite in contrast to the Soviets' use of newly ordained politicians in the Soviet-created governmental agencies. They had already organized such help, and were seeking more, in their zones. But the Western leaders never seemed to recognize at the time of the conference that the political tasks of the council had indeed been preempted for the Soviet Zone by the secret formation of the new central ministries. Nor did they see beyond their hopes for a unified economy in the four zones, even though the separate Soviet Zonal economic program that wholly undermined their plans was then at least half accomplished.[24]

The Westerners left Potsdam at the beginning of August far more suspicious of Stalin and his schemes than they had come. Yet they left continuing to believe that Germany, without the part east of the new Soviet-created Polish frontier they reluctantly came to accept as lost, if only tacitly conceded at Potsdam, would be treated as a single economic and political unit under the Control Council. They seemed to believe still that their original plans would ultimately prevail. They still thought that Germany's future political and economic system, with its mandated democratic institutions, would develop from the Council's decisions alone, and eventually flourish under its control. But this regime and these institutions would come into being only when all powers agreed they were feasible.

Privately ignoring his allies, Stalin continued to pursue his plans ding his antifascist Bloc parties, tied closely to Karlshorst, own existing local and central governments. He seemed to assume that the Control Council, or the Western leaders, would in time come round to seeing matters his way. Probably he expected that the parties and his other agencies, of which so many to suit every Soviet organizational purpose were then being developed, could be used to mobilize public opinion, including a powerful Communist party in the West, against the foreign military governors in the Western zones when the proper time for that move arose.

So, predictably, the Soviets made another vain effort to interject the matter of Stalin's government-in-waiting into conference-level politics by bringing up the key all-German government issue at the next opportunity, the Council of Foreign Ministers' meeting in late September. This reiteration of the same Soviet theme reemphasized Stalin's undiminished, though publicly unarticulated, determination to gain further influence, and ultimately sway, over all Germany. And beyond Germany, the Kremlin no doubt kept well in mind, lay the rest of exhausted postwar Europe.[25] But Stalin was in effect already undoing his grand plans by ordering the relentless Sovietization of his zone of Germany. The more he moved toward Soviet economic and political control in the Soviet Zone, the more he widened the gap between the zone and the rest of Germany that he wanted to control. Perhaps no one then quite knew that the separation was increasing geometrically with every passing day.

It must be stressed here again that the new Western leaders Stalin met at Potsdam were very much tougher minded and more skeptical than their predecessors had been at Teheran and Yalta. Even before the conference at the Cecilienhof, incoming Prime Minister Attlee and Foreign Secretary Bevin had reasonable doubts about the whole Soviet enterprise in east central Europe, as President Truman most assuredly also had. Their professional advisers, too, were far more critical of the Soviets than many of the wartime advisers in both London and Washington had been. The intelligence information the President and Prime Minister were by then getting from their advisers would necessarily have encouraged all kinds of legitimate doubts about Soviet behavior all over Europe.[26]

Moreover, Truman and Attlee, as neophytes in diplomacy, were prone to listening. Both were experienced in domestic politics, and Attlee had somehow managed to operate successfully in Churchill's shadow all through the war. But they did not have to unload the psychological baggage of earlier failed cooperation with the Soviets, cooperation Churchill and Roosevelt had maintained desperately even when it seemed to meet no fair response.

The flagrant differences between Eastern and Western values and concomitant behavior consistently cropped up at the conference table in Stalin's tricks and devices, which aggravated the Western participants and delayed the conduct of conference business. The way in which Stalin brought up his central German government platform almost out of the blue, without reference to the lengthy and tedious discussions on postwar German issues that had been going on ever since Yalta, was but one example of his whole manner; he seemed to interrupt whatever point was under consideration by interjecting matters that demanded careful consideration (in this case one that the others thought had been temporarily resolved months before). This sort of interruption and the extraordinary assertions and demands with which he responded to legitimate questions about his machinations with reparations, borders, and expulsions kept the conference away from productive challenges to Soviet behavior in Europe, or from business in general. When challenged on an issue, Stalin would frequently respond with some barefaced lie, such as saying that there were no Germans left east of the Oder–western Neisse line, so their existence there could not pose a problem to the Poles. Only the diplomatic courtesy of the conference table permitted such extravagant assertions to pass unchallenged.[27]

All the Western participants, new as well as old, were fully aware of Stalin's prevarications, and they found Molotov a hopeless negotiating partner. Here again, they did not voice their skepticism, except occasionally when Stalin challenged them head on.[28] Privately, however, they had grave doubts about the man Attlee called "a slippery customer," and about his intentions. And, now that the European war was won, they were not bound by the same pressures that had governed the attitudes of their predecessors.

Part of this radical change in Western attitudes, beyond that derived from the different states of mind the new leadership brought to the conference table, had to have come about just because these conferees met in the geographical middle of the area of dispute. At earlier meetings in Soviet-sanitized milieus far distant from the places discussed, the Westerners could concoct fanciful plans for the future while both ignorant of and, in their zeal to end the war in harmony, emotionally beclouding the future's likely realities. In the different circumstances at Potsdam, postwar reality, the Red Army, the NKVD, and Stalin's German agents were all about. At Potsdam, Stalin slowly cut away at his perceived wartime character: by proving himself unreliable when it came to the reality at hand, he made himself suspect about those realities out of sight. And the presence of his agents gave the Westerners a profound sense of the nature of Continental political geography and its connection with Soviet political and military power that earlier negotiators could only imagine.[29]

The evidence of Soviet deceptions and the Soviet state's different political and social values fell steadily into place at every level and locale of Western Allied–Soviet encounter over the summer of 1945. The Westerners saw for the first time, at first hand, the giant propaganda banners, the posters with their blown-up and retouched photos of the vozhd' and his Kremlin subalterns, the oversized signs and symbols expressing Soviet power hanging everywhere among the ruins of Berlin, doubly absurd in the ravaged landscape. These were the standard Soviet trappings, long familiar in the Soviet homeland and soon familiar in the vaster empire, but, at the time, strikingly new to the West; even the Americans, in election years, had not seen such public displays of personalities and affirmative slogans. The Westerners were astounded, too, by the newly put up, obviously permanent victory monuments and memorials, all of which proclaimed the magnificence of the Soviet victory, the power of the Soviet armed forces, the grandeur of Soviet leadership, and the eternal correctness of its thinking. All stood out against a background of complete disaster.[30]

In the light of recent encounters and discoveries, and in sight of a world they had helped turn upside down, the Western leaders at this point had to make a quick reassessment of their wartime planning for a long-term, vindictive treatment of defeated Germany. It was evident that the Germans were already paying a colossal price for the war their leader had inspired. It was now clear that although the Western powers were already having to help meet that price, imposing a higher price on the Germans would only mean that the West would have to pay more of it themselves. They were already paying heavily for the consequences of Soviet reparations and territorial policies, insofar as these deprived the Germans of foodstuffs and productive employment and drove more refugees into the Western zones and sectors.[31]

In these circumstances, the American and British leaders discovered at last the urgent need to establish their own protective diplomatic and economic lines. They had to define a limit to further unilateral Soviet encroachments. And they had to do something to make it impossible for Stalin to redesign at will any previously made agreements with the West that he did not like. They had to maintain Western space and prerogative while at the same time hoping for a turnabout in Soviet behavior that would help to keep alive for their war-exhausted and heavily propagandized peoples the façade of United Nations unity.[32]

Their decisions, taken ad hoc at the Potsdam Conference in the light of what these leaders then knew, add up in retrospect to necessary, practical stands that developed out of the conferees' actual experience in the heart of defeated Germany. Some of these decisions mirrored changes of attitude; others came as the result of private resolutions, made quietly, perhaps desperately, on how to deal with Stalin in the future. Many were seized upon in the effort to wind up the dreary business in the war-sodden environment and go home before there was a head-on collision that would drag out the conference and, certainly, demolish the Westerners' illusions and hopes for peace. Even Stalin at that time may have felt the need to preserve some illusions, if only temporarily. But if he thought he could gain something from sitting on longer at Potsdam, Truman and Attlee were impatient to return to domestic affairs. So, almost inevitably, the rudimentary notion of territoriality, reflected in the several armies in place along lines fixed earlier for far different purposes, came to cast the limits of influence of East and West for years to come.

To Stalin, whatever emerged from the hectic circumstances in vague resolutions surely appeared to assist his way of ultimately gaining his expansive ends de facto. The vagueness appeared to leave open the possibility of his taking even more, once the Western leaders had gone home. In many cases, for example, that of the population expulsions and the arrangement of Poland's northern border with the USSR, they did just that.

Stalin had gained the impression from Roosevelt at Yalta that the American forces soon would leave Europe. Once they were away,

Stalin would feel easier: he always seemed to think that his long-term power to create mischief, in particular to paralyze action, to the west of Soviet lines in Europe was far greater than it truly was. Out there, he believed, the local Communists held the power to disarm their governments whenever the Foreign Bureau in Moscow sent the signal.[33] He had been harboring such dreams and fancies for many years. But, in fact, the schemes were not even tried, for Stalin was manifestly too cautious and too much preoccupied with other domestic and foreign problems, even in later postwar years, to move on a number of difficult fronts at a time.

The disagreements at the round table in the Cecilienhof were papered over by hopeful communiqués and a final statement stressing agreement, but the main result of the conference was that the Westerners gave up—they hoped not permanently—the firm effort at cooperation that had held the wartime alliance together. They had found it increasingly difficult to maintain the façade of cooperation. The only real points of agreement then were those to disagree and to postpone decisions, and to draw firmer lines both delimiting and more specifically assigning authority. With the separation between the Westerners and the Soviets, the wedge directed at the heart of the alleged unity of the wartime United Nations fell firmly into place and the first formal moves toward the postwar division of Germany were taken.[34]

One obvious and practical upshot of the separation implemented at all Western Allied levels in the summer of 1945 was that the Soviets were to be excluded from regular interventions beyond Soviet zonal borders in Germany. Their irregular interventions, kidnappings, and political manipulations that were supposed to help hold whatever power and places they did have inside the Western sectors of Berlin continued for years. But, in return for helping to fix the grounds for zonal separation, the West in effect conceded the Soviets a quid pro quo, the right to do as they chose within their own lines. That meant, too, that the West abandoned their expectations of an all-German governing body that would cooperate to hold sway in all the pre-1938 German territory. The organization itself, the Allied Control Council, had come into being. But its role was sharply diminished by the de facto concession to the Soviets of total sovereignty in all the German territories occupied by the Red Army in return for the implicit Soviet recognition of the final Western say in

all the German lands to the west: the Westerners had thus effectively conceded the limitations of the Council's authority.

It is doubtful that anyone at the conference systematically reflected on the long-term consequences of the limits that were gradually, but definitely, being set.[35] Stalin certainly did not. He was
determined to move onward, violating agreements, implicit or written, as far as possible, and he was still confident that he could move
west. His agents in the eastern sector of Berlin were even then working full-time toward that goal when they were not distracted by implementing their plans for the Soviet Zone. Probably Stalin did not
sense, in his obtuseness, the extent of the rebuff or the determination behind it strongly founded on the psychological sense of territoriality, however senseless the local limits of that territoriality.[36]

Not knowing Stalin's grander plans, the Western leaders plainly
hoped the standoff would not last. Truman, upon his return home,
continued desperate efforts to find modes of cooperation with the
Soviets. But his and British orders left behind for those on the scene
who had to deal with the Soviets there established the lines for the
confrontation to come.

What started as a sharpening conflict over Germany replaced, in
the summer of 1945, the wartime conflict over Poland as the focus
of Big Three antagonism. At Potsdam the Polish situation had been
resolved by Western recognition of Stalin's personnel as its government and the Western Allies' implicit surrender of their interest in
the German lands to the east of the Oder–western Neisse line. Here
again, the Westerners simply conceded what they could not control.
At the same time, however, they grasped that quid pro quo by reinforcing the existing zonal and sector borders in Germany and Austria as the prospective limit of the Soviet-style regime. If Stalin
hoped to change that limit while the Allied armies remained in
place along it, he would have to confront them directly. He was too
cautious to make such a move; and in any case, he had a different
vision of the future. He would triumph in the West as a result of the
erosion of Western strength behind the lines.

Stalin's proposal for a German central government had been enormously important to his vision. Because it was prospectively of such
enormous portent for the future political organization of Germany,
the Soviets and their German friends repeatedly brought it up in
postwar forums. Stalin's plans for Germany needed the extension of

these agencies, managed from his sector of Berlin, in the same way that they needed the all-German political parties, also managed from his sector of Berlin. These two parts of his scheme would work together to gain him control of German-speaking central Europe, for he had the same goal in mind for Austria. In a way, it was the plan of all those new governments Stalin had founded since the Finnish war of 1939. Therefore Stalin's failure to get more power in Germany at Potsdam marked a critical moment in Big Three history. The prize he had in mind was the grandest yet, and for the first time in the East-West negotiating encounters he was stymied. His German agents were denied the advantageous access to the Western political arena that they needed in order to take power there, as the vozhd' required of them.

In fact, the clever and far more labile policies pursued by Ulbricht, and even by local Soviet commanders who conferred with and helped him, were meanwhile booking many important local successes needed for the achievement of long-term Soviet goals for Germany. By spreading their intellectualized dreams of a peaceful future guaranteed by the antimonopolist Red Army, and of a post-fascist Europe beyond strife, they had already captured the opinion of much of Germany's guilt-ridden population, particularly the hopes of many anti-Nazi intellectuals, artists, writers, and filmmakers. The Soviets were successfully farming the "intelligentsia" and intellectuals—a tactic that almost always brought them important successes. They had invested much in the organization of societies, like a League of Democratic Women, a Chamber of Artists, a League of Culture, and the Free German Trade Union, that they meant to control. These groups, at first liberally managed, and enlisted in the vaguely pacifist antifascist front Moscow was supporting all over Europe, soon recruited countless sincere anti-Nazis for their ranks.[37]

Yet, even then, as often as not, directions from Moscow annulled or set aside the positive effect of this important work. The Soviet bureaucracy was as remote as Stalin himself from life outside the Soviet system, and evidently still as ignorant as they had been in 1939 of states of mind and political-social behavioral standards and expectations beyond the Kremlin's traditional reach. Stalin in 1939 had expected the Finns to rally to the Soviets and overthrow their own government upon a signal from Moscow. Similar preposterous expectations lay behind much of Soviet policy in east central Europe

STALIN IN THE HEART OF EUROPE   155

in the early postwar days. And because the Red Army and NKVD in eastern Germany possessed the force to make the revolution happen there, at whatever cost, Stalin could still, for a time, continue to hold rosy expectations about western Europe.

The Kremlin's overriding of local initiative and local information was to occur time after time in Germany, where the Soviets, in spite of all their misdeeds, really did have strong initial support and capable local leaders. Stalin's ultimate failures in Germany to secure the goals won to the east, eastward beyond the reach of Western eyes and armies, were therefore almost inevitable. The fault lay in the intrinsic frailty of the awkward and chaotic centralized tyrannical state, riddled with spies, that "execrable" system Stalin fostered and directed.[38] And to a degree also, the fault lay in Stalin's compulsion to take charge of every portfolio and to intervene in the tiniest details of his satraps' conduct. Thus the blocks set up at the Potsdam Conference to Stalin's purposes in central Europe reflect his personal failings and those of the institutions he nurtured, just as the successes to the east, measured by his standards, reflect his skills, and the dreadful force they had created.

Stalin apparently did not expect the Westerners to respond to his unilateral political moves in Germany in the way they did, but in fact the Western powers soon realized, once the experience of the confrontation at Potsdam was absorbed, that they could not allow the Soviets to organize and sustain the only political life in Germany while the four-power Allied Control Council struggled mightily just to set the basic mechanisms for its own functioning.[39] The Soviet political apparatus was going to function at Stalin's direction regardless of whatever governing mechanisms the Control Council finally arrived at, and the French were going to be grasping and vengeful, until they too, some years later, at last got the Soviet point. That being true, the British and American commanders had to counter the Soviets by permitting political activity in their zones and sectors.

In the fall of 1945, the Germans in much of the west got a freer hand from their occupation authorities to begin the development of their systems of politics. Free local elections were announced for the American Zone for January 1946.[40] It was the last thing the Stalinist cadre in the eastern sector of Berlin wished to see. Stalin in fact had, in his haste and ignorance and obtuseness joined to the inevitable cruelties of the Red Army and the NKVD, provoked the early rise of his own organized political opposition. It developed spontaneously, was soon relatively open and emphatically anti-Soviet, in fixed enmity to the guided Soviet zonal politics then directed out of Soviet headquarters at Karlshorst (when not directly by telephone from the Kremlin). Stalin and his Soviet helpers, "a bludgeon in one hand, a rubber truncheon in the other," had moved too quickly and too awkwardly.[41]

Stalin had done the same at the Potsdam Conference. As a result, the Soviets' Bloc parties and the other organizations prepared to secure Soviet influence, an eminent success story for the Soviet cause and its propaganda in the early days of the occupation, were, within a few months, to confront the spontaneously developing rival political structure set in a freer western German political environment. West of the forward line of the Red Army the Westerners were soon making it clear that they intended to superintend alone. Ulbricht and his group, with Stalin acting from his director's seat in the Kremlin, in the months to come continued to forge ahead systematically with their schemes to expand the net of their influence in the German west. Relying on the force of persuasion and the other controls usually available to the Red Army, they would harden their power, while gradually purging all opponents in their own zone. But every such step they took at home to secure themselves all the more firmly against the blossoming free politics of the West only decreased their political appeal and influence out there.[42] The focus of the comparatively open and politically competitive Berlin political environment slowly established by the presence of all four powers in the city soon became the main circle of light on Soviet behavior projected out to the world.

One further observation on matters centered on that focus on Berlin must be added to finish this set of historical reflections on Stalin's role in the coming of the Cold War. The history so far told has brought us topically and chronologically through the Potsdam Conference. It ended in the first days of August. With its end came the breakup, now if not then evident, of wartime inter-Allied unity, as well as the long abiding appeasement of Stalin.

After the Soviet blockade and final division of Berlin during the arch confrontations of the Cold War of the late 1940's and 1950's, many tears and lamentations, and much pain and expense, were registered over the city's regrettable and dangerous situation, its remoteness and its lack of secure corridors to the west. The lack of foresight and of Western leadership that brought about this mistake have been much condemned. But surely, in some respects, the accidental isolation did pay off handsomely in critical times. The Soviet breaking of channels of information wherever the Red Army came in east central Europe in the aftermath of the defeat of the Germans kept the West from knowledge of the tragedies of Sovietization there. But at least, until the building of the Berlin Wall in 1961, the presence of Western observers in their sectors of Berlin gave us out here, all over the world, one window on the East and minute-by-minute proofs of the Soviet Union's techniques, strategies, and programs for the Europe it took over. Those proofs could be sent out quickly from Berlin, first via photograph, news film, and radio, later, by television, all over the world within range of Western Allied information. Without the watching post that Berlin, as the hub of the Western confrontation with Stalin, became in the late 1940's, in the first years of the obvious Cold War, the Soviet system of obfuscation, lies, and disinformation would have kept us a great deal more ignorant of its continuing expansionist designs and yet more naively open to its dissimulating propaganda. The crudeness and brutality that could be witnessed daily over many years during the confrontation of East and West in Berlin, even the televised building of the infamous Wall itself, with all the often public human tragedies it involved, were proof of what others could only assert verbally of less visible corners of the Marxist-Leninist bloc.

Few generalizations about mass behavior hold like the following. It really does take a kind of seeing to believe, for comfortable people, like those in the West, will resist uncomfortable encounters with distressing information. They may compel sacrifices few would ever wish to make. Yet the sight of repeated injustice, if undeniable, ultimately bestirs even many of the most comfortable. Public campaigns effectively broadcast audio-visually in recent times on behalf of various sufferers in many parts of the world have strikingly confirmed and reconfirmed this behavioral observation. And that is why the eye into the East that Berlin then afforded was so important.

The joyful and sustained emotional charge recorded far beyond Germany after the breaching of the Wall in November 1989 testifies to how strongly Berlin as the symbol of the Cold War had become embedded in Western consciousness. Without that threatening line of the Soviet presence and the open window in Berlin, the West would have been the more innocent and prone to ignoring what was otherwise reported. And this was so mainly because of the large-scale failure, a failure that persisted even to the end of Soviet power, of Western media to open other wide and straightforward channels of vision in the Marxist world once that in Berlin was closed.

Moreover, the very same media have since shown a failure to search out and preserve an abiding historical memory of their terrible reportorial failures of 1939–45. Too often journalistic todays, constantly interrupted by a quest for novelty that undermines focus and memory, are born without the light of yesterday. It should be clear by now that reportorial failings together with the frailties of Western wartime leaders contributed greatly to the Soviet triumphs at the expense of those peoples who did not want to become part of Stalin's realm in eastern Europe.[43] The journalistic history of these events all too often repeated itself whenever the East-West conflict afterward took fire.

SUMMARY AND EPILOGUE

BY THE MIDDLE of 1945, the Red Army was ensconced in the heart of Europe. Stalin's countless legions, battle-proven, were in charge of the great historical capitals, Warsaw, Berlin, Vienna, Budapest, and Prague. In six years, they had come out from defeat before the frozen Mannerheim Line, from ragged, tyrannized Muscovy to these once splendid centers of European culture. With their arrival there in the course of the wartime destruction of half of Europe, the ultimate nihilism of crazed Adolf Hitler's secularized Armageddon had been almost realized. At the same time, Stalin's and Molotov's Bolshevik expansionist scheme for Europe, driven by a similar secular Manicheanism, was itself already half realized.

In enfeebled postwar western Europe, and in seemingly omnipotent, victorious, confident America, leaders still misunderstood Stalin's purposes, though suspicions that these were not benign were sharpening. Yet these leaders, and opinion makers, still widely broadcast Soviet propaganda views of Soviet life and purposes. And all over, in shattered Europe and in optimistic America in the early summer of 1945, the dominant mood was one of relief that the war in Europe was over and that before long, given the combined Allied strength, the war in the Pacific would also be over. If the battle promised to be long and bloody, victory seemed certain.

The conditions for Cold War had developed with the coming of the hot war in 1939 and the Nazi and Soviet dictators' deliberate disarrangement of the Versailles system. Once Hitler and Stalin had smashed the territorial settlement of World War I, any falling out between these two evil allies resulting in the defeat of one by the other would have required the construction of some kind of new political and geographical order. Assuredly, however, it would not have been one that pleased Great Britain and France and the nations that profited from Versailles, or the United States, isolated though many of its citizens still were from concerns about the European and world balance of power.

In spite of the incredible wartime disaster that had befallen the Soviet peoples from Stalin's conniving with the Hitler Reich toward achieving his fanciful Marxist-Leninist schemes, Stalin continued to pursue the disingenuous and destabilizing policies he had directed in Europe, if only ideologically, long before and during the pact with Hitler. From 1941 to 1945, he puffed up easily won Western hopes for his future good behavior. He made small shows of good faith, dissolving the Comintern and dragging out high-sounding pseudo-democratic and liberationist jargon, but these were only superficial acts deliberately concocted to mislead those who, lacking geopolitical understanding, were yet carried away with the moralistic passions of war.

As it became gradually more obvious to the Westerners that Stalin was bent on achieving goals that were unacceptable to them and disadvantageous to their nations, they did their utmost to ignore, and to conceal from themselves and from their publics, what was really happening in the increasingly confrontational situation in central and east central Europe. Who knew what the consequences might be? In the end, as so often happens, death and political chance shifted the problems to others to resolve. Were the Western wartime leaders not themselves the victims of the same sort of self-delusion and appeasement that had overcome other Westerners before them who had been frightened by Hitler's berserk tactics and then had been accused, by Churchill and others, of self-delusion?

Stalin's program, at once both ideologically and militarily expansionist, could only begin to develop after Hitler opened up to him prospects of incredible gain at a presumably small cost. The pact of 1939 set the conditions for the coming of war, and then Cold War, both begun with the assault on the uneasy post-Versailles European order. Stalin started his campaign to hold onto his first set of spoils when he insisted in 1941 on keeping the territorial and some of the human booty he had acquired by allying himself with Hitler.

In 1939 and 1940, Stalin in collaboration with Hitler had begun his plan of uprooting and transferring European populations. He continued these works during the war after he allied himself with the Western powers. As the fight went on, Stalin's agents diverted for his population moving Soviet equipment as well as equipment supplied for the war against the Germans by the Western Allies, equipment that had been paid for by the sacrifices of the patriotic Western nations and had been drawn from their stocks at no inconsiderable cost to their own war efforts against both the Germans and the Japanese. In the course of fighting on several fronts, the Western leaders, if they knew much about these forced transfers, turned a blind eye. In the summer of 1945, the Western Allies began to see the awful evidence of some of these forced transfers. Perhaps then the Western leaders suddenly realized what Stalin had done at their expense and at the expense of the suffering peoples. But Stalin, far from really caring what the Westerners thought, or even at that point being able to stop what he had done to advance his plans, passed on much of his share of the burden of caring for the helpless, diseased, and starving refugees.

Indeed, long before 1945, while the wartime "grand alliance" appeared to flourish, numberless additional conditions for postwar open Cold War confrontation had been set. Beyond the curtain of lies and misinformation supplied by Soviet journalists and all too frequently uncritically passed on by journalists from the West, Stalin prepared to plant his political and economic control wherever his armies touched on the victorious march toward Berlin. He sharply advanced the coming confrontation by suddenly demanding of his new Western allies, at Teheran in December 1943, that he be given, as a "trophy" of battle, a bit of German territory—which would move the borders of his state of eight million or so square miles a little farther west, taking one of the bits of wartime booty that he had once, in all likelihood, promised his Polish servants. He then went on to organize with these Polish political unknowns whom he was preparing to install as the postwar government of Poland, a reward at someone else's expense to quieten their complaints of his betrayal.

Stalin's offer to compensate the Poles with far more extensive, different German lands went well beyond the planned reward to the Poles he had earlier set with his allies. He correctly doubted that the Westerners would approve the transfer of these additional lands to the Poles, so it was necessary for him, in 1944–45, to conceal his actions from his allies. While he pushed the Polish borders west and south, he gradually prepared to transfer the power of government to Moscow. The claims of the London exile group, successor to the Warsaw government Stalin had attacked in 1939, had had the support of Great Britain and the United States, and originally of Stalin as well, when he needed Western help most. Stalin then unilaterally enfranchised his own Polish government, despite Western Allied resistance. So when, at Yalta, Stalin directly confronted the West on the border issue, bringing out the new map for which he alone was responsible, the negotiations that followed led to the undoing of all previous agreements on Poland's western borders.

But these were simply the issues underlying some of the undeniable conflicts inevitably produced during the war by Stalin's regularly disingenuous and ruthless modus operandi that began even before August 23, 1939. For Stalin had never given up the grand international plans he and Molotov had hatched when they first joined hands with Hitler, even then hoping for, and expecting, the latter's demise. And all his success in duplicity and the military prowess his armies had so effectively proved, if at terrible human cost, only sharpened his appetites and underpinned his hubris. Stalin had colored a postwar Europe red in 1939. He meant to have it his way.

Stalin's works had slowly begun to unsettle the Western leaders when they gradually learned how he used the Red Army, which had arrived at the fringes of once independent east central Europe in early 1944, to eradicate opposition, beginning once again in Poland, and to send its parliamentarians and underground heroes to Soviet prisons and camps. Stalin had developed this program between 1939 and 1941 for the territories he took in collaboration with Hitler and had carried it out wherever the Red Army advanced, and after the war he applied it in all the Red Army–occupied lands.

If the Westerners even after 1944 still did not know the extent of Stalin's doings, such as the secret clauses of the pact with Hitler and the realignment of the Polish borders to suit himself, they were increasingly watchful. As the two fronts drew together in the middle of Europe and East-West encounters became more frequent, the atmosphere grew more and more tense. Once the allies from East and West met in Berlin and Vienna, Western wartime dissatisfaction, earlier willingly put aside, was first enhanced, then became suspicion; suspicion increased as facts massed.[1] Shocking evidence arose from absolutely incontrovertible proofs of Soviet misconduct right before Western eyes. In 1944, the Soviet failure to help the Poles in the Warsaw uprising had been a distant matter, though the uprising was costly in lives and matériel to both Britain and the United States. At Yalta, in early 1945, Roosevelt and Churchill had still believed that Stalin's suddenly presented new map for Germany could be amended. Andrei Vyshinskii's March 1945 coup d'état in Bucharest happened in a place Churchill had already conceded to Stalin. The kidnapping and later judicial murders of Poland's anti-German underground leaders could perhaps be excused, even if the Soviet method of justice appeared somewhat severe, because of the Poles' alleged anti-Soviet deeds. A person needing to do so might believe that these actually had occurred as Stalin and his journalists reported.

Yet Western leaders from the late spring of 1945 could no longer overlook the suddenly abundant Red government indignities, some of them directly attributable to Stalin, for example, lying and deceitful tricks played on former comrades in arms and his utterly false accusations of Western deceit. Stalin himself was the master of that kind of lie. His high-handedness (to say the least) eventually had to become undeniable.

In the middle of Europe in 1945, everyone on hand to greet the Soviet liberators heard of Red Army brutalities ranging from gang rape to kidnapping and mass execution, undertaken wherever it camped. They encountered lesser Soviet indignities visited on ally and former foe alike, thefts done in the name of "reparations." Western soldiers at first thought the wildest of the stories to be the probably exaggerated complaints of the whining defeated, but skepticism yielded as these deeds undeniably continued before the very eyes of the representatives of the Western Allied powers, and even in their own occupation backyards, in Berlin and Vienna. There, too, were the hordes of desperate expellees and other trekkers from the east and the west, women, children, and the old—the expellees, at least, indisputable evidence of Stalin's population shuffling. And the Western leaders themselves came to destroyed Berlin on a modest victory tour. They heard the stories, saw the treks, too.

Harry Truman and Clement Attlee, who first appeared in three-power diplomacy at Potsdam, soon grew increasingly impatient. Their predecessors' earlier commitments to faith in Stalin had helped to create the situation they faced in the summer of 1945. But it became quite evident in the course of the Potsdam Conference that they had no real alternatives except to abandon that faith, to deal with Stalin on his terms, those of confrontation. Surely it was easier for them, not carrying the baggage that had burdened their predecessors, to put aside the previous policies of appeasing Stalin, to make the terrible choice for confrontation then, even before the war in the Pacific was over.

The Western governments, for good reason, had uneasily watched Stalin's carrying out of the Yalta agreements on the seemingly intractable Polish government issue. When the subject of Poland's borders inevitably came up again at the Potsdam Conference, circumstances this time clearly marked them as another fait accompli. On the Polish issue and elsewhere in these negotiations, Western reaction to Stalin's arrogance was almost palpable. President Truman's sometime pre-Potsdam suspicions of the Soviets notably quickened, and Churchill's successors also met Stalin head on. It was now certain that Stalin was not going to dominate the decisions on the future of Germany in the way that he had dominated decisions on Poland.

At Potsdam the Western leaders for the first time drew important symbolic limits to preclude further easy Soviet advance. It is true that their presumed need for Soviet help in the war against Japan kept them from emphasizing their quite sharply defined disagreements. Only over many months after Potsdam did Truman and Attlee find themselves gradually forced to give up all their illusions of a cooperative and peaceful reconstruction of Europe. After a time, the symbolic limits in central Europe became the real ones of police and armies ready for action.

Thus the Cold War, viewed historically as confrontational acts and consciously undertaken responses, developed when the two sides came together geographically. At last, suspicions became undeniable, and the range of possible palliative explanations of, and placatory responses to, Soviet behavior grew smaller and smaller. With the Red Army mounted across the center of Europe, Potsdam marked the first major diplomatic stage in the development of the Cold War as a conflict, a new historical epoch of confrontation.

Yet the conclusions then drawn, the lines then in fact set, if scarcely articulated, by key Western leaders and diplomats, were not at all shared by their nations. Most people in the West still deeply believed that all reasonable people must be committed to finishing the war against the Japanese as allies acting in harmony. They hardly doubted that a lasting peace, the former allies living in that same harmony, would follow. The democracies, in 1945, had already fought, however reluctantly, for that peace against the Nazi terror. Misled by political and opinion leaders, some of whom misled themselves, the people of the Western democracies had supposed that Stalin would now conduct himself like the responsible and moderate leader of a nation that had been an ally. But moderation was not a Stalin ideal, nor was peaceful world harmony. Indeed, Stalin's plans for Asia after the battles to come were evidently not dissimilar, if perhaps less systematically formulated, from those he had for Europe.[2]

Once again, reluctantly, the democratic peoples would have to confront an expansionist dictator. But democratic peoples are slow to move against other nations. They must be moved by an overwhelming flow of information, even misinformation, to do so. In this instance, the flow soon developed, and the source was, of course, Germany, where the clever, but ultimately too hurried and too heavy-handed program of Stalin and his German Communist followers was beginning to take shape. Out of sight behind wartime cover in Romania, Poland, Hungary, and Bulgaria, as well as in the now unhappy, reingested Baltic countries, Stalin had done just about as he liked; and he had succeeded, too, in planting a Soviet-designed regime in Austria.

And so, only after the war, slowly but inevitably, the mass of democratic peoples were pulled along by their leaders and by gradually increasing, in some cases reluctantly accepted, knowledge of the unfair, crude, often downright brutish acts of the Soviets. For Stalin was the last person, except perhaps Hitler had he been alive, who might have been expected to carry out a subtle, careful program of expansion in the sharp light of the international journalistic focus and other Western attention then fixed on postwar central Europe.

The journalistic focus professionally followed the drama and "human interest" there, as ever news interest develops. Many journalists on hand soon learned that matters were other than many of them had earlier been led to believe, especially by their professional

confreres writing in wartime from the Soviet side of the front. Moreover, the Soviets in Berlin and Vienna were under the watchful eyes
of thousands of American and British (and later French) soldiers,
who had had to fight that war for what they had been led to believe
would be an enduring peace and a coming universal democracy
among the United Nations. Then they, too, met the Red Army in
the middle of Europe.

But in the public mind especially, the truth leading to the confrontational state developed slowly. The people of the Western democracies had resisted leaving the peace of the 1930's until Hitler
crudely compelled them to do so. In 1946, one year after World
War II ended, 74 percent of the American public that was polled said
that the United States and the Soviet Union were equally to blame
for the global misunderstandings that had developed; on the basis of
the information they had, they still supposed the victims and crooks
alike responsible for the crimes. Even in January 1947, a few months
before President Truman at last dramatized direct opposition to the
Soviets in Europe with his announcement of aid to Greece and Turkey, 43 percent of Americans asked still gave their questioners to
understand that they believed the Russians could be trusted. Sea-
soned observers have learned over the years that there are questions
and questions, polls and polls, but there is probably more than a
modicum of truth in these figures.[3]

The striking thing is that these opinions were still held well after
the Soviets had virtually duplicated their sack of half of Europe in
the course of their advance against the Japanese in Asia, and even
after Stalin had officially revived the doctrine of international revolution. By the end of 1946 the Soviets were solidly fixed in the northern half of the Korean peninsula and had reannexed or reoccupied
old tsarist territories long since held by the allied Chinese and
enemy Japanese. They also randomly seized several Japanese-held
islands. Some of this land taking had actually been conspired in
by Franklin D. Roosevelt, to be sure. Thanks to President Truman,
however, who at Potsdam quickly sized up the real nature of Soviet
behavior and, moreover, had the power to do something about what
he had learned, the Russians were at least blocked from taking part
in the occupation of Japan and from occupying more than half of
Korea.[4]

More than anything else, these major Soviet setbacks in Asia were
the result of the new awareness of what the Soviets really wanted.

It was not yet evident to everyone that the Soviet urge to rearrange the social order, with its pervasive atmosphere of fear and occasional outbursts of savage behavior, essentially derived from the rot at the Soviet center.[5] Truman's knowledge of the atomic bomb, which he knew he could dispose in generosity or in threat, may well have helped to stiffen his hand against the Soviets in the summer of 1945. If so, it helped rescue the Japanese, its chief victims, from the division of their nation in the manner that befell the Germans and the Koreans.

The inevitable first moment of militant and military confrontation finally had to come. Once the concentration on wartime issues was put aside, the irrationality of Stalin's appetites and his disingenuous manipulation gradually became ever more obvious. For years after 1945, he held on to his power in the Soviet state as his personal varieties of madness took more and more control over him; a similar madness had struck Hitler before and during the war. The clues to Stalin's puzzling behavior are still not wholly clear, but certainly the erratic and bullying domestic and international manifestations of his state of mind were sufficient at last to convince all types of utterly disparate nations and improbable partisan coalitions, from Marxist Social Democratic secularists to the Pope of Rome, to join against him.[6] By the time of the beginning of Stalin's blockade of Berlin in the summer of 1948, the confrontation was no longer just diplomatic; it had become economic, with the Marshall Plan and German currency reform, and military as well.

In 1948, army confronted army in the center of Europe around Berlin, but in stalemate. Each side, just recently released from the terrors of modern war, feared the consequences of new military action, although Stalin, who had recklessly squandered Soviet soldiers and civilians all during the war, probably only feared the consequences of losing. Air forces fought the only battles in the course of the famous Airlift into Berlin, in the strange games we now call dodg'em and chicken, in the skies over Germany.[7] There were casualties, but no real war. Finally the propaganda defeat the Soviets sustained in trying to freeze and starve by means of blockade two million Berliners became too great. Stalin gave up the armed battle on that front, as he had given it up in Finland in 1940, when he came to fear he might meet further opposition he did not want to face. In 1948, he also suddenly faced a new, and for him, dangerous front in Yugoslavia: an independent-minded pupil and former ally who balked at Stalin's, and general Russian, schoolmasterly arrogance. Having discovered the future, the Soviets wanted, indeed, "history" required, that they bring their version of it to all peoples, even to those who did not want it.

It must have been just about then that Stalin shifted some of his attention to Asia, where the fronts between East and West were still less well defined and the opportunities for fruitful expansion therefore greater. The bloody invasion of South Korea in 1950 he helped to sponsor was the first major result. As always before, Stalin had carefully chosen a point of weakness, and again, as before, he tried to conceal his own hand in the business.[8] By this time, by American, and many other Western imaginings, even the power of his hand was such that he hardly needed to stir it to bring a swift, often poorly calculated, reaction , even overreaction. This hardened public reaction introduced a new period of the Cold War, in which the Western leaders and their now very much aroused democratic peoples, led by the Americans, frequently responded with as much irrational hostility to every move of the Soviets as they had once responded to them with exaggerated outbursts of friendship and understanding.[9] Surely one of the undeniable lessons of contemporary history is that the traditions of democratic isolation set few useful guides for the conduct of foreign affairs.

Stalin, though aged, paranoic, physically ill, stumped, and blocked, hacked wildly at both the weeds and the flowers in his own, allegedly beloved, garden. He had so far failed in his thrust westward and, unlike the Tsar Alexander I, had never reached Paris. He turned inward, as his sense of caution always had dictated, to face plots, probably imaginary, and to build great bombs, much aided by the lore supplied from purloined secrets and captured German scientists, to match those of the Americans. He continued to dream that he might confront the West once again, join with Molotov, or a successor to Molotov, once more in coloring the European map, and more beyond, red. Certainly the enormous weapons of terror and violence he had cocked were quite ready for use at the time of his lonely death, superintended only by a field veterinary, in 1953.[10]

REFERENCE MATTER

ABBREVIATIONS

AAN	Archiwum Akt Nowych
AMZV	Archiv Ministerstva Zahraničních Věcí České Republiky
AÚTGM. BA	Archiv Ústava Tomasa G. Masaryka, Benešův Archiv
BA	Bundesarchiv
DBFP	*Documents on British Foreign Policy*
DDF	*Documents diplomatiques françaises*
DGFP	*Documents on German Foreign Policy*
FO	Foreign Office
FRUS	*Foreign Relations of the United States*
HA	Archive of the Hoover Institution
IS	Sikorski Institute and Polish Museum
IWM	Imperial War Museum
KC	Komitet Centralny
KPD	Kommunistische Partei Deutschlands
KRN	Krajowa Rada Narodowa
KSČ	Kommunistická Strana Československa
LC	Library of Congress
MID	Ministerstwo Informacji i Dokumentacji
MSZ	Ministerstwo Spraw Zagranicznych

MZV	Ministerstvo Zahraničních Věcí
NK "FD"	National Komité "Freies Deutschland"
NKID	Narodnyi Kommissariat Inostrannykh Del
NKVD	Narodny Kommissariat Vnutrennykh Del
PAN	Polska Akademia Nauk
PAP	Polska Agencja Prasowa
PKWN	Polski Komitet Wyzwolenia Narodowego
PPR	Polska Partia Robotnicza
PRO	Public Record Office.
PURKKA	Politicheskoe Upravlenie Rabochii-Krest'ianskoi Krasnyi Armii
RGAKFD	Rossiiskii Gosudarstvennyi Arkhiv Kinofotodokumentov
SBZ	Sowjetische Besatzungszone
SMAD	Sowjetische Militäradministration in Deutschland
SPD	Sozialdemokratische Partei Deutschlands
SUA	Státní Ústřední Archiv v Praze
TASS	Telegrafnoe Agenstvo Sovetskogo Soiuza
TJP	*Teheran, Jalta, Potsdam*
WFD	Wytwórnia Filmów Dokumentalnych
WW	Wydział Wschodni
ZPA	Zentrales Parteiarchiv
ZPP	Związek Polskich Patriotów

NOTES

For titles of works cited in part or by author's name only, please consult the Bibliography, p. 235.

INTRODUCTION

1. The strange, and certainly purposeful, way in which the Soviets under Gorbachev acknowledged Stalin's involvement in the Katyn Forest Massacre (Gorbachev himself was oddly involved in the public news event) was sharply observed by Horst Bacia, in *Frankfurter Allgemeine Zeitung*, Apr. 17, 1990, p. 3. Information from a variety of sources in the West continues to suggest how reluctant some post-Soviet archivists still are to allow access to various archives. For background information on this point, see Kramar, "Archival Research in Moscow."

2. The chief of the Polish government-in-exile, General Władysław Sikorski, discussed the possibility of Soviet expansion with British Prime Minister Neville Chamberlain and Foreign Secretary Lord Halifax at some length in his first visit to London in the fall of 1939 ("Sprawozdanie z wyzyty w Anglii") ["very confidential"], 1s, A10. 1/1. Sikorski, well aware of the "efficacious bolshevization" that the Soviets were then pursuing in their half of occupied Poland, was apparently following up on conversations between Chamberlain and Halifax and the Polish foreign secretary, August Zaleski, a month earlier (Oct. 11, 1939). In these talks, Halifax spoke optimistically of the possible effects of Soviet intervention in the war, and he laid stress on the rift that he seemed to see already developing between Germany and the Soviet Union. Chamberlain was less optimistic, expressing honest fears of the war ending with permanent bolshevization of Ger-

many (see reports of meetings of Zaleski with Halifax and Chamberlain, Oct. 10, 1939, ibid. A12. 49/WB/15). Sikorski promised to send Chamberlain and Halifax more details, seeing this "as the first important effort toward the establishment of common war aims." Whether or not he did this, Churchill, Chamberlain's successor, like most other Westerners, neglected the rich sources on Soviet behavior that his Polish allies were able to provide on the subject, and only gradually began to realize the extent to which his Soviet policy had failed. During Churchill's prime ministership, the Foreign Office was certainly aware of the possibility that the Red Army might end up in the middle of Europe (see "Notes on a Discussion in the British Foreign Ministry," Nov. 19, 1941, in Bracher and Jacobsen, eds., *Deutschlandpolitik*, p. 958), but there is no evidence the notes were passed along to the Foreign Secretary or that there was any contingency planning, either early on or later, when the matter became urgent.

3. *Pravda*, Nov. 3, 1987. Gorbachev suggested that the secret protocol to the Pact was a Western falsification because, allegedly, no copy was now to be found in the Soviet archives. See [Mikhail S. Gorbachev], *Inteligencja wobec nowych problemów socjalizmu*, p. 88. But the documents have recently (1990) been published in Russian in USSR, Ministerstvo inostrannykh del, *God krizisa (sentiabr' 1938–sentiabr' 1939). Dokumenty vneshnei politiki SSSR 1938–1939 gg.*, 2: 319–21. See also my article, "History as Past and Current Politics." Obviously, what Gorbachev originally believed, however much he understood of the dimensions of Stalin's foreign crimes, was that it was tactically necessary to move forward today, and to reserve looking back for tomorrow. But the debate over Stalin in the Soviet Union soon generated its own momentum. For an early appraisal, see Nies, "Die Stalin(ismus)-Kontroverse in der Sowjetunion."

4. See, for example, Kennan, "The View from Russia," p. 28.

5. This point was made earlier by Aleksandr M. Nekrich, "Perestroika in History: The First Stage." The last Soviet president also had a faithful core of historical jesters at his beck and call. For example, asked by the editors of *Voenno-istoricheskii zhurnal* to look into the question of the introduction of Red Army units into the Baltic states in 1939 and 1940, I. N. Venkov went right into the archives then wholly forbidden to the rest of us and came up with documents and text supporting the Soviets' peaceful purposes ("Dopustit' razmeshchenie voisk"). The series of articles in which this one appeared was titled, "In Search of the Truth."

6. From Khrushchev (p. 40): "Whatever Stalin said was correct; they were the words of genius. He said all that was necessary in the interests of revolution, in the interests of victory and anything else of importance."

7. Sokolov, p. 110.

8. For example, David Irving, in *Hitler's War*, pp. 12–13, 15, 54, 71–73, 136, 270–71, 509, 630–31.

9. United States Ambassador Averill Harriman, months after he had first taken up his Moscow post, still held to a variety of this position; see Pastusiak, p. 104.

10. This writer has for some years been looking into pre-August 1939 diplomatic records from Great Britain, Poland, Czechoslovakia, Germany, and France to see what their embassies and central analytical diplomatic stations were offering political leaders at home as information on Soviet behavior and purposes. The conclusion expressed above is firm, though based on this still incomplete research. On the development of U.S. policy, see Mark, "American Policy Toward Eastern Europe."

11. See Kennan, *Russia and the West Under Lenin and Stalin*, and Ulam, *Stalin: The Man and His Era*.

12. Letter of Jan. 26, 1945, USNA, RG59, Records of Charles Bohlen, 1942−1952, Bohlen Correspondence, box 3 ("Personal Correspondence, 1942−1946").

13. Tucker, *Stalin in Power*; Conquest, *Stalin: Breaker of Nations*; Laqueur, *Stalin: The Glasnost Revelations*.

14. Lundestad and Watt, neither one American, have made the same point earlier.

15. See, for example, Ryerson, "Questions of Bias." But there are countless other writings and masses of textbooks in American history that Ryerson does not discuss. The same misinformation has also been spread by a number of European writers.

CHAPTER I

1. The confusion of interpretation is well illustrated by the way in which the Foreign Office summarized the comments of Lord Chilston, the British ambassador in Moscow, and others in various British diplomatic posts at home and abroad, on Stalin's published remarks of Feb. 14, 1938; see PRO, FO371, 22288, N819, N898, N923, N963. Various voices in the Polish foreign office and foreign service were quite as inconsistent as British observers: see AAN, MSZ, WW, 6664. These Polish diplomatic records were captured and taken out of the country, however, first to Germany and then to the Soviet Union, and there are a number of obvious gaps in the documentation.

2. Quoted in Ikonnikov, p. 53. The reader who consults Lenin's speech of September 20, 1920, the stenogram of which was recently published ("Ia proshu zapisyvat' menshe"), will see how closely Stalin meant what he said, for he followed in Lenin's footsteps of the Polish campaign in 1920 in carrying out his own plans in the aftermath of the Hitler-Stalin Pact. Lenin proposed to annex a large part of eastern Poland, "Sovietize" (Lenin's terminology) the rest of Poland, put the Red Army on the borders of Sub-Carpathian Ruthenia to march into Hungary, and, no doubt, with Poland "Sovietized," to put the Red Army on Germany's borders, too (pp. 16−27).

Since, after the Treaty of Versailles, Germany was virtually demilitarized and the army it had was required to keep 100 km. from its borders, Weimar Germany would have been wholly hostage to Soviet whims. In 1939, Hitler, proposing the infamous pact to Stalin, opened the path for the Soviet drive to the west and put the Soviets on Germany's borders, both of which the victory of the Poles at the Vistula had blocked in 1920.

3. For example, the Polish ambassador in Moscow discounted even as late as May 1939 Stalin's interest in foreign revolution: see Grzybowski to MSZ, Moscow, May 16, 1939, AAN, MSZ, ZSRR, 6696. Even earlier, in 1935, the French chargé informed Paris that the Soviet government was not in the least interested in world revolution and that the Comintern was dying (see Carley, p. 160). Prewar American diplomats and the press were similarly naive. In 1940 many saw the Soviet occupation of the Baltic states as defensive, just as the Soviet propaganda line suggested (reported by Mal'kov, pp. 50–52). The argument has recently been raised that Trotsky himself was only retrospectively a Trotskyite; see Wohlforth, p. 40 n. 14.

4. Stalin piously disavowed his interest in bolshevizing other nations or taking other nation's territories, although forcible bolshevization was clearly his mentor Lenin's modus operandi; see Lenin, "Ia proshu zapisyvat' menshe," esp. pp. 16–27. Stalin himself, in 1925, had this to say about bolshevizing Germany: "The most favorable revolutionary conditions will be when an internal crisis in Germany and the decisive growth of the power of the German Communist party come together with serious complications in the camp of its external enemies" (meaning, of course, the Versailles victors). Although Stalin carefully did not name the "complications" he was expecting, we would perhaps not have to jump far to conclude that he meant an international war, as Leninist doctrine had fixed; see Stalin in "Tov. Stalin o perspektivakh GKP i o bol'shevizatsii," *Pravda*, Feb. 3, 1925, p. 1. Yet Stalin was now saying that he had no intention of exporting the revolution (an example from 1943 quoted by Firsov, "Stalin und die Komintern," p. 120). Soviet diplomats repeated the line: for example, Davidson to Orme-Sargent, Mar. 1, 1941 (PRO, FO371, 29464, N791): one of his officers heard it from the First Secretary of the Soviet Embassy in London, who got it straight from Stalin. The research department of the Foreign Office repeated these stories uncritically. Presumably they did not know when they wrote "The USSR and the Principles of the Atlantic Charter" (Feb. 3, 1944, PRO, FO371, 43332, N744) that Stalin had just proposed taking part of Germany as well. One Foreign Office worker opined (c. May 26, 1944) that the Soviets would not be likely to support movements by the extreme left because they were now "nationalist and satisfied"; he added that he had recently heard that the majority of French Communists were Trotskyites, by which he apparently meant that they were at the opposite pole from Stalin. Duff Cooper, in Algiers (May 25, 1944), reported to London

that Rene Massigli, a de Gaulle foreign policy adviser, thought "Russian foreign policy had undergone important change and was now mainly directed to the maintenance of order in Europe" (PRO, FO371, 43335, N3224). Still another example of wartime disbelief in Stalin's Trotskyite internationalism in the West is contained in a British document entitled "Probable Post-war Tendencies in Soviet Foreign Policy as Affecting British Interests" (Apr. 29, 1944, PRO, FO371, 43335, N1008): "After Stalin's victory over Trotsky . . . the aim of spreading bolshevism or of fomenting world revolution for its own sake was abandoned." (Ironically, it was Stalin who cast this definition of the term Trotskyism: see Tucker, *Stalin as Revolutionary*, pp. 340–62.) This document was prepared by the policy planners of the British Foreign Office for its use and that of the War Cabinet, including the Prime Minister and Foreign Secretary. In the same document, the authors expressed their confidence that Stalin's 1939 expansion to the west was "defensive." In the United States, Charles Bohlen's memorandum of Dec. 15, 1943 (dated in pencil, USNA, RG59, Bohlen Correspondence, box 3), on the subject of Soviet intentions makes no suggestion of Soviet expansion westward. Even as late as April 1950, Bohlen was suggesting that Stalin would take no major risks toward international revolution that would imperil his domestic regime (quoted by May, p. 13). Bohlen was even then literally correct, though in fact more than slightly misstating the issue. For what was a major risk? The Berlin blockade? The war in Korea? If not these rash moves, what, then, less than a grand march in any direction of the Soviet army, was a major risk? On the background of the war in Korea we now have much new evidence pinning down Stalin's hortatory, and the Soviet Union's participatory role. See Weathersby, pp. 21–32; Kramar, p. 34; Chen, pp. 18–31. Two writers, one a Russian defector with considerable higher military access during his time in the Soviet Union, pioneered in putting together the story of Stalin's bolshevizing thrust to the west. But they, Grigorii Tokaev (writing in 1951) and Carl O. Nordling (much relying on Tokaev and writing in 1984), have been largely ignored and are rarely cited in the vast literature on the early Cold War. It is quite clear that the actual experiences Tokaev relates, which are confirmed in the main by other sources, make him a believable reporter on the Soviet system and Stalin's war plans.

5. The assessment of Stalin and his program (with the key exception of the attribution to him of aspiring to international revolution) outlined in this chapter follows in a number of respects early accounts like that in Ulam, *Stalin*, and in Kennan, *Russia and the West Under Lenin and Stalin*, p. 330, and also in Kennan's 1944 analysis, "Russia—Seven Years Later," p. 65. It was more recently, in the earlier days of glasnost', strikingly reinforced by Medvedev, "O Staline i Stalinizme," pp. 166, 171–73 (Stalin: "monstrously cruel," "a sadist," a "new tsar"). None of these authors par-

178 NOTES TO PAGES 15 – 17

ticularly emphasizes ideological force in the formation of Stalin's expansionist plans. Not so the most recent volume of Stalin's biography from Robert C. Tucker, *Stalin in Power: The Revolution from Above, 1928– 1941*, which gives up-to-date background and maintains the same argument that follows in this text with respect to Stalin's Russian nationalism (for example, p. 568) and his quest for a German alliance, and offers an interesting psychological approach to understanding Stalin's motives derived from his external behavior (p. 573). See Stalin's own words in his book *The Foundations of Leninism*, chapter entitled "The Nationalities Question," and also as reported by "Historicus," pp. 187–93, 199, 203–9; Tokaev, pp. 23– 24; and Tucker, *Stalin in Power*, p. 511; see also, Wohlforth, p. 42. One of Stalin's rare openly expressed reflections on his own character was a comment he made to American Ambassador Averill Harriman (in 1944) with respect to the dangers of writing things down: "I am a cautious old man" (Harriman papers, LC, Churchill-Stalin Conference Record, conversation no. 8, Oct. 17, 1944). Stalin's Trotskyite plans are now revealed in intra-Comintern and interparty discussions following the Hitler-Stalin Pact recorded in the ZPA, Wilhelm Pieck Nachlass, 36/528 and 36/540, in the newly opened records of the former German Communist Party, at the former Zentrales Parteiarchiv (the former central archive of the Zentralkomittee of the former East German Communist Party, the Sozialistische Einheitspartei Deutschlands). The archive, now a part of the Bundesarchiv, is now called Stiftung der Parteien und Massenorganisationen der DDR. Volkogonov (p. 10) cited the first hint of Stalin's interest in a *Drang nach Westen*. Hitler himself perceptively assessed the traditional Muscovite aspect of Stalin's otherwise Bolshevik expansionist program. See Bregman, pp. 84–85.

6. For two eyewitness descriptions of central Russia in 1940 from British diplomatic representatives in Moscow that suggest eloquently the poverty, disorganization, and wretchedness of life in Stalin's Russia out beyond the major cities, see PRO, FO371, 24856, and 14891, N6421. George Kennan, in the U.S. embassy in Moscow again late in the war, sent along a similar report to Charles Bohlen (Sept. 29, 1944), to complain that the Soviet Union had not changed for the better since his prewar time there; USNA, RG59, Bohlen Correspondence, box 3.

7. Tucker, *Stalin in Power*, p. 573.

8. See Molotov and V. G. Dekanozov in U.S. Congress, Select Committee on Communist Aggression, *Third Interim Report*, pp. 341–44, 450–63; also, Stalin and Molotov, Oct. 2, 1939, Transcript of the meeting of Munters, etc., with Stalin, etc., USNA, T1244, reel 5.

9. For estimates of Soviet military weaknesses and obsolescent aircraft in the aftermath of the purge (1938), see Committee of Imperial Defence memo, "The Air Forces of the USSR," January 1938; also British air attaché

C. Hallawell (Moscow), "Report of a Conversation with the German Military Attaché," Feb. 8, 1938, saying that in his opinion the Germans do not "overrate the power of the Soviet Union," and that the Red air force lags behind those of the West; PRO, FO371, 22292, N165 and N730. From 1939: Firebrace (British military attaché in Moscow) to Moscow chancery, Jan. 24, 1939, reporting the opinions of German military attaché General Koestring; Ambassador Seeds (Moscow) to Halifax, Feb. 8, 1939; Firebrace, "Report on the Red Army," Mar. 7, 1939, PRO, FO371, 23688, N489, N1003, N1542.

10. Although many diplomats then, and authors since, have accepted the notion that Stalin would have come to the aid of the Czechs had the French stood firm in 1938, the bulk of the evidence and the most powerful arguments by now clearly fall on the other side. See, for example, Pfaff, "Prag und der Fall Tuchatschewskii"; Tucker, *Stalin in Power*, pp. 514–25; Hochman, pp. 149–69; Suda, pp. 154–57; Nordling, pp. 15–29; and Rupnik, p. 133. Two recent articles by Igor Lukes may well put to rest the argument in favor of Stalin's interest in collective security at the time of Munich; see Lukes, "Stalin and Benes," and "Benesch, Stalin, und die Komintern." Some contemporaries who were closely involved, like Edvard Taborský and Polish Foreign Minister Beck, were also doubters: see Taborsky, pp. 56–63, and Cienciała, *Polska polityka zagraniczna w latach 1926–1932*, pp. 217–18; see also, Jordan, p. 274. So were French diplomats: see Coulondre, Moscow, to Bonnet, June 10, 1938, DDF 10: 7, and other reports of the same month and surrounding months; Lamarle, Prague, to Bonnet, Aug. 23, 1938, 10: 788; Bonnet, Paris, to Payart, Aug. 31, 1938, 10: 900; and Payart, Moscow, to Bonnet, Sept. 2, 1938, 10: 938. See also Duroselle, pp. 339–40, 354–55. For British doubts, see Fraser to Phipps, Paris, Dec. 22, 1938, PRO, FO371, 22915, C1503; report of a conversation of A. Gwatkin, Foreign Office, with Baltrusaitis, Lithuanian Ambassador to the Soviet Union, June 1, 1939, PRO FO371, 23697, N2752; and Strang, *Home and Abroad*, pp. 149–53. For a general background of the negotiations in Moscow from one of the British representatives, see Strang, *The Moscow Negotiations*. Polish diplomats in Prague, Berlin, and Moscow were especially disdainful of Moscow's role in the Czech crisis, seeing the Soviets up to encouraging war by pushing the Czechs to stand fast against the Germans and at the same time offering no substantial military support. Polish Ambassador Papée in Prague, usually well informed, told Warsaw that both Beneš and the Czech general staff felt betrayed by Stalin in the crucial days of September 1938: see Papée to MSZ, Sept. 20, 21, and 23, 1938, in AAN, WW, Poselstwo w Pradze, 5431. For international doubts about the Soviets, see Lubieński, Paris, to MSZ [?], Apr. 7, 1938; for Czech doubts, Papée, Prague, to MSZ, Sept. 6, 1938, ibid., WW, Poselstwo w Pradze, 5430; and E. Raczyński, London, to MSZ [?], May 4, 1938, both in the HA, Ambassada RP w Paryżu, box 7; E. Raczyński, London to MSZ, Sept. 18, 1938, AAN, WW, Poselstwo w Pradze 5430, and also Oct. 7,

1938, ibid., MSZ, WW, 6664. A useful background is the recent study by Jürgen Pagel on prewar Polish-Soviet relations, esp. pp. 134–35, 150–51, 160–63, 202, 212–19. President Beneš, though not trustworthy as a reporter, stated in his published memoirs that he was certain that the Soviets could not have helped him any more than they had helped Spain, which would have been a catastrophe for the Prague government (Beneš, *Mnichovské dny*, p. 321), and he confided much the same to Czech Communist Party chieftains in Moscow during the war, emphasizing far more than in the later memoirs the division in the country, and bringing up the military inadequacies of the army. See "Poznámky k zápisu o rozmovách s presidentem dr. Benešem," Dec. 13 and 15, 1943, SÚA, KSC, Fond c.100 24, 172, 1526; also Jordan, pp. 280, 315 n. 12, 320. All later efforts of Beneš and of his close adviser, Hubert Ripka, to claim that the Soviets, unlike Britain and France, had been loyal to him in 1938, must be seen in the light of these statements and the strange history of his wartime cozying up to Stalin; see, for example, among many, Beneš in conversation with a Polish-exile Foreign Ministry colleague reported in Kulski to Roberts, Sept. 9, 1943, AAN, Ambasada RP w Londyniu, 1493. In his *Memoirs* (pp. 40–43), Beneš reversed himself to say that Czechoslovakia *was* prepared for war in 1938, and he paints a picture of Soviet willingness to help at that time. Here he puffs up the Soviet Union as reliable while attacking Britain and France. One gathers that he was writing for his own internal consumption as well as for posterity. Not for nothing was he referred to as the "Czech Machiavelli" (quoted by Taborský, p. 24). For British unpreparedness in 1938 compared with 1939, see Litvinov-Hudson conversation notes, Mar. 22, 1939, in USSR, Ministerstvo inostrannykh del, *God krizisa*, 1: 317–18, Potemkin-Hudson conversation notes, Mar. 27, 1939, 1: 335.

11. Numerous documents show the skepticism about Moscow's intentions. See Papée, Prague, to MSZ, Mar. 26 and 28, and Apr. 4, 1938, AAN, WW, Poselstwo w Pradze 5428, Sept. 20 and 23, 1938, ibid., 5431, and Sept. 30, 1938, ibid., 5433; Łukasiewicz, Paris, to MSZ, Sept. 25, 1938, ibid., 5432; R. Raczyński, Bucharest, to MSZ, Sept. 23, 1938, ibid., 5431; E. Raczyński to MSZ [?], May 4, 1938, Ambasada RP w Paryżu, HA, box 7. Also, Newton, Prague, to FO, Mar. 19, 1938, PRO, FO371, 22286, N1622; Vereker (Moscow) to Foreign Secretary Halifax, May 16, 1938, PRO, FO371, 22288, N2519, and Vereker to Halifax, May 31, 1938, reporting the words of German military attaché Koestring, who discounted the possibility of Soviet aid to Czechoslovakia in the event of a German-Czech confrontation, and said that the Soviet army was too weak to act and that the only reason the Germans had gone ahead, in March 1938, to occupy Austria was that they had no fear of the Soviets because of the weakness of the Red Army (PRO, FO371, 22289, N3329); also, Chilston to Halifax, Oct. 18, 1938, 22289, N5164. See also, Douglas, "Chamberlain and Appeasement," pp. 84–85; Herndon, pp. 311–

12; Hochman, p. 159; Jordan, p. 276; also H. Phillips, pp. 162–63. For Beneš's estimate of Soviet help, see his *Mnichovské dny*, pp. 321–22. For reports from the German embassy in Moscow, see DGFP, series D, 1: 900, 918, and 2: 838, 847–88; of particular importance: Schulenberg, Moscow, to the Foreign Ministry, Sept. 23, 1939 (pp. 897–98), Sept. 26, 1939 (pp. 946–49), and Sept. 29, 1939 (pp. 998–99).

12. Grzybowski, Moscow, to MSZ, Mar. 29, May 25 and 31, 1938, AAN, MSZ 6664, and ww; Poselstwo w Pradze 5428, and May 31, 1938, AAN, MSZ, Ambasada RP w Berlinie 56; Jankowski, Moscow, to MSZ, Sept. 6, 1938, ibid., ww, Poselstwo w Pradze 5428; Łukasiewicz, Paris, to MSZ, Sept. 13, 1938, ibid., 5430; Papée to MSZ, Sept. 29, 1938, ibid., 5438. See also, Pagel, p. 213. For a note from the French ambassador in Moscow, see Coulondre, pp. 142–63; for the Germans: Schulenberg, Moscow, to Foreign Ministry, Sept. 23, 1938, DGFP, series D, 2: 897–88; and Moltke, Warsaw, to Foreign Ministry, Sept. 24, 1938, DGFP, 2:922.

13. Firsov, "Arkhivy Kominterna," p. 31.

14. Grzybowski, Moscow, to MSZ, Mar. 25, 1938, AAN, MSZ, ww, Poselstwo w Pradze 5428.

15. Grzybowski, Moscow, to MSZ, Apr. 29, 1939, Ambasada RP w Paryżu, HA, box 8; Nadzhadov, p. 47; Semiriaga, "Eshche raz o krizisnom gode, 1939," pp. 121–22; Rosenfeld, pp. 298–99. Also, Nekrich and Heller, pp. 117–22. It was probably true, as Stalin himself told German Ambassador Schulenberg, that all the efforts of the Western powers could not have won him for their constellation in 1939 (see the notes of Schulenberg on his conversation with Hitler, Apr. 28, 1941, in Jacobsen, ed., *Der Zweite Weltkrieg*, p. 209). Publicly, however, Stalin gave out via Foreign Minister Litvinov denials of his interest in the German pact (see Gryzbowski, Moscow, to MSZ, Apr. 29, 1939, Ambasada RP w Paryżu, HA, box 8), the latter terming the notion "fantastic." Only two months earlier, Litvinov had told the Czechoslovak ambassador that he saw no reason why the Soviet Union and Germany could not work together (see Fierlinger, Moscow, to MZV, Feb. 14, 1939, AMZV, 4-70-114). For background, see H. Phillips, pp. 161–65. Viacheslav Datschitschew (Dashichev) has made the point of Stalin's Neanderthal understanding of European history and tradition, and his quest for the German pact, in "Der Pakt der beiden Banditen," also in "Planungen und Fehlschläge Stalins am Vorabend des Zweiten Weltkrieges," and many times since, most recently in Soviet historical journals. See also the article by Pietrow-Ennker. A much earlier source is Tokaev, p. 28. Molotov in his infamous speech to the Supreme Soviet of October 31, 1939 (*Pravda*, Nov. 1, 1939, p. 1), stressed the point that British and French guarantees had not availed the Poles in 1939.

16. Vereker (Moscow) to Collier, Foreign Office, Feb. 21, 1939, PRO, FO371, 23677, N902. Several times in 1938, notes from the French ambas-

sador in Moscow and other French observers to the Quai d'Orsay described Stalin's quest to join up with Hitler: see, for example, Coulondre (Moscow) to Bonnet, Oct. 4, 1938, *DDF*, deuxième série, 11: 28; and Oct. 18, 1938, deuxième série, 12: 277. Stalin's flirtation with the Führer was not at all subtly conducted, although the odd lack of historical writing on the subject until more or less recently might indicate the contrary. Litvinov was letting out broad hints of Soviet collaboration with Germany and of Germany's finding satisfaction for its expansionist expectations by moving westward, not eastward, in February 1939 (see Fierlinger, Moscow, to MZV, Feb. 14, 1939, AMZV, 4-70-114). American President Roosevelt had been informed of Stalin's hints to the Germans dropped in his famous speech of March 10, 1939 (on the eve of Hitler's already much rumored march into Czechoslovakia), but publicly he discounted the possibility of a Nazi-Soviet rapprochement. See Polish Ambassador Potocki's report from Washington, D.C., to the Polish Ministry of Foreign Affairs, Mar. 14, 1939, AAN, MSZ, ww, Poselstwo w Pradze, 5436. Other Polish diplomats likewise reported the story home. See Kruszyński, Stockholm, to MSZ, Feb. 14, 1939; Zarański, Vienna, to Ambasada RP w Berlinie, May 24, 1939; Ambasada RP w Berlinie 21; and Sokolnicki, Ankara, to MSZ, June 28, 1939, AAN, MSZ, ww, 6655. See Nadzhadov, p. 48; also H. Phillips, pp. 154, 160, 165–66.

17. See Stalin's reflections on October Revolution day, 1939, expressed to his intimates, in Institut Marksizma-leninizma pri TsK KPSS, "Komintern i sovetsko-germanskoi dogovor o nepadenii," p. 211; also, Firsov, "Arkhivy Kominterna," p. 26. For an early suggestion, from 1938, of Stalin's hopes of dividing Poland with Hitler, see Lukes, "Benesch, Stalin und die Komintern," p. 350.

18. George F. Kennan interview of May 30, 1972, with J. K. Zawodny, p. 226; Kennan, "Russia—Seven Years Later," p. 64; R. Weber, pp. 285–86; Nekrich, *"June 22, 1941,"* pp. 305–22; The Anglo-French diplomatic effort was launched some days before Hitler marched into the remnant of Czechoslovakia with a surprise, symbolic visit of Prime Minister Chamberlain and much of his cabinet to a reception at the Soviet Embassy in London; see Maiskii, London, to Narkomindel, Mar. 2, 1939, *God krizisa,* 1: 246. For more on the diplomatic rush given the Soviets, see Maiskii, London, to Narkomindel, Mar. 15 and 16, ibid., pp. 274–75, 292; Surits, Paris, to Narkomindel, Mar. 15, 1939, ibid., p. 276; Litvinov-Hudson conversation notes, Mar. 23 and 25, 1939, ibid., pp. 317–19, 324–27; Potemkin-Hudson conversation notes, Mar. 27, 1939, ibid., pp. 335–37; also Schulenberg, Moscow, to Foreign Ministry, June 5, 1939, in Sontag and Beddie, p. 20. For the background of British diplomacy, see Manne, "The British Decision." On the disillusion of the British delegates with their early hopes from the Moscow parlays, see Jankowski, Moscow, July 4, 1939, to MSZ, HA, Ambasada RP w

Paryżu, box 8. For background from the chief British negotiator, see Strang, *The Moscow Negotiations*.

19. For Stalin in charge of Soviet foreign policy, and Molotov as his only collaborator, see Sokolov, p. 110. Molotov later recalled that one task he had as People's Commisar for Foreign Affairs was "to broaden as far as possible the borders of the fatherland. And, it seems, we and Stalin didn't do badly at this work"; quoted in Resis, ed., p. 8. Details of Krėvė-Mickievičius are in U.S. Congress, Select Committee, *Third Interim Report*, pp. 340–44, 450–63. For the striking parallels between Stalin's moves to expand the USSR's borders during World War II and the intended expansion of Russia to the west in World War I, see Smith, pp. 11–14, 20, 49, 86–88, 94, 102–3, 105, 108. For background on the pact and the documents, see Suziedelis; see also, the editors of *Lituanus*, "The Molotov-Ribbentrop Pact: The Documents"; and Hass, pp. 89–96. On Hitler's decision for the pact, see Zoria and Lebedeva, p. 125. Hitler cynically viewed the pact as a tactical maneuver: see Überschär, pp. 573–75. Stalin had predicted in 1934 that the assailants of the USSR in a future war would collapse and that revolutions would break out in some of the lands of Europe and Asia (Schroeder, p. 617). This was clearly another one of Stalin's Aesopian references to what he had had firmly in mind for years, following directly in spiritual father Lenin's footsteps. See Lenin, "Ia proshu zapisyvat' menshe."

20. For the first hint of the plan, see "Komintern i sovetsko-germanskoi dogovor o napadenie," p. 206. Molotov, nine months later, blurts out the grand scheme: Myllyniemi, p. 126; Sommer, *Das Memorandum*, pp. 115–17. The original revelation in English of part of the plan is in U.S. Congress, *Third Interim Report*, pp. 342–43, 450–63. V. G. Dekanozov confirms Molotov: *Third Interim Report*, pp. 402, 462–63; Myllyniemi, p. 126; more from Andrei Zhdanov, Myllyniemi, p. 133; also Tokaev, pp. 29–30; Ślusarczyk, p. 28; Sommer, *Das Memorandum*, pp. 120–22. The chief, but not the only, reporter of the scheme was Professor Vincus Krėvė-Mickievičius, vice-premier and foreign minister of the government first set up in Lithuania in June 1940 to please the Soviets, and a former dean of Kaunas University; his Soviet bona fides are set down by one old friend of the Stalinists, Anna Louise Strong, in Strong, p. 120; and by Soviet history writers at the very top: Akademia nauk SSR, pp. 185, 254. Just as important, Krėvė-Mickievičius was at this time privately confiding in Thomas Preston, of the British Legation in Kaunas, details of his interviews with Molotov and V. G. Dekanozov. Preston, whom the exiled Poles later described as "very pro-Soviet," hence untrustworthy (see "Race Matters in the Soviet Zone of Poland," IS, A9, V. 8d), found Krėvė a "kind, well-meaning academical person." Krėvė's reported thoughts were given in confidence to Preston, perhaps because of the latter's alleged views, on occasions both before and after Krėvė's visit to Moscow. Among other liberal notions and hopes Krėvė held before

his departure for Moscow (July 2, 1940) was the notion that the Soviets had missed the opportunity to attack Germany before it had finished with France. But upon his return a few days later, after the meeting with Molotov, Krėvė was evidently downcast. He said "with great emotion" and "in strictest secrecy" that Lithuania would soon be incorporated into the USSR. This confirms part of what the other sources named above tell us he had heard from Molotov. Furthermore, Krėvė said that though he did not know how the end of Lithuanian independence would come, it was already determined, and with the end of Lithuania's independence, a strict Soviet regime would rule. He also put a far more desperate emphasis on the foreign situation than he had given in conversation with Preston before his trip to Moscow: though he had always believed, and still did, that war between the Soviets and Germans was inevitable, "he had been assured by M. Molotoff that all Russia's military moves had been made with the complete agreement of Germany, who had expressed her complete disinterestness therein." This certainly indicates that Molotov had told Krėvė the truth, but Krėvė, shaken, could not bring himself to tell Preston the whole tale he had heard from the Soviet foreign minister, which he reported several times elsewhere only later. In any case, he was by implication letting Preston know that he had been disabused of his early idealistic notion that the real purpose of the Soviet occupation of the Baltic states was pursuit of the war against Germany, and he no longer spoke of the liberal domestic changes in Lithuania he had hoped to effect with Soviet help. See Preston to War Cabinet, June 26 and July 5, 1940, PRO, FO371, 24671, N5889 and N5943. Supplemental and independent confirmation of much of what Krėvė reported, from an NKVD defector who went with Andrei Zhdanov to Tallinn when Dekanosov came to Kaunas, can be found in the report of "Petrow," pp. 11–14; and the more extensive accounts in "Les Souvenirs d'un agent soviétique"; also from Nikita S. Khrushchev in Khrushchev, pp. 99–100. Molotov's insistence on the Rhine battle to come as the scene of the great Western-German stalemate conducing to the proletarian revolution in the West was repeated by two different higher Soviet military figures quoted by Tokaev (pp. 72–73) on two different dates between 1939 and 1941. Tokaev does not appear to have been familiar with Krėvė's story when he wrote. Stalin and Molotov, in their imaginings, appear to have thought that the Maginot and Siegfried lines would cause a stalemate, which would have to be broken by throwing men against the two military walls in the style of the Somme offensives of World War I, hence Molotov's emphasis on the Rhine.

21. How often the Soviet chieftains both privately and publicly embroidered their hopes for others is reflected in the fact that an American representative in Peking reported to Washington on June 20, 1940 (USNA, microfilm 982, reel 25), that an American newsman had it from the Soviet representative, Nikitin, in charge of the embassy there, that the Soviets

made the agreement with Hitler "in the hope that the resultant war between Germany and the western allies would bring about the mutual exhaustion of both sides leaving Russia safe from external menace in Europe."
The American minister to Estonia and Latvia, John C. Wiley, wrote from
Riga to Loy Henderson, Sept. 7, 1939, that he had heard that the Soviets
wanted a long drawn out war in the West (in LC, Loy Henderson Papers).
Even American FBI chief J. Edgar Hoover, claiming "one of the highest Russian sources," had got wind of the larger plan by June 1940 (Hoover to A. A.
Berle, June 17, 1940, USNA, M982, R25). A later, Soviet source reported by
Karl Erban is "Věc: rusko-německý pomer," London, June 19, 1941, AMZV,
4-70-114. All these sources, I think, establish that the Soviets were in this
case not holding their secrets very tightly. Tokaev (p. 71) suggests why, ex-
plaining how reports, originally concocted at the top of the Soviet hierarchy,
filtered down through the party echelons. He, in effect, helps fix the Kremlin, in this case by analogy, as the place where these particular plans origi-
nated. The same method of distribution accounts for the number of reports
we have, for they are the inevitable leaks. Foreign Minister Litvinov had
already outlined compatible Soviet expectations at the time of the Czechoslovak crisis in 1938. And Beneš saw the Soviet aim, with the conclusion
of the Pact in the summer of 1939, as encouraging war for social revolutionary purposes with a view to intervening as soon as the other powers were
weakened; see Lukes, "Benes, Stalin und die Komintern," pp. 350–53. What
Nikitin in Chungking reported might have been the line put out to the local
diplomats, but only the former part was true if we are to believe Molotov.
He, like Stalin, was an amazing combination of candor and deceit, ready to
organize each story with truth and falsehood for the benefit of his current
audience. A striking example of the two of them at work is in a report of
the conference with Latvian Foreign Minister Munters in Moscow, in which
Stalin fantasizes about a number of his favorite subjects to the captive audience, including philosophy, history, and ethnology, and about the need for
Soviet sailors to avail themselves of the services of Latvian women when in
port, and says that Munters need not try to complain to the Germans
(whose behavior and plans he describes at length) about current Soviet pressures on his country. Stalin: "Ribbentrop is a sensible man" (transcripts of
meetings numbers 1 and 2 with Stalin and Molotov in the Kremlin, Oct. 2
and 3, 1939, USNA, microfilm 1244, reel 5).

Soviet and post-Soviet historians have recently reported finding Stalin's
plan for the war sketched out in several places, with parts or all of it mentioned by L. M. Mekhlis, E. S. Varga, and Andrei Zhdanov (the latter, from
1941: "We have already entered on the path of a policy of attack"), all of
whom were part of, or close to, the Kremlin inner circle, between 1939
and 1941. See Volkogonov, p. 10; Semiriaga in "17 sentiabria 1939 goda,"
pp. 14–15 (includes the Zhdanov quote just above), and in "Sovetskii soiuz

i predvoennyi politicheskii krizis," pp. 54–61; and Spirin, p. 95. Soviet defector Grigorii Tokaev told much of it even earlier: pp. 72–73; see also Firsov, "Stalin und die Komintern," p. 120; and (on Varga), Duda, p. 159. Finally, Walter Ulbricht, a German Communist boss close to the Comintern leaders, suggested in a party information meeting in Moscow that the westward thrust of the Red Army after the collapse of the warring powers was one anticipated outcome of the war ("Politischer Informationsabend am 21. 2. 1941," in ZPA, Pieck Nachlass 36/528). My own earlier evaluation of some of these materials is given in "Stalin's Plans for World War II." For other reports suggesting that the original Soviet line (almost identical to that employed in Poland in 1939) used during the occupation of the Baltic states in June 1940 was to portray the invasions there as "defensive" (or "offensive" against the Germans), see PRO, FO371, 24761, N5833, N5889 (another, from Riga; and another conversation of Preston's, this time with the Lithuanian chief of staff). About the same time the American ambassador in London reported that he had heard the same (PRO, FO371, C7376). Important ideological and political background supporting the notion that Stalin's *Drang nach Westen* was nothing new in 1939 is in Kaplan, pp. 3, 91. My article "Stalin Plans His Post-War Germany" established Stalin's determination to move Communist Party influence and control into Western-occupied, postwar Germany; it seems undeniable that this plan represented a continuation of his plans of 1939–41, adapted to the changed circumstances. On the psychological drive to betray secrets and widen the circle of intimates, see my article "When Plans Fail." Whatever the compulsion, the notion that the Kremlin held such secrets well will not stand. For example, nine months before Stalin moved to take Bessarabia and Northern Bukovina in June 1940, and just one month after the pact was signed with Hitler, the Soviet ambassador in London was letting out information, which he had no reason then to know, about the changes to come involving Romania. See Beneš notes, "Rozhovor s Majským," Sept. 22, 1939, AÚTGM, BA, EB/L 101.

22. U.S. Congress, *Third Interim Report*, pp. 342–44, 459; Firsov, "Arkhivy Kominterna," p. 28. Several authors, writing earlier, have suggested that Stalin actually had a firm date, or at least a firm military plan, for the attack west, which would be directed against the Germans. Certainly the Soviet military was making contingency plans in the spring of 1941 (see "Schukows Angriffsplan"). This proves little, however, since all military staffs presumably make contingency plans. On the plan, see Gor'kov, "Gotovil li Stalin uprezhdaiushchii udar protiv Gitlera v 1941 g.?" Some of the most controversial assessments of Stalin's intentions in making the Pact are in Suworow (Suvorov), *Der Eisbrecher*, pp. 61–67; on his findings and other evidence to the point, see chap. 2, n. 21; and Topitsch, pp. 7–8, 14–16. The most substantially researched version of the argument is Joachim Hoffmann's "Die Angriffsvorbereitungen der Sowjetunion 1941," in Wegner, ed.,

Zwei Wege nach Moskau. See also, Semiriaga, "Sovetskii soiuz i predvoennyi politicheskii krizis," p. 61. Suvorov is challenged, to be sure on the basis of limited sources and research suprannuated by other findings and revelations when published, by Gabriel Gordetsky, in the same Wegner-edited volume mentioned above: "The notion that Stalin had in mind an attack on Germany is 'absurd'" ("Stalin und Hitlers Angriff auf die Sowjetunion," p. 362). But Gorodetsky is praised, and his opinion ratified, at least with respect to 1941 and 1942, by Dallin (pp. 20, 28), who neither cites the recent Russian-language accounts nor deals with the primary sources, many of them available when he wrote; Dallin also omits any mention of Krėvė-Mickievičius and Soviet defector Tokaev, who presented the earliest versions of Stalin's war plan, Tokaev arguing that Stalin planned to attack Germany and Finland in August 1941 (p. 34). It therefore appears that the notion of a Soviet attack to the west in 1941, or 1942, is not quite so absurd, even if the date, which perhaps depended on the circumstances as Stalin perceived them, remained open. Was the Soviet army in an attack position on June 22, 1941? It is a point well established by other evidence, such as Czech analyst Karel Erban, writing for his exiled foreign minister, London, June 18, 1941, AMZV, 4-70-114; and by military historian V. A. Semidetko, pp. 29–31. Like the notion that Stalin conducted a "defensive" policy before the war (suggested as if there were no possible challenge to the notion by Haslam, p. 106, and by others), the idea that he actually planned an attack to the west assaults the received thinking of countless historians and other writers.

23. ZPA, Pieck Nachlass. 36/540. Wilhelm Pieck, German Communist leader and a member of the central direction of the Comintern, wrote of Stalin's September 1939 introduction to his new, post-Pact elucidations, "of great historical significance"; "stirring . . . analysis"; "unshakeable logic and clarity." See also, "Komintern i sovetsko-germanskoi dogovor o nepadenii," pp. 210–15. The developed line is most completely expressed in "Zum Bericht im Sekretariat am 30. 12. über die deutsche Frage," and Pieck's notes of Dec. 26, 1939, both in ZPA, Pieck Nachlass, 36/540. On Stalin's "policy of peace," see "Veränderungen in der internationalen Lage seit Paktabschluss" (probably 1940), Pieck Nachlass, 36/497; and detailing the virtues of the aid to Germany, "Zur deutschen Aussenpolitik von Versailles bis zum sowjetischen-deutschen Pakt" (draft of a *Flugschrift*, Feb. 28, 1940), in ZPA, Ulbricht Nachlass, 182/225. Molotov evidently believed that Germany could ultimately be brought to its knees by the Western Allies (U.S. Congress, *Third Interim Report*, pp. 342, 402). Ulbricht, in the talk to party comrades in February 1941 cited in note 21 above, suggested that the inner circle at that time already believed that Germany was weakening. The opinions of Molotov and Ulbricht perhaps derived from the prediction of E. (Jenö) Varga (Stalin's favorite economist at the time) that Germany's eco-

nomic resources would quickly decline as the war progressed: see Duda, pp. 152–53. The scheme of aiding the Germans in order to prolong the war is restated in Erban, "Věc: rusko-německý pomer," London, June 18, 1941, AMZV, 4-70-114. See also, Tokaev, pp. 72–73.

24. See U.S. Congress, *Third Interim Report*, pp. 342, 459. On the connection of Stalin's European and Asian policies, see Drechsler, pp. 42–45; and H. Thomas, pp. 40, 66.

25. Piekalkiewicz, p. 57. The photo is in the Ribbentrop Collection in the Hoover Archive.

26. One can speculate on what might have happened had the British known that Stalin definitely intended to enter the conflict against the Poles on Germany's side. To what extent would the British and French commitment to the Poles then have held, and how would it have been worked out? On Stalin's fear of being identified with the Germans, see Fleischhauer, *Diplomatischer Widerstand*, p. 30.

27. Cienciała, "Polska w polityce brytyskiej i francuskiej w 1939 roku," pp. 169–70. Stalin on Poland: "Komintern i sovetsko-germanskii dogovor o nepadenii," p. 206. On Hitler's fear of a two-front war, see Speer, pp. 72, 227; Fleischhauer, *Der Pakt*, 540 n. 8; Binion, pp. 61–65; Rosenfeld, p. 299. Stalin allegedly calculated that he was releasing Hitler from the threat of a two-front war, but took the chance in his imagining that the war would bring down the whole European political house of cards. Meanwhile, Soviet propaganda lauded the Pact as a "mighty step toward the strengthening of peace" (Tokaev, p. 30). Only a few diplomats saw Stalin's plan for the war clearly: Pagel, pp. 269–72, 287–88.

28. Who now recalls this division?—an augury of the grotesque division of Berlin that came later.

29. Nekrich and Heller (pp. 354–55) maintain that Stalin even furnished the Germans direct military support, including a submarine base at Murmansk in 1939 and 1940. The American government does not seem to have learned about this until after the war; see Reinhart to Durbrow, Nov. 10, 1945, in USNA, RG266, entry 1, box 5.

30. On Stalin's lack of preparedness, see Rzhevskaia, "V tot den', pozdnei osen'iu," p. 169. For an older and somewhat outdated though sound account of the background of the war, see Hofer; an older introduction to the research question and an important bibliography are in Jacobsen, *Zur Konzeption einer Geschichte des Zweiten Weltkrieges*. Hitler gives witness when receiving the new Soviet ambassador in Berlin, Aleksandr A. Shkvartsev, on Sept. 3, 1939, of the discussion in the Molotov-Stalin-Ribbentrop talks of the first demarcation line in *God krizisa*, 2: 360. One mark of Stalin's strange sense of humor to be noted: the Poles thought the new ambassador was "a Jew by birth," saying that this was a "great sensation" in Moscow diplomatic circles ("Dla A.T.E.," Warsaw, Sept. 2, 1939, AAN, MSZ, WW,

6664). Presumably the German embassy in Moscow also knew this, and either deliberately did not pass the word along to Berlin, or (far less likely) the Führer sufficiently overcame his fears of catching the "Jewish bacillus" to give Shkvartsev an extremely friendly and respectful personal reception in the name of the newly discovered German-Soviet friendship. Hitler remarked, "In a few weeks hence I shall stretch out my hand to Stalin at the German-Russian frontier and with him undertake to redistribute the world": *DBFP*, 3d series, 7: 258.

31. Piekalkiewicz, pp. 182–86; J. Gross and I. Grudzińska Gross, pp. 3–12; Garliński, pp. 39–41. The most complete account of the war itself is in Liszewski, *Wojna Polsko-Sowiecka 1939 r.* Interesting Soviet fables on the attack told by one of its generals are in Sandalov, pp. 39–44, including General Sandalov's proud defense (p. 39): "All of us faithfully believed in the wisdom of the Central Committee of the Communist Party." The Poles monitored Soviet broadcasts for a number of days after the war began: "Raporty z nasłuchu radia radzieckiego [1939]," AAN, MSZ, WW, 6664.

32. Bennett, p. 187.

33. Piekalkiewicz, pp. 127, 132, 141, 158–61, 170–72.

34. See *Pravda*, Nov. 30, 1939; Garliński, pp. 46–47; Weinberg, *Germany and the Soviet Union, 1939–1941*, p. 58. For Molotov on the alleged defensive nature of the pact, see U.S. Congress, *Third Interim Report*, p. 455.

35. For a description of the general British ignorance of eastern Europe, see Rothwell, p. 158. Churchill, who believed World War II to be a continuation of World War I, had a fixed notion that tsarist Russian contributions to the Allied cause in World War I ought to be credited to the "Russians" in World War II: see Churchill to Roosevelt, Feb. 20, 1944, in Kimball, ed., *Churchill and Roosevelt*, 2: 738. Churchill later said that he had merely tried to make the best of a bad thing in his dealings with the "odious" Soviets, but his words and behavior to 1945 deny this: see Churchill, *The Gathering Storm*, p. 339, and *The Hinge of Fate*, p. 393. For a very balanced assessment of Churchill, see James, "The Epic Concluded." According to Lawlor, "Britain and Russian Entry into the War," Churchill's later foreign secretary, Anthony Eden, was far more prone than Churchill to seeing matters from the Soviet standpoint; PRO materials on British-Soviet relations from the winter of 1941 through the spring of 1942 make this failing especially evident. A very divergent view, full of praise for Churchill (and, by contrast, especially hard on Roosevelt) as the only statesman who saw the Soviet danger from the beginning, seems at odds with the facts presented here and below: see Wheeler-Bennett and Nicholls, pp. 289–90.

36. On Roosevelt's persisting naïveté in handling the Soviets, see Kennan's "comment" to the article, "Allied Leadership in World War II," p. 31: "When [it came] to foreign policy, a very superficial man, ignorant, dilettantish, with a severely limited intellectual horizon." In 1938, Roosevelt

was enthusiastic about and strongly recommended the viewing of the pro-Communist Joris Ivens's propaganda film *Spanish Earth*, which greatly simplified the complex issues of the Spanish Civil War. Many of Roosevelt's chief advisers were equally blind to the potential Soviet danger. See Schwartz, for example (p. 57), on Sumner Welles.

37. One of the British rationalizations in September 1939 for doing nothing about the Soviet attack on the Poles was to recall the Curzon Line, in effect, their own uninformed design, thereby compounding their ignorance. This rationale the Soviets respectfully noted. See Kitchen, p. 2. For Chamberlain and Halifax on the Curzon line, see E. Raczyński, "Notatka sprawodawcza . . . z rozmów A. Zaleskiego w Londyniu," Oct. 12, 1939, in S. Stanisławska, ed., p. 112.

38. A leader in *The Times* ("from a correspondent," but presumably by Professor E. H. Carr, then the newspaper's leader writer on most such subjects), dated May 16, 1945, implicitly approving the recent Soviet annexation of the Czech province of Ruthenia, shows how ignorant even Slavicists were about the demography of the region: "The Russians, Ruthenes, or Ukrainians (they have been called all three)" live in Sub-Carpathian Ruthenia. The Ruthenians are "the most westerly branch of the Russian race."

39. On Stalin's success in hoodwinking the British, see Gorodetsky, *Sir Stafford Cripps' Mission to Moscow, 1940–1942*, p. 13. On the birth of the Curzon line, see Hooker, "Lord Curzon and the Curzon Line," and Kimball, ed., *Churchill-Roosevelt: The Complete Correspondence*, 2: 684n. Churchill devotes a chapter to Curzon in his *Great Contemporaries* (rev. ed., 1938). One striking symptom of the failure of the British and American press is the ratio of articles carrying information on Nazi-occupied Poland, 1939–41, to those bearing on Soviet-occupied Poland. Besides the indexes of *The Times* (London) and the *New York Times*, one can consult the summary in "The Weekly Review of Polish Issues in the Press of Great Britain," compiled by the Polish government's Ministry of Information in London (in Polish). Its records are in IS, MID, A10, 5, 15. A later thoughtful reflection on the subject of the perils of journalism in the USSR is Winterton's *Report on Russia*.

40. Weinberg, *Germany and the Soviet Union*, p. 56. Hitler and Ribbentrop were vainly trying as late as September 28, 1939, to get back from Stalin the oil-rich areas of southeastern Poland, which these blunderers apparently realized they had forgotten to include in their original take: see Piekalkiewicz, p. 220.

41. It must be recalled that Churchill's frequently deprecated chief, Prime Minister Neville Chamberlain, regularly scourged for Munich, gave even then at least some thought to the prospect of such a disaster. See Introduction, n. 2.

42. Piekalkiewicz, pp. 220–23; Sword, "The Division of Poland," chap. 2, n. 38.

43. At the outset of the negotiations, Ribbentrop was apparently pressing for a German-Soviet division of Latvia—again, to great German military advantage in the case of a later German attack on the Soviet Union—and had earlier imagined German military forces advancing in agreement with the Soviets as far as Reval (Tallinn): see DBFP, 3d series, 7: 259. Yet by this time he was willing to give up even Lithuania. Even so, Stalin apparently did not claim all that Hitler, hopelessly arrogant, was willing to offer: the Führer was at the outset of the negotiations even willing to give him Istanbul and the Straits (Hofer, pp. 118, 123). After the second set of negotiations, Ribbentrop was absurdly delighted with himself (Weinberg, *Germany and the Soviet Union*, p. 58), despite his realization that Stalin was getting rid of his Polish problem (Pagel, p. 303). See also, Topitsch, pp. 40–41, and Mazur, pp. 139–45. The fact that Stalin seemingly frivolously gave part of Poland back as a hunting preserve (Speer, p. 232) tells much about the character of both men.

CHAPTER 2

1. Cienciała, "Polska w polityce brytyskiej i francuskiej," pp. 181–82; Sandalov, pp. 39–40; Piekalkiewicz, p. 162. A rather up-to-date Polish diplomatic background is in Batowski.

2. The dimensions of chaos and disorganization in internal Soviet structures at that time are reflected in the summary article by Fitzpatrick, pp. 368, 372.

3. Weinberg, *Germany and the Soviet Union*, pp. 55–57; see also the article by Langner, pp. 193–94.

4. Piekalkiewicz, pp. 205–25.

5. Kaslas, *The Baltic Nations*, p. 219. Elsewhere (*The USSR-German Aggression Against Lithuania*, p. 309), Kaslas says that the Swedes "proved to be one of the most notorious fair weather friends in recent diplomatic history," as the other Scandinavian and Baltic states also learned.

6. German newsreels were then still under the Ufa label. They were produced in many languages for distribution abroad, as were the famous feature-length *Feldzug in Polen* and, from Goering's Luftwaffe unit, the film of the destruction of Poland's cities and defenses from the air, *Feuertaufe*. *Feldzug in Polen* was made in several versions (one shown in the United States), those in the Bundesarchiv (Koblenz) and in the archive at the Wytwórnia Filmów Dokumentalnych (Warsaw) being significantly different in sound track.

7. American cameraman Julian Bryan was in Warsaw from a few days after the war began until September 21. He managed to smuggle his film through the German lines, and back in the United States he produced a

documentary film, *Siege,* on the horrors of the Nazi bombardment. *Siege* was turned out in many languages. Although Bryan actually did not use some of the worst scenes of destruction, the film was shocking, and it stimulated the fears of civilians all over the world about the new weapons of mass terror. This is something the media do well, as we have learned over time. A copy of the film and a number of its outtakes are in the archive at the Wytwórnia Filmów Dokumentalnych in Warsaw.

8. Kaslas, *La Lithuanie et la seconde guerre mondiale,* p. 86; Kaslas, *Baltic Nations,* pp. 225, 228, 231.

9. Hofer, pp. 146–47; Weinberg, *Germany and the Soviet Union,* p. 86.

10. See Rzhevskaia, "V tot den'," p. 169, on the fear of Nazi attack and the lack of preparation even as late as 1941.

11. Weinberg, *Germany and the Soviet Union,* p. 87.

12. *Pravda,* Nov. 3, 1939 (p. 3), compared the stubborn Finns to Poland's Colonel Beck, who "provoked the war with Germany." See also, Misiunas and Taagepera, p. 25; Myllyniemi, p. 126; Weinberg, *Germany and the Soviet Union,* p. 143; Tucker, *Stalin in Power,* p. 604; Semiriaga, "Voina kotoruiu stydno vspominat'," p. 77.

13. Myllyniemi, p. 154.

14. Garliński, p. 47; Gorodetsky, *Cripps,* p. 11; Weinberg, *Germany and the Soviet Union,* p. 87, all mention Hitler's suggestions for peace with the West. For Stalin's haste and technique of crisis building, see Spring, pp. 216, 219; for Stalin's plans, see Mastny, p. 27 (quoting Khrushchev); Sommer, *Botschafter Graf Schulenberg,* p. 81. Enthusiasm of the Soviet peoples for the Finnish war manifested, authentically, it appears, in the celebrations of the return of the Red Army in Leningrad in 1940, is shown in the film *Liniia Mannergeima,* in the RGAKFD Archive, Krasnogorsk. See also the account of the successes of Stalin's nationalist propaganda line as represented in film, theater, and print, reported by Tucker, *Stalin in Power,* pp. 574–75.

15. Spring, p. 209; Vihavainen, pp. 315, 317n.; Weinberg, *Germany and the Soviet Union,* p. 90; Semiriaga, "Voina kotoruiu stydno vspominat'," pp. 72–79; Werth, p. 67; Schwartz, p. 13. For press coverage, see *Pravda,* Nov. 29, 1939, pp. 1–2; *Moscow News,* Dec. 4, 1939, p. 4. For the development of the new Soviet propaganda line, see ZPA, Pieck Nachlass, NL36/540, and "Komintern i sovetsko-germanskii dogovor o napadenii" for analysis of aspects of the contemporary line, see Thompson, p. 396, and Raack, "Poor Light on the 'Dark Side of the Moon'."

16. Rzhevskaia, "V tot den'," p. 170; on the external effects of the Tukhachevskii affair, see Hochman, pp. 131–35. Hitler, observing the Soviet failures in Finland, jumped to the conclusion that the Red Army was weak; see Überschär, pp. 573–75. Further details of Stalin's purges of the officer corps are in Kuznetsov, "Generaly 1940 goda." On Finland, see Schwartz,

p. 28; on Stalin's faith that the Finns would jump to join the "happy family," see Salmon, p. 98.

17. The first Soviet-published acknowledgment of Stalin's plans for Finland is in Vashchenko, p. 30; see also the article by Noskov; Semiriaga, "Voina kotoruiu stydno vspominat'." On Poland, see Ozimek, chap. 3.

18. The Soviet forces were of course made up of many nationalities, not just Russians, but in the public opinion of 1939, it was the Russians who got the credit and blame for all that the Soviet Union did.

19. For mass public sentiment for the Finns in Britain, see Kitchen, p. 11. See also, Seeds to Foreign Office, Dec. 6, 1939, PRO, FO371, 23678, N7134, and in the same, the Foreign Office asking the Committee for Imperial Defence for "studies on various ways of going to war with Russia." Yet the Soviet apologists, including J. B. Haldane, G. B. Shaw, Jawarharlal Nehru, and John Steinbeck, continued to support Stalin in his demands on Finland (Vihavainen, p. 317 n. 8). *Pravda*, Dec. 4, 1939 (p. 1), just after the Soviet attack on Finland, reported the support of G. B. Shaw, who, not alone among British intellectuals, thought that the Finns would not have resisted had they not been supported by the United States. On the notable lack of U.S. aid, see Schwartz, pp. 18, 23, 27.

20. For Churchill's interest in the Scandinavian campaign, see Colville, pp. 103, 287. An interesting theory is noted in Weinberg, "The Nazi-Soviet Pacts," pp. 179, 184. See also the articles by Parker and by Dilks; for Soviet knowledge of the British-French plan, see Noskov, p. 14; and for background, Millman.

21. Woito, pp. 108–21. Recalling the oft-cited Oxford Union debate of 1934 as an index of the persistence of antiwar sentiment among the contemporary *jeunesse dorée*, a *Christian Science Monitor* poll of the Harvard University student body taken on May 25, 1940, indicated that 91 percent of those polled were unwilling to fight fascism, and that 62 percent opposed helping the Allies; cited by Petropoulos, p. 42.

22. The Soviet arms budget in 1941 was 43.4 percent of the total state budget. On Stalin's fears of the West, see Semiriaga, "Voina kotoruiu stydno vspominat'," p. 78; N. and V. Baryshnikov, p. 45; and for the background of the urgent rearmament program of 1939–41, see Ziemke, "Stalin as Strategist"; Perechnev; Ivashov, p. 13. None of the authors clarifies just when, in 1939, the speeded rearmament program began. On the pell-mell rush to rearmament and the dispersal of industry eastward after the Finnish disaster, see the brief article by Anfilov; see also Rotundo, p. 280.

23. For details of the new armaments, see Ivashov, pp. 14–17; Spirin, p. 94; Rotundo, p. 280; Ziemke, "Stalin as Strategist," p. 175; Tucker, *Stalin in Power*, p. 609; Kumanev, p. 6. The 1940 (or perhaps 1939) May Day parade seems to be in part used in the Soviet Central Newsreel Studio production *Boevye Budni* (1940), USNA, 111M52911R, reel 6; the 1941 parade is com-

plete in *The First of May* (1941), USNA 111M52939R. Viktor Suvorov argues that Stalin would have been ready to attack Hitler in 1941 ("Yes, Stalin Was Planning to Attack Hitler in June 1941," p. 73); Joachim Hoffmann suggests 1941 or 1942.

24. Semidetko (p. 30) describes a fascinating discovery: the Soviet troops on the White Russian front in June 1941 were in an attack position. Perechnev, on the other hand, maintains (p. 49) that the Red Army was rapidly moving toward the German border, implying that this was for defensive purposes, but was not yet, on June 22, in position. See also, on Stalin's dreams of a *Drang nach Westen*, Semiriaga, "Sovetskii soiuz i predvoennyi politicheskii krizis," p. 61. For Stalin's agents in the West, see Cecil, p. 175.

25. Myllyniemi, p. 155; Weinberg, *Germany and the Soviet Union*, p. 90.

26. Myllyniemi, p. 157; Schwartz, pp. 47–42, 47–54, 58 on the development of Finnish relations with Germany and the further breakdown of those with the USSR. The quotation is from E. R. Lingemann, commercial secretary of the British Legation, Mar. 19, 1940, PRO, FO371, 24795, N4211. The Leningrad scenes of wild celebration are recorded in the film *Liniia Mannergeima* (1940?), at the RGAKFD, Krasnogorsk.

27. Gilbert, 6: 213–306; Churchill, 1: 543–48; Butler, pp. 90–104, 109–12. Stalin, after the Finnish war no doubt looking to further his sinister interests in Finnish affairs and business, had denied Finland a defensive pact they wished to try to conclude with Sweden and Norway. Such a pact would have made the German plans for war in Scandinavia far more risky, for in attacking Norway, Hitler would have had to take on Sweden and Finland too. Such an alliance might have brought Hitler up against the Soviets as well, since they had staked out Finland as theirs. Thus Stalin probably helped deliver Norway to the Germans. According to Weinberg, "The Nazi-Soviet Pacts," p. 186, Stalin actually aided Hitler militarily during his Norwegian campaign, and, as Schwartz (pp. 40–42) notes, helped to blockade himself from support from the West in the Nazi-Soviet war to come.

28. "Petrow," in *Lithuanian Bulletin*. Proof that the Soviets had had the takeover of the Baltic states in mind since the agreements with Hitler comes from witnesses who saw maps (labeled "first edition, 1939") of the three states with the names of Soviet republics. This was reported by, among others, Karl Selter, a member of the Estonian government until 1939, who saw maps that were captured when the Soviet armies hurriedly fled before the Germans in the early summer of 1941; reported in U.S. Congress, Select Committee on Communist Aggression, *Fourth Interim Report*, pp. 1433–34. Other accounts are in Myllyniemi, pp. 133–38, and Kaslas, *La Lithuanie*, pp. 18–21.

29. For Soviet occupation and population policy in the Baltic countries, see: Latviešu, pp. 5–36; Bilmanis, ed., pp. 232–33; Vardys, ed., pp. 67–68; Rann, pp. 149–56. Alleged documentary scenes of dispossessing the middle

class and replacing them with workers at the Soviet takeover in 1940 are shown in the Soviet film *Soviet Lithuania* (c. 1941, perhaps reedited shortly after the war), USNA 242MID5149, reel 1.

30. The Lithuanians already had good reason to fear the Soviet takeover. When they received the Polish city of Wilno as a gift, provided by the Germans and handed over by the Soviets after a month of their occupation in late October 1939, the economic conditions there were reported to be "appalling." This followed the Soviets' "wholesale loot of the Wilno district." See Preston (Kaunas) to Foreign Office, Oct. 19 and 25, 1939, PRO, FO371, 23689, N5479 and N5639. For the despairing description of the same in 1940, see Preston to War Cabinet, July 31, 1940, ibid., 24761, N6045.

31. Galienne (Tallinn) to War Cabinet, July 24, 1940, PRO, FO371, 24761, N6045.

32. On Soviet plans, already in the works in September 1939, for the complete takeover of the Baltic states and their addition to the list of Soviet republics, see U.S. Congress, Select Committee, *Third Interim Report*, pp. 340–44, 450–63; Myllyniemi, pp. 122–33; see also, Langner, p. 197; Latviešu, p. 15.

33. Myllyniemi, pp. 118, 125–26; Raack, "Stalin's Plans for World War II"; USNA, T1244, reel 5: transcript of Munters meeting with Stalin and Molotov, Oct. 2, 1939; Misiunas and Taagepera, p. 25; clocks forward to Moscow time: Walter Leonard (Tallinn) to Secretary of State, Aug. 6, 1940, USNA, T1244, reel 5. Stalin knew little history, and, like Hitler, knew what he did know faultily. He did like to make parallels between himself and his misbegotten vision of Ivan. See Kobrin, p. 5.

34. Stories, recently established as correct by revelations from the Comintern archives (see chap. 1 above, citations from the Pieck collection in the ZPA), even then abounded in diplomatic circles that Stalin hoped for a long war in the west and was dismayed by the defeat of France. See, for example, John C. Wiley (Riga) to Loy Henderson, Sept. 7, 1939, LC, Loy Henderson papers; Smyth (Peking, story from a Soviet diplomat), to Secretary of State, June 20, 1940, USNA, M982, reel 25; J. Edgar Hoover (from a high Russian source) to A. A. Berle, June 17, 1940, USNA, M982, reel 25: Soviets will intervene in the war when the warring powers weaken. One American press watcher in Moscow noted the fact that, just as Paris fell, *Komsomolskaia Pravda* of June 14 published information indicating a sudden reconsideration of Soviet policy toward the proletariat's participation in the anti-Nazi war: Thurston (Moscow) to Secretary of State, June 15, 1940, USNA, M982, reel 25.

35. Harry S Truman expressed this thought in June 1941; see Mastny, p. 306; and Gaddis, *The United States and the Origins of the Cold War*, p. 198.

36. Weinberg, *Germany and the Soviet Union*, pp. 101–5; Gafençu,

pp. 48–84. On Finland and the Soviet Union after the March peace, see Krosby, pp. 26–27, 30, 34, 57–67; Weinberg, *Germany and the Soviet Union*, pp. 126–28; Schwartz, pp. 39–56.

37. Kaslas, *The Baltic Nations*, pp. 247–51. The complete archival documentation of the Lithuanian sale has been published by Kaslas in English translation: *The USSR-German Aggression Against Lithuania*, 133–307, and Kaslas also describes it in his article "The Lithuanian Strip." For a recent account exploiting the Soviet documents, see Gorlov, esp. pp. 26–27.

38. Gorodetsky, *Cripps*, p. 52.

39. Weinberg, *Germany and the Soviet Union*, pp. 142–44; Topitsch, pp. 86–88; Kaslas, "The Lithuanian Strip," p. 221. Gafençu (pp. 111, 116) notes that rumors were rife in Moscow in late 1940 that Stalin was preparing to take all of Finland as soon as the opportunity arose. For Hitler's resolve for the campaign in the Soviet Union, see Goerlitz, ed., *General Feldmarschall Keitel*, pp. 242–46.

40. For Churchill among those putting a good light on Soviet expansion in the Baltic in the fall of 1939, see Salmon, p. 113; Nordling, p. 98; Lane, pp. 145–46.

41. Roosevelt, in controlled wrath, at the time called Stalin a dictator allied to another dictator, and, in effect, a bully. Churchill was quoted in *The Times* as warning as late as March 5, 1940, that a Finnish defeat might mean "a return to the dark ages." Both remarks are in Derek Spring's film *The Soviet-Finnish War*, released by the Inter-University Film Consortium in the U.K. in 1978.

42. Sword, article in *Polityka*; Kowalski, pp. 52–59.

43. Hanak, pp. 49–50; Boyle, p. 147. Earlier, Chamberlain and his foreign minister, Lord Halifax, had determined not to trouble the Soviets unduly over their taking half of Poland, and in October 1939 Halifax in the House of Lords appeared to justify the Soviet invasion as essentially anti-German. Both Halifax and Chamberlain made it clear that they would not declare war on the USSR just because of its war on Poland.

44. Gilbert, 6: 99.

45. ZPA, Pieck Nachlass 36/740. For background, see Dallin, pp. 27–29.

46. Resis, pp. 422–24; Gorodetsky, *Cripps*, pp. 1, 12, 15–17; Kitchen, pp. 7–8, 11, 16, 18, 21–22, 36, 41–42; Miner, pp. 38, 42–43, 51–57. The picture one gets from the accounts in Gorodetsky, Kitchen, and Miner (in spite of Gorodetsky's apparent sympathy with the unusually uninformed, fellow-traveling Cripps) is that of a British diplomacy à la Keystone Kops, with conflicting opinions among the Foreign Office professionals, multiple and well-placed Soviet agents inside the system, and such distrust on the part of Churchill, Cripps, and other leaders, of the British professionals in the "Northern" (Russian, etc.) section of the Foreign Office, and of British

politicians of their ambassador, whoever he might be, in Moscow. Cripps, a staunch supporter of the Soviet Union throughout the 1930's, believed the Red Army invasion of Poland was a benefit to the Polish peasants in freeing them from their landlords (indeed it freed many of them as completely as is possible by freeing them from life itself). He was outraged by the Labour Party's condemnation of the invasion. He also supported the Soviets in their demands on Finland, which he thought were justified because the Soviet Union was a workers' state that needed to protect itself (*Pravda*, Dec. 4, 1939, p. 1; Vilhavainen, p. 317 n. 8). William Seeds, who preceded Cripps as ambassador in Moscow, was also sympathetic to the Soviet ideals, and believed that the lands the Soviets seized in eastern Poland had a Russian, or "nearly Russian," population (Bethel, p. 379). Archibald Clark-Kerr, who was on the British Moscow staff during most of the war years, was regarded by some as a Soviet agent (see Glees, *The Secrets of the Service*, p. 211; Glees also comments on the naïveté of the Foreign Office). See also the policy planning documents of 1944 cited in Chap. 1, n. 3 above. For more on this ineptness of British diplomacy of those times, see Manne, "Some British Light." Gilbert describes Churchill's unawareness of the Soviet danger and misunderstanding of Soviet behavior as no more than anti-German (Gilbert, 6: 99–100, 105–12), and he says that Churchill, blind to the danger to the Poles (and to all Europe) from the east, did his utmost to encourage them to stand against Hitler, and made it clear that his main concern was Germany (Gilbert, 5: 1112). In late August 1939, after the Nazi-Soviet Pact was published, Churchill feared that the Poles would not persist in standing fast, which meant to him that Chamberlain would be ready to make concessions to the Germans, though he, Churchill, was ready for war. Unfortunately, Britain was not. See Cienciała, "Polska w polityce brytyjskiej i francuskiej w 1939 roku," p. 173; Kennan interview in Zawodny, pp. 226–27. Churchill's earlier anti-Bolshevik remarks were actually collected by the Germans for propaganda purposes and published: see *Mon allié, Staline*, and other language editions in the Hoover Institution Library, Stanford, California. De Gaulle, quite understandably, was obsessed with the German enemy, and quite as blind as the British to the prospective Soviet danger; see Zaks, "'Wolna Francja' i Polska w latach 1943–1944," pp. 99, 105, 109, 114.

47. For Roosevelt's views, see Bennett, p. 187. Many members of the Labour Party became passionate supporters of the Soviets, and of Stalin, during the war, having, with the aid of a massive Ministry of Information propaganda effort, conveniently put aside their memories of 1939–41; see Weiler, pp. 8, 58. On Western Allied responses to the Soviets being, in effect, precast before 1941, see Kennan, *Russia and the West*, pp. 331–33; Weinberg, "The Nazi-Soviet Pacts," p. 188.

CHAPTER 3

1. The film is available in the complete file of the wartime German newsreels at the Bundesarchiv in Koblenz. Soviet cameramen may also have filmed the parade, but the film, if shot, was never shown publicly in the USSR.

2. See Raack, "Nazi Newsreels for the General Gouvernement," and Raack, "Nazi Film Propaganda and the Horrors of War."

3. Partial descriptions of the terrible situation in the USSR under Stalin first began appearing in the Soviet press only a few years ago. For early examples, see the anonymous article, "Beriia"; and Burlatskii, "Khrushchev. Shtriki k politicheskomu portretu." Walter Laqueur summed up the early evidence in his book *The Glasnost Revelations*.

4. Karl Marx made this point in his indictment of British diplomacy toward traditional Russia in his "Revelations from the History of Eighteenth-Century Diplomacy." See Wittfogel's "'Einleitung zu Marx' 'Enthüllungen zur Geschichte der Diplomatie im 18. Jahrhundert.'"

5. For Polish attention to developments in the Soviet Union, see Stone, pp. 167–83.

6. This point is easily established with respect to information contemporary to events by a comparison of the relevant indexes of the *New York Times* and *The Times* (London) for September 1939–June 1941. The survey of the entire British press made by the Polish government Ministry of Information (in London, 1940 on) shows nearly 100 articles pertaining to the Nazi area of conquest to one article about the Soviet area. See IS, MID, A10, 5, 15 ("Przegląd tygodniowy spraw polskich w prasie Wielkiej Brytanji"). The next several paragraphs in the text describing the situation in Poland under Soviet occupation follow the account in Gross, *Revolution from Abroad*, pp. 17–70. Gross, a sociologist, has made a well-considered analysis on the basis of the multiple historical sources in the archive of the Hoover Institution, Stanford, California, and his account authenticates the much earlier one by Roman Umiastowski of the Soviet attack and occupation of eastern Poland in *Russia and the Polish Republic, 1918–1941*, esp. pp. 239 and 239n., 242–44, 253, 256. The most recent and concentrated account of the beginnings of the underground resistance to Soviet rule is Węgierski, chap. 1. For a splendid contemporary summary of the work of the Soviets in just one moderately sized Polish town, Przemyśl, and its surrounding region, see IS, MID, A9, III, 2A/19 ("Miasto Przemyśl i Powiat Przemyśl"). See also, Pinchuk, *Shtetl Jews Under Soviet Rule*.

7. The Soviet accounting for its attack, "to take under protection the life and property of the population of the Western Ukraine and Western White Russia," and the course of the brief war that followed are summed up in one short paragraph in an 885-page Soviet history of World War II. See Platonov,

ed. *Vtoraia mirovaia voina, 1939–1945*, p. 168. Lubachenko, pp. 127–38, gives a brief account of the Belorussians under Polish rule. As of not so long ago, some Soviet authors were still telling the same old rescue story to account for the attack on the Poles. See the article by Antosiak.

8. Garliński, p. 40; Piekalkiewicz, p. 213.

9. Pobóg-Malinowski, 3: 107; IS, MID, A9, III, 2A/19 ("Miasto Przemyśl i powiat Przemyśl"), p. 19.

10. Garliński, pp. 53–55; Gross, *Revolution from Abroad*; Gross, "Wybory." Misiunas and Taagepera, p. 26, note that in the Baltic elections it was specifically denied that the eventual goal was incorporation in the Soviet Union. For the fate of the Belorussians under Soviet rule, see Lubachenko, pp. 139–45.

11. In German-occupied Poland, Jews when asked their names had to add either "Israel" or "Sarah."

12. Stefan Jędrychowski in Syzdek, ed., *Wanda Wasilewska*, p. 164.

13. The main centers for pro-Soviet Poles during the occupation were Białystok and Lwów (see Kersten, p. 31; Garliński, pp. 55–56). Almost all direct communication between the conquered cities in the Soviet zone of occupation, as well as all outside communication, soon vanished in keeping with the rigid centralized organizational scheme. See Jędrychowski in Syzdek, ed., *Wanda Wasilewska*, pp. 162–63. Remarkable evidences for the incredible social and infrastructural changes, based on the required visible acceptance of the Stalinized Soviet value system, beyond those described by Gross and Umiastowski, are in three films showing scenes from Lwów. The first of these, *Jewish Life in Lwów* (in Yiddish; copy at the National Center for Jewish Film, Brandeis University, Waltham, Mass.) shows street scenes of daily life in prewar Lwów, probably 1938–39. The second film was made by Soviet filmmakers, directed by the famous Alexander Dovzhenko, who were sent in soon after the occupation to make propaganda films for Soviet audiences. Dovzhenko's *Osvobozhdenie* (Liberation) of 1940 (copy at the Wytwórnia Filmów Dokumentanych, Warsaw) concentrates on the Soviet parades and rallies described by Gross and Umiastowski, one reviewed by Khrushchev, in the fall of 1939. But it also includes, as incidental background, views of the city as it looked before the Soviet nationalization and forced depolonization that began in December 1939 and January 1940: capitalist advertising and entrepreneurial shop signs still intact, and in Polish. These background details are an interesting contrast to what is shown in the German newsreel *Deutsche Wochenschau* (German Weekly newsreel, no. 556/1941, in the Bundesarchiv, Koblenz) that was made in early July 1941, just after Ukrainian nationalist and German units arrived in Lwów for its next "liberation." Behind the allegedly happy crowds there are visible changes, and the clothes people are wearing are also in marked contrast to the still respectable and often smart costumes of the people casually filmed

as background in 1938 or 1939. The film evidence underscores the Soviet emphasis on ridding Poland of bourgeois values. It wanted to show the good Soviet people the falsity of capitalist extravagances such as women's permanents, stylish dressing, French cognac, cigarette holders, chandeliers, the tango, elegant restaurants, street advertisements, postchivalric, gentlemanly attentions to females, etc. Soviet director Mikhail Romm's post-occupation feature film *Mechta*, completed in 1941, about the liberation, makes much the same point. Romm also noted in print how such capitalist "excesses" struck him when he arrived in Poland along with the baggage of the Soviet occupation forces. The Soviet occupation of Wilno, which the Red regime took over briefly in September and the greater part of October 1939, before it was handed over to the Lithuanians, was in many ways similar to the occupation of Lwów. One Lithuanian report noted that after just one month of Soviet rule the population in the Wilno area looked simply terrible (Łossowski, pp. 66, 68). After the Red Army left, the population, overwhelmingly Polish, having witnessed what they imagined was a typical foreign occupation, rushed out to buy whatever remained in the shops for whatever their remaining Polish currency would buy, apparently expecting from the Lithuanians a ridiculous second Soviet-style devaluation of the Polish currency, the *złoty*.

14. Kolski, in *Nowe Widnokręgi*, pp. 149–45; this outrageous paean to Stalin was excised in post-Stalinist times from Kolski's collected writings, *W służbie ludu pod sztandarem* KPP. A recent thoughtful analysis with important bearing on literary politics in occupied Poland and Stalinist purposes is Czajkowski, "Soviet Policies in the Literary Sphere: Their Effects and Implications," read at a School of Slavonic and East European Studies conference, London University, Apr. 13, 1989.

15. Gross, *Revolution from Abroad*, pp. 87–222; see also, Gross, "Wywózki do Rosji"; and Garliński, p. 57. For a "People's Polish" bland version, substantially reduced to a debate over numbers, see Kersten, pp. 32–40. Later, Stalin also began to deport Ukrainians and, to the delight of Hitler, Jews; see Bregman, pp. 84–85. Comparative information for the Baltics is in Misiunas and Taagepera, pp. 38–43, and Vardys, ed., pp. 67–68.

16. Stalin saw nothing wrong about massive population shifts as a way of remaking society, like mass murder and mass starvation of "socially dangerous elements." Pinchuk, "Jewish Refugees in Soviet Poland, 1939–1941," tells the story of the train cars of voluntary Jewish repatriatees, one going east and one west. They meet at a demarcation line station. One group's shout at the other, "You're insane, don't you know where you are going?" is identically, and just as vociferously, returned by the other (p. 153).

17. In spite of this the Soviets deliberately turned over Jews and others to the Gestapo during this period of Nazi-Soviet collaboration. See Buber-Neumann, pp. 52–63.

18. Friedman, pp. 6–10; Lewin, pp. 136–37; Stehle, p. 412; Tennenbaum, pp. 115–16; see also the article by Prus. For the Poles greeting the Germans, see Weinstein, p. 93. Jews were attacked in Wilno in October 1939, after the month-long Soviet occupation there (see Łossowski, p. 82), and under the German occupation similar situations developed in the Baltic countries. Except for Lithuania, these countries had smaller Jewish populations than Poland. In Lithuania Jewish Communists and pro-Soviet collaborators formed a high percentage of the total population; see Misiunas and Taagepera, pp. 60–61.

19. Kettenacker, "The Anglo-Soviet Alliance and the Problem of Germany, 1941–1945," p. 436.

20. Laqueur, *The Terrible Secret*, pp. 196–208; Frei; Penkower, pp. 59–147, 295–96.

21. The story of Churchill and Eden in their first extended negotiation on the Polish question, and of Roosevelt's role therein, is one that has not yet been substantially told. The interested reader will find much of it in PRO, FO371, 29655, 32833, 32877–79, 32880, 32882. One of the most trenchant descriptions of Churchill's tragic self-deception vis-à-vis Stalin and his slowly growing dependency on an uninformed Roosevelt, who represented increasing weight in the alliance scales, is in Seaton, pp. 518–20. For an analysis of Churchill's blind optimism and his refusal to take into account the prospective postwar power relationship in settling political questions, see Ben-Moshe, "Winston Churchill and the 'Second Front,'" pp. 531–32. The reader may judge Churchill's naïveté as reflected in his early approach to Stalin, whom he had no reason whatsoever to trust, with respect to the postwar dismemberment of Germany (see Maiskii, London, to Narkomindel, Dec. 5, 1941, in Ministerstvo Inostrannykh del SSSR, *Sovetsko-angliiskie otnosheniia*, p. 182). Stalin could easily have used this information against the British in his wartime secret negotiations with the Germans.

22. Molotov told Anthony Eden in December 1941, "In the absence of a frontier agreement there is no sound basis for relations between Great Britain and the U.S.S.R."; see Eden, p. 341. Terry (pp. 58–59, 127,245–60) suggests (incorrectly) that there is no real certainty about just what Stalin wanted territorially of, or offered to, Sikorski just then. Miner, writing later and documenting from the British archives, says that Stalin's demands put to Eden included the restoration of the Soviet Union's 1941 frontiers, which he referred to as the "Curzon Line," and he also says that Stalin proposed that the Poles be compensated with East Prussia and, even then, all of Germany up to the Oder River; see Miner, pp. 186–251. On the Polish issue, Miner can be supplemented by consulting the PRO files cited above in note 21. For Sikorski's own hopes and illusions, see Bruce Lockhart to Halifax, Sept. 12, 1940, PRO, FO371, 24292, C9969; and "Sprawozdanie z podróży

Generala Sikorskiego na średni wschód i do Rosji," Dec. 1941 (?), ıs, A12 49/sow/2.

23. Wheeler-Bennett and Nicholls and many other British historians are not given to finding fault with Churchill. Wheeler-Bennett and Nicholls, indeed, extol Anthony Eden and Churchill, and damn Roosevelt (pp. 289, 290, 297). They quote Churchill, writing later on the border issue: "We could not force our new and sorely troubled ally [i.e., the Soviet Union] to abandon . . . regions on her frontier which she had regarded for generations as vital to her security" (ibid., pp. 30, 35). Bethel, *The War Hitler Won*, though he writes perceptively about the Hitler-Stalin campaign against Poland in 1939, still shares Churchill's limited version of Stalin's European aims (pp. 325–30, 351). Most assuredly, the British could not force the Soviets to relinquish Poland, but neither could they force the Germans out of Poland, though they had, in effect, gone to war for that purpose and had dragged the French in with them. Certainly, in 1941, they held some negotiating strengths vis-à-vis Stalin. And with Roosevelt then so sympathetic to Churchill, their influence in the United States was also very large. See also, Kacewicz, p. 224; Takayuki, p. 154.

24. Long before Churchill was in office, the Chamberlain government probably accepted the "Curzon" line of thinking—a line made easier because it was likewise traditionally preoccupied with Germany as enemy and caught up in British (Curzon's) historical residues. Well before June 1941, the British were indicating to Stalin that they would happily recognize de facto Soviet conquests coming out of the Hitler-Stalin Pact in return for a more neutral Soviet stance vis-à-vis Hitler (Kacewicz, pp. 79–85). See Seaton, pp. 162, 166–67; and Karski, pp. 16–20. Perhaps even more disreputable were the games Free French leader Charles de Gaulle played with Sikorski. De Gaulle was, like Churchill, obsessed with the German enemy and unmindful of the potential Soviet danger, yet he constantly played the old French trump card, France's historical friendship and support of the Poles, even while tacitly supporting Soviet claims to its gains in Poland as a result of the 1939 pact and denying the Poles any wartime diplomacy in areas that did not have Stalin's support. Always stressing Poland's right to expand westward at the expense of the Germans, he undoubtedly meant thereby to fix precedents for France's right, the gist of its postwar policy, to expand France's borders eastward at the expense of the defeated; see Zaks, "'Wolna Francja' i Polska w latach 1943–1944."

25. For Roosevelt's early abandonment of the Polish issue to the British, see "Memo of a Conversation between Welles and Polish Ambassador Ciechanowski," Washington, D.C., July 8, 1941, usna, RG59, Lot 59, 396, box 4.

26. Kacewicz, pp. 151–52, 154, 157, 219; Hooker, pp. 137–38; Harbutt, p. 38. Churchill kept expressing himself privately about the prospective

dangers of Soviet influence in a postwar Europe (Harbutt, p. 50), but he never did anything about it, even by way of tactful suggestion of the problem to Roosevelt.

27. See Kennan's description of Roosevelt in Chap. I, n. 36 above. Churchill's similar conviction, uttered in a conversation with Molotov, May 21, 1942, was "We should win the war, and after the war, Great Britain, Russia and the United States would share the responsibility for guiding the forward movement of the world." See PRO, FO371, 32882, N2901.

28. Terry, pp. 58–59, 127; Miner, p. 186.

CHAPTER 4

1. The Soviet government said that it subscribed "to the common principles of policy set forth in the Declaration" and promised "to co-operate to the best of their ability in giving effect to them." Its representative then went on to say that while the "practical application of these principles will necessarily adapt itself to the circumstances, needs, and historical peculiarities of the participating countries," the Soviet government would state "that a consistent application of these principles will receive the most energetic support on the part of the government and peoples of the Soviet Union" (quoted in Wheeler-Bennett and Nicholls, pp. 36–37, 43). Churchill took this deliberately opaque wording to mean that the Soviets had approved the Charter. Perhaps something was also lost in the translation, but it is clear that, after having renounced the agreements with Germany dividing Poland, any exclusion that might have been read into the above words did not cover that nation. And finally, even if someone still wants to read it as exonerating Stalin, it is more than obvious that the declaration in the long run meant nothing to him. He went on to take far more territory (from Germany, Czechoslovakia, and Finland) than he had held in 1941, and went on to try to take even more.

2. "Declaration of the Governments of the U.S.S.R. and the Polish Exile Government," Dec. 4, 1941, quoted in Bracher and Jacobson, eds., *Deutschlandpolitik*, p. 582.

3. James, *Anthony Eden*, p. 259. The Soviet line on the history of Polish-Soviet relations was considerably different. See Kalenychenko, pp. 75–79; and Vengerov, p. 72. Vengerov insists that Anders' guilt was genetic—he was a "German by birth." The Anders army was evacuated beginning in March 1942: Łuszkiewicz, p. 25. The London Poles began pressing the issue of withdrawing to Iran in November 1941, when they first realized how much the Soviets were stonewalling on equipping and provisioning the army and in locating thousands of captured officers. See "Notatka z konferencji (with Soviet Ambassador Bogomolov)," Nov. 6, 1941, IS, A12, 49/sow/2.

4. Mastny, pp. 39–45; for Churchill and intelligence, see Wright, p. 231.

5. Many of the most influential American journalists and newspapers could be relied on by the British to cooperate in keeping information the Foreign Office wanted kept secret kept that way. They included Walter Lippmann, Arthur Krock, and the *New York Times*; see Halifax to Foreign Office, Apr. 12, 1942, PRO, FO371, 32878, N1921, Apr. 23, 1942, ibid., N2130, May 10, 1942, ibid., 32880, N2464, and "First Meeting . . . with Molotov," May 21, 1942, ibid., 32882, N2901. The Western press correspondents could only get out of Moscow to the front when permitted to do so, that is, conducted on tours; usually they were briefed on the spot by representatives of the Soviet government. Much of their reportage was, therefore, little more than a repeat of what the Soviet official press stated, though this was never then, so far as I have read, made clear. Worse yet, at least three representatives of the British press, including one from the conservative *Times*, and also from the *Sunday Times*, the liberal *News-Chronicle*, and the left-leaning *Manchester Guardian*, were either Stalinists or radically pro-Soviet. One was later employed by the Moscow-directed Poles, and another was the voluntary postwar Moscow resident and writer of anti-Western diatribes mentioned in the text. See H. Thomas, pp. 199–200, 217–18, 511–12. One Briton, shocked by what he saw and heard in the Soviet Union when he went in with the Beaverbrook mission in 1942, only privately reported the anguish he felt at having "to remain dumb in the face of abuses and injustice." The later British ambassador, Clark-Kerr, a determined friend of the Soviets, did all he could to keep the journalists in line and away from expressing anti-Stalinist positions (Darman, p. 165). *The Times* leader writer, E. H. Carr, who was responsible for most of that newspaper's editorial intelligence on the Soviets, regularly misconstrued eastern European affairs to Stalin's advantage, justifying, for example, on July 25, 1940 ("Russia on the Baltic") the Soviet takeover of the Baltic states. He also presumably wrote the column of May 16, 1945 ("From a Correspondent"), another example from many, supporting Stalin's takeover of the Czechoslovak province of Ruthenia. Much of the work of the British correspondents also appeared in the American and Canadian press. The most infamous American correspondent, of course, was Walter Duranty, in Moscow in the 1930's. See Crowl, and also De Mowbray, for information on the intertwining of the British press, TASS, and Soviet-friendly agents in the British ministries. For background on the heavy British censorship, see Bell.

6. Rothwell, pp. 152–53, 156, 158, 163, 165. For Ambassador Halifax's view of the American "Liberals, who . . . profess to admire Russia," see Halifax to Foreign Office, Apr. 12, 1942, PRO, FO371, 32878, N1921.

7. The anti-Polish sentiment was catching, as in the case of Canada (whose press shared journalists with Britain and the United States); see Létourneau, p. 54. Much later, New Zealand Premier Fraser, on a visit to London, sadly noted the propensity of "Anglo-Saxons" who wanted good

relations with the Soviets to see all the difficulties of Polish-Soviet relations caused by the stubbornness of the Poles (Fraser conversation with Arciszewski, etc., London, Apr. 12, 1945, IS, A12. 45/15 III).

8. See Wandycz; Taborský, chap. 4; Zaks, "'Wolna Francja' i Czechosłowacja (1940–1944)," pp. 109–10; HA, Taborský Collection, box 6, all from Edvard Beneš: "Telefonogram do Parize," Jan. 11, 1940; "Rozmluva s polským ministrem zahr. věcí," Sept. 4, 1941; "Rozhovor se Sikorskim . . . 23 January 1942," and "Rozmluva s Molotovem . . . 9 June 1942." See also: "Zaznam o rozhovoru Masaryka s vysl. Bogomolovem," June 15, 1942, AÚTGM, BA, EB-L104; and Sikorski's warning, c. Mar. 26, 1942 (passed by Kulski to Eden), HA, Mikołajczyk Collection, box 19, See Kisielewski for background to the lively current discussion of Polish-Czechoslovak interwar and wartime relations.

9. Ślusarczyk, p. 160; AAN, PPR 190/I-14.

10. See Jerzy Putrament, in Syzdek, ed., *Wanda Wasilewska*, pp. 253–54; and Stefan Jędrychowski, in ibid., pp. 163–65; Wasilewska's picture, in Soviet uniform, is between pp. 128 and 129. The newsreel shots are in the Soviet newsreel, *Soiuz Kinozhurnal*, no. 20 (1943). See also, Vengerov, pp. 64–65; and Kalenychenko, p. 95.

11. Jędrychowski, in Syzdek, ed., *Wanda Wasilewska*, p. 171; see also, Dilks, ed., *Cadogen Diaries*, p. 516n.

12. See *Soiuz kinozhurnal*, no. 40-41, 1943; Bolesław Drobner, in Syzdek, ed., *Wanda Wasilewska*, pp. 148–49. The ZPP's first official public meeting was held June 8, 1943. Even in late November 1941, when Wasilewska first emerged as a champion of Polish independence (no mention of her Soviet citizenship or her role as deputy of the Supreme Soviet), she listed only those Polish places as candidates for liberation that were in the German area of occupation; see *Izvestiia*, Dec. 2, 1941. On the design of the Soviet-friendly groups and committees, see Edward Osóbka-Morawski in Syzdek, ed., *Wanda Wasilewska*, pp. 183–84. Wasilewska's fascinating memoirs, edited by Felix Tych, are "Wanda Wasilewska. Wspomnicnia (1939–1944)."

13. The London Poles did not miss the significance of the founding of the NK "FD" as the German equivalent of the ZPP, the Titoists, and the earlier governments formed in the Baltic countries and Finland: see, Derwiński, pp. 226–28. Eden, if anything more determined than Churchill to appease Stalin, termed one British cleric who wrote him about his fears that the NK "FD" might become exactly what it did, a "pestilent priest" and discounted the information (Glees, *Exile Politics*, p. 194). For Stalin's direct hand in the founding of the NK "FD," see Heider, pp. 17–18. Stalin expressed his preference for an old leader to his chief Polish agent, Bolesław Bierut, in Moscow, October 1944, in "Protokul [sic] z posiedzenia KC [PPR]," AAN, KC PPR, 295/V/1. For the remark on a social democrat (in this case, *Polska Par-*

tia Socjalistyczna, referring to Osóbka-Morawski) we can "work with," see "Protokul [*sic*] z posiedzenia Biura Politycznego," Dec. 14, 1944, ibid.

14. Jędrychowski, in Syzdek, ed., *Wanda Wasilewska*, p. 172; Putrament, in ibid., p. 259; Włodzimierz Sokorski, in ibid., p. 158; Polonsky and Drukier, p. 12. A. M. Cienciała noted that Stalin was already recruiting for a planned Polish division in the Red Army in 1940; see Cienciała, "The Question of the Polish-Soviet Frontier in British, Soviet, and Polish Policy in 1939–1940: The Litauer Memorandum and Sikorski's Proposal," p. 314. This may derive, she suggests, from the thought having crossed Stalin's mind after the fall of France that he might soon have to deal with the Germans—on the territory of "former Poland" east or west of the demarcation line. See also, Zaks, "Stosunki polsko-radzieckie w 1943r." Ślusarczyk (p. 193) uses the rather odd expression "activated themselves" apparently to explain the sudden cascade of deeds among the Poles in Moscow in early 1943.

15. Rothwell, pp. 15–17, 176; Babiński, pp. 246, 255. British Permanent Foreign Office Undersecretary Sir Alexander Cadogen called the Poles (1944) "incurable idiots." By the spring of 1943, Roosevelt was apparently willing to yield on the Polish border in the east and to concede the Soviets the Baltic states and their Finnish claims (see Dilks, ed., *Cadogen Diaries*, 7: 519, April 1943), which perhaps explains his outrage over the Poles' demands for an investigation of Katyn: "[they are] fools. I've no patience with them" (Larson, p. 82 n. 40). The *New York Times* publicly reported Roosevelt's antipathy to the London Poles, Dec. 10, 1944 (4B, p. 11).

16. Seaton, pp. 512–15. The Soviets of course denied any intention to set up their own government for Poland: Kacewicz, p. 157; also, pp. 147 and 147–48 n. 29. *New York Times* correspondent Raymond Daniell reported from London, May 1, 1943, that Stalin had denied that he had a plan to set up his own Polish government, but the scheme did not elude the better informed Free French representative in Moscow, who two months earlier had reported what he thought were Stalin's plans (Zaks, "Stosunki polsko-radzieckie w 1943," p. 127). Elbridge Durbrow, of the State Department, wrote to Loy Henderson, Apr. 9, 1943, that the Soviets "may desire to cause a break with the Polish government-in-exile and set up a Moscow-controlled 'Free Poland',"; see USNA, T1244, reel 3. One suspects the hypothesis was never presented to President Roosevelt, however. According to *Nowe Widnokręgi*, no. 4 (1942), p. 4, the Nazis described Sikorski and Anders as tools of the "Judeo-Bolsheviks" in the Kremlin.

17. Christer S. and Stephan A. Garrett, pp. 439–40, report a shocking example of Roosevelt's censorship of anti-Soviet news conducted for him by Alan Cranston, later Senator from California. For an analysis of much American press coverage for those days, showing many pro-Soviet judgments expressed by the *New York Times*, the *New York Herald-Tribune*,

the *Washington Post,* and the *Washington Star,* see "Information Published on the Murder of the Polish Officers in the Katyn Forest; April 1943–July 1944," in LC, Harriman Collections, no. 187. The official British wartime censor had already silenced all discussion of the Soviet-Polish frontier in the British press: memo from G. D. Thompson, chief press censor, Mar. 2, 1943, in IS, MID, A10, 5, 13 ("Sprawy prasy 1943"). Even before the German attack on the Soviet Union in June 1942 the British government had restricted BBC broadcasts about the Soviet zone of occupation in Poland: see Brandes, p. 148.

18. Kacewicz, pp. 168–82, traces the development of Churchill's policy of appeasing the Soviet Union. On the development of British (and American) appeasement policy with respect to the Polish borders, see Brandes, and for beginnings of appeasement by Eden and Churchill, particularly with respect to the Baltic states, Miner. Nordling (pp. 60–61) notes an earlier occasion on which Stalin demanded the resignation of members of a foreign government (the Finnish government, in 1940) he did not approve.

19. Eden, p. 496.

20. For Poland as the main subject of discussions, see Ambassador Harriman quoted by Schlesinger, Jr., p. 41; Roosevelt-Stalin meeting (Bohlen minutes), Dec. 1, 1943, U.S. Department of State, *FRUS,* The Conferences at Cairo and Teheran, p. 594. For Secretary of State Hull's apparent disappointment at Roosevelt's behavior, see Halifax to Foreign Office, Jan. 19, 1944, PRO, FO371, 43359, N447; see also, Mastny, p. 141; Eden, pp. 489–90. Ironically, Czech President Beneš was among those most willingly gulled by Stalin's speech on the subject of the rights of small nations and did not inquire in response about the historical examples of Soviet respect, for example, for the rights of the Baltic nations.

21. Glees, *Exile Politics,* p. 221.

22. On the Roosevelt-Stalin talks of Nov. 29, 1943, see Fischer, ed., *TJP,* pp. 48 and 84n. For Roosevelt warned by former Ambassador to the Soviet Union William C. Bullitt, see Bullitt, ed., pp. 591–99.

23. Acquiring a "trophy" of battle, whatever the cost, was typical Stalin-Soviet thinking. Stalin claimed a vaguely defined northeastern portion of East Prussia around Königsberg for "Russia" as an "ice free port." But the port at Königsberg is not ice-free. He also argued quite sophistically that the area was originally "Slavic." He wanted, he said, Königsberg as a bit of war booty, and he suggested that the tsarist "Russians" had been deprived of it by losing World War I (Fischer, ed., *TJP,* pp. 84–87). Although Stalin claimed this area as Slavic (but never as Russian, though it was later to be annexed to the former RSFSR), it was originally populated by Prussians, who were related linguistically to their neighbors the Lithuanians. Stalin later told his friendly Poles, when he pushed his demand for what he had first promised them, that he needed the territory "symbolically" and that there were his-

torical reasons for the territory's going to "Russia." On his Polish friends, who (no more than the English-speaking allies) did not attempt to challenge his fraudulent history, see Spychalski, p. 203. See also my recent article on the subject, "Stalin Fixes the Oder-Neisse Line."

24. See the untitled document (probably Churchill to Stalin, January 1944), HA, Mikołajczyk Collection, file "Russian-Polish territorial settlement 1944–1945," box 35.

25. The Poles first suggested taking over East Prussia, but the area of expansion westward was gradually broadened, then connected to the idea of compensation for any losses in the east. See Raczyński-Halifax conversation, Nov. 15, 1939, IS, PRM, 3; and "Tekst ostateczny memorjału . . . [Sikorski to Roosevelt]," Mar. 20, 1941, AAN Ambasada RP w Londyniu, 1506; see also, Leeper to Strang, Nov. 25, 1939, PRO FO371, 23131, C19288; and "Memo of the Polish Exile Government on War Aims" (Nov. 1940), in Bracher and Jacobsen, eds., pp. 225–27. See also: Brandes, pp. 61–62, 107–8; Bethel, p. 381; Szaz, p. 98; Simon, pp. 243–55. Roosevelt, mindful of the Polish vote, was very worried that the transfer of eastern Poland to Stalin would become public before the 1944 election; Churchill assured Roosevelt that Stalin would not tell his secret before the election, thereby putting Roosevelt in Stalin's debt; see Karski, p. 24.

26. AAN, PKWN, microfilm 23153, "Protokoły posiedzień PKWN," for July 19–26, 1944. Number 8/52, Aug. 18, 1945, of "Protokoły posiedzień Rady Ministrów Rządu Jedności Narodowej," t.2, ibid., RJN, gives a relatively candid account, presumably for the new members of the Polish government, of the effort to cover up the border changes Stalin had agreed to since the preceding July. For Stalin in command (of all the details) see "Protokul [sic] z posiedzenia KC . . . , 9 October 1944, [and the same of] 14 December 1944," On the organization of the government, "Protokul," Oct. 22, 1944: AAN, KC PPR, 295/V/1. See also, Ważniewski, pp. 9–10.

27. The pro-Soviet Poles actually proposed to Stalin at the time that he name them the government, but he deferred this, apparently on Molotov's advice, until January 1, tactfully reserving the bad news for later for his British and American allies. See Osóbka-Morawski, in Szydek, ed., Wasilewska, pp. 183–86; also the article by Osóbka-Morawski in Pobrzeże. Pravda (July 26, 1944, p. 1) let it out that the KRN (National Homeland Council) "of Warsaw" announced the formation of the PKWN in Chełm, in Poland, but this was completely untrue. All the negotiations leading to the founding of the committee were conducted in Moscow, and Pravda simply wanted to make it appear that the PKWN was a spontaneously formed, native organization. Stalin and Molotov had moved to found a Polish government, under a cover name, just after Teheran in late December 1943. They said nothing about this, of course, at the conference. See Syzdek, "Sprawa

powołania Polskiego Komitetu Narodowego w Moskwie (grudzień 1943–styczeń 1944)," pp. 84, 88.

28. For Churchill's assurances to the cabinet, see Ben-Moshe, *Churchill: Strategy and History*, p. 305. For Churchill's later private use of the same term, somewhat embellished, and others, to the Poles, see "Rozmowa z Churchillem," Nov. 2, 1944, HA, Mikołajczyk Collection, box 32.

29. The British position papers (certainly more extensive than what I have found on the same topics from the American side) include a memo by Eden, "Soviet Policy in Europe," Aug. 9, 1944, PRO, FO371, 43336, N4957; and from the Post-Hostilities Planning Sub-Committee, "Effect of Soviet Policy on British Strategic Interests," June 6, 1944, ibid., 43884, N3791.

30. Excesses of the Red Army, continuing in 1945, almost a year after it had entered what Stalin accepted as Polish territory, are noted in "Protokół z plenarnego posiedzenia KC . . . 20–21 May 1945," in Kochański, *Protokół obrad*, and "Wyciąg ze sprawozdania Województwa Poznanskiego . . . August 1945," AAN, KC PPR, 295/VII/267.

31. Rzeczpospolita, Aug. 4–6, 1944.

32. Ibid., Aug. 14 and 15, 1944; Polonsky and Drukier, p. 45. The reports given to the PKWN on the talks with Mikołajczyk and his group by Bolesław Beirut and others, no doubt carefully chosen, clearly show direction from above. Even the wording is similar to that used by Stalin and Molotov, talking to Beirut and that group in advance, to suggest the outcome of the talks so that they would pick up the line they were to take. See AAN, PKWN, microfilm 23153, "Protokoły posiedzenia PKWN . . . 9 August 1944."

33. On Stalin and Warsaw, see Zawodny, chaps. 7, 10, 11.

34. Rzeczpospolita, Aug. 15, 1944, p. 1, and various comments in August, September, and October 1944; *Izvestiia*, Oct. 3, 1944, p. 4.

35. Spychalski, p. 203; "Protokoły posiedzenia PKWN . . . 9 August 1944," AAN, PKWN, microfilm 23153.

36. Spychalski; Lehmann, pp. 33–34; Raack, "Stalin Fixes the Oder-Neisse Line." At Teheran, Stalin had not contradicted Churchill when he named the prospective Polish take at the expense of the Germans (East Prussia and the area of Silesia around Oppeln) except to demand the Königsberg area plus Memel (part of Lithuania, 1919–38). He said that if he got these rewards, he would accept Churchill's definition of the Polish borders. Obviously he did not mean it, because earlier in the conference all had agreed on the western Polish border at the Oder River, which lay far beyond East Prussia and Oppeln Silesia. See Fischer, ed., *TJP*, pp. 86–87. Stalin must have agreed with his Muscovite Poles just after his return to Moscow from Teheran that Stettin had to go to them, most likely in compensation for their letting him have Königsberg without a fight. For he had already told the University of Chicago economist (later economic theorist of Polish communism) Oskar Lange, when he visited Moscow in the spring of 1944, that

he had (since Teheran) changed the agreed-upon Polish border to include the port of Stettin. See Mikołajczyk's report of his conversations with Roosevelt and Lange, June 7, 1944, IS, A12, 49/15 II. The head of the Polish division of the Foreign Office's political intelligence department heard the same from a London Polish representative much earlier; see McLaren-Zerański conversation report, Mar. 9, 1944, ibid., A12, 49/15 I.

37. According to Spychalski (p. 203), Stalin knew that he was giving the Poles more than Churchill had agreed; he even told them he was certain Churchill would not know that there were two Neisse rivers and would think he was referring to the Neisse River some 200 kilometers east of the Lusatian Neisse. See also: Skrzypek, pp. 192–95; and further details in Tusiński, pp. 45–46, 50; Nazarewicz, p. 72; Raack, "Stalin Fixes the Oder-Neisse Line"; and Zabiełło, p. 172.

38. The formation of U.S. policy toward the Poles is outlined by Kacewicz, pp. 202–3. See also, Churchill to Roosevelt, Mar. 7, 1944, in Kimball, ed., *Churchill and Roosevelt*, 3: 29. The Lublin Poles, helping Roosevelt's and Churchill's fantasies about Poland's future government by suggesting for the benefit of the Westerners that they would welcome Mikołajczyk as premier of the new Polish government, were therewith effectively contributing to the split in the London Polish camp that Churchill hoped would occur. See *Manchester Guardian*, Aug. 30, 1944, and the *New-Chronicle* (London), Aug. 31, 1944. See also Góra and Kochański, pp. 98–99. Roosevelt and Mikołajczyk had evidently discussed the minimum area of Polish territory the latter thought his colleagues would accept in the east: Lwów and part of Galicia surrounding it; Mikołajczyk had told Czech President Beneš that even before Beneš went to Moscow in December 1943 (Taborský, p. 108). For an interesting discussion between the PKWN and Mikołajczyk and Grabski, from London, see Mroczkowksi and Sierocki, eds., pp. 109–53.

39. See *Rzeczpospolita*, Sept. 4 and 10, 1944. The same discussions were held with the chiefs of the Lithuanian SSR. For Stalin's gradual conversion of the PKWN into a government, see NKID to Australian Embassy, Aug. 23, 1944, in Khrenov et al., eds., *Dokumenty*, 8: 203. See also, Pożarskas, p. 49.

40. Eden, p. 563. The British liberal journalist at the conference in Moscow apparently took it all in and reported it as if everything said were the gospel truth—or perhaps the censor doctored his story to make it appear so. In any event, he sent out the Soviet-sanitized version: *News-Chronicle* (London), Aug. 30 (p. 4) and 31 (p. 2), 1944. The PKWN never had any intention of allowing Mikołajczyk to become premier with any power, and after he had abandoned his leadership of the London government, they quickly found a reason for not offering him that role. Both Stalin and Molotov helped their PKWN bosses organize, keeping all-important portfolios in their government-in-becoming in their hands. See Grzędziński, ed., pp. 150–51.

For the organizational word from the Kremlin, see "Protokul [sic] z posied-zenia KC . . . 22 October 1944," AAN, KC PPR, 295/V/1.

41. Kacewicz, p. 206 and 206 n. 57; Siracusa, "The Meaning of Tolstoy," p. 452: Stalin said, "Silesia would go to the Poles and parts of East Prussia," etc., on October 10, 1944, at 9:00 P.M.; News-Chronicle (London), Dec. 19, 1944 (p. 4), quoting Pravda.

42. Harriman to Roosevelt, Oct. 14, 1944 (p. 203); to Romer (p. 204); and Mikołajczyk to Harriman, Oct. 16, 1944 (p. 204) in U.S. Department of State, FRUS, The Conferences at Malta and Yalta. See also, Harriman to Secretary of State, Moscow, Dec. 19, 1944, USNA, T1244, reel 3. Harriman, who probably had no notion of the private arrangements on the Polish borders that Roosevelt had made with Stalin at Teheran, got some of the information on what Stalin wanted to include from the London Polish delegation, which held discussions in Moscow with the PKWN leaders in August; see Zyblikiewicz, p. 14.

43. The arrangements at Quebec and the earlier talks show to what extent Churchill and Roosevelt had lost sense of the history of Europe, which up until 1870–71 was marked by the enduring conflict of the peripheral powers over the European center. For a discussion of this point, see Wheeler-Bennett and Nicholls, pp. 182, 296–97. These authors sharply criticize Roosevelt but heap praise on Churchill and Eden (p. 289). Roosevelt had only the smallest notion of the geography he was rearranging and was quite wrong in his presumptions regarding Stalin's state of mind; this is clearly established by Edward Stettinius, recalling Roosevelt's conversations with Mikołajczyk of June 1944; see Stettinius, Jr., p. 85. One must remember, however, that at about the same time Churchill was insouciently parceling out Palestine: see Cohen, p. 307. On the Morgenthau Plan, see Kimball, Swords or Ploughshares, pp. 36, 47, 101.

44. For the October 1944 discussions in Moscow, see Tsakaloyannis, "The Moscow Puzzle"; News-Chronicle (London), Dec. 16, 1944, p. 4. For additional diplomatic background, see Zaks, "Stosunki polsko-radzieckie w . . . 1944 roku," p. 122.

45. Pravda, Dec. 13 and 18, 1944 (each, p. 4).

46. The agreements with the White Russian SSR, Sept. 9, 1944, with the Ukrainian SSR, Sept. 9, 1944, and with the Lithuanian SSR, Sept. 22, 1944, are in Khrenov et al., eds., Dokumenty, 8: 213–19 (p. 219 n. says 1,500,000 Poles were returned to Poland from the USSR). See also, "Protokoły z posiedzenia . . . TRJN, 13 February 1945," AAN, TRJN, t.1; Protokoły z posiedzenia . . . RJN, no. 2/46 of July 7, 1945, AAN, RJN, t.2; "Polacy znad Wilii, Niema, Narwi, i Bugu," p. 157. For Khrushchev's insistence that the Poles be put out of the Ukraine by Jan. 15, 1945, see Polish Government (London) Airgraph, Nov. 23, 1944, IS A10. 5. 19; Rzeczpospolita, Feb. 3, 1945, p. 3; Parsadanova, pp. 192–93. Krystyna Kersten says that the official govern-

ment bureaus to deal with the issue were first formed in the spring and summer of 1945 (p. 92); see also, Dushyck, pp. 10, 18, 28. For the PKWN's diplomatic record, see "Protokul [sic] z posiedzenia KC . . . 22 October 1944," AAN, KCPPR, 295/V/1; for opposition of the London Poles to Stalin's vast territorial grants in Germany, see Roberts-Zerański conversation notes, London, Dec. 28, 1944, HA, Mikołajcyzk Collection, box 32. The PKWN leaders in Moscow pleaded with Khrushchev, in Stalin's presence, to try to humanize the behavior of Soviet border guards and other officials toward the Poles who were being forcibly evacuated; see "Protokól z posiedzienia KC PPR . . . 14 December 1944," AAN, KC PPR, 295/V/1.

47. Kersten, pp. 94−98; Cavendish-Bentinck (Warsaw) to Bevin, Oct. 10, 1945, PRO, FO371, 47129, N14734. The PKWN complained for the Western public about the terrible food disaster facing Poland, but never suggested how much of it had been created: *Manchester Guardian*, Oct. 2, 1944, p. 5. See also, IS, MID, A10, 5, 19 (Airgraphs), Dec. 1, 1944, on the reports of agricultural chaos. The chaos was directly related to the forced agricultural land reform and the "transferences," as even the Polish subalterns of Stalin admitted. See Kochański, ed., *Protokół obrad*, pp. 8, 9, 32; also, "Protokół z plenarnego posiedzenia KC, PPR . . ., 11−12 July 1945," and "Protokół z wspólnego posiedzenia CKW PPS i KCPPR . . ., 28 September 1945," in AAN, PPR, 295/II-3 and 295/III-3, respectively. The Poles had a desperate need for UNRRA assistance after the war; the significant aid that went to them, to be sure, could not be sent to the rest of starving Europe. Predictably, the Ukraine, as well as Russia itself, was also racked by famine in the first postwar year. See Burlatskii, "Ispoved' reformatora," p. 11. Stalin told Churchill at Moscow in October 1944 that no further changes in the eastern Polish border could be imagined because the Soviets had a collective agricultural economy, whereas the Poles would establish a private farm economy; a few months later, in Berlin, Mikoian, his agent, was also testifying to the virtues of a free market for postwar Germany.

48. See U.S. Department of State, *The Conferences at Malta and Yalta*, and U.S. notes, ibid., p. 511; Eden to Churchill (Bohlen notes), p. 509; Eden, p. 575.

49. This idea was expressed by Georges Bidault, quoted in the *New York Times*, Dec. 22, 1944, p. 5.

50. Fischer, ed., *TJP*, p. 146. It was not until the spring of 1945 that Churchill allowed his suspicions of the Soviets to arise in print, but Alexander Cadogen, Britain's Permanent Undersecretary for Foreign Affairs, wrote his down in early 1944: "They *are* swine" (quoted by Kacewicz, p. 177 n. 5). See also, Seaton, pp. 516−17.

51. Churchill and Eden had unsuccessfully tried the same (including bringing up Lwów) at Moscow in October 1944. Stalin allowed them to carry on—and, at least for Eden, the carrying on apparently involved consid-

erable moralistic hand-wringing—without denying their plea, never telling them he had already decided matters (Kacewicz, p. 196; on Eden and Lwów, see Darman, p. 175). Churchill only weakly supported Roosevelt's timid proposal at Yalta: Lukas, pp. 131–32, 135, see also, Davis, p. 177.

52. "Protokul (sic) z posiedzenia KC . . . 9 and 22 October 1944," both in AAN, KC PPR, 295/V/1.

53. Churchill had heard about Stettin in October, but he must have known that Roosevelt had not accepted it; see Ushakov, p. 44.

54. *Rzeczpospolita*, Feb. 5, 1945, p. 3.

55. See Zaremba, "Wyzwolenie Szczecina w 1945 r. na tle sytuacji między-zynarodowej"; Vosske, *Die Vereinigung der KPD und der SPD in Mecklen-burg-Vorpommern*, pp. 23–27. The most complete account of the Stettin takeover is Zaremba's Ms. in 13 vols., "Szczecin 1945. Dziennik wydarzeń i dokumenty historyczne" (c. 1960), in the Biblioteka główna PAN, in Warsaw.

56. Polonsky, ed., pp. 281–82. Stalin had a propensity, not unusual, to use as examples in an argument what was currently held secret in the other half of his mind. Charles Bohlen, who with Harry Hopkins was in Moscow in May 1945 on a mission for President Truman, recorded the information about Stettin in a memo dated May 28, 1945 (U.S. Department of State, *FRUS, The Conference at Berlin, 1945*, 1: 49); Stalin mentioned Stettin as a place from which the Germans were fleeing westward, thereby simply abandoning the territory to the Poles and making it unnecessary for the Poles to drive them out. (Stalin used the same general argument at Potsdam with respect to eastern lands from which the Germans were fleeing.) Bohlen at the time did not understand the issue of the German and Polish frontiers: he later maintained in his memoirs (p. 189) that the frontier issue was not important at Potsdam, and mistakenly noted in retrospect that whatever border issue there was, it was the Polish eastern frontier (Bohlen, p. 226). Stettin was no doubt on Stalin's mind in late May 1945, before the Potsdam Conference, presumably because of the debate going on in Stettin between the rival claimants, one of them being unacceptable to the West. Stalin also blurted out to Bohlen and Hopkins the name of the German General Krebs, a name unknown to Bohlen and Hopkins and perhaps not very familiar to Stalin himself (though it is not inconceivable that he remembered him as one of Germany's prewar military attachés in Moscow). However, Stalin knew that Krebs's corpse had been found in Berlin along with those of Goebbels and Hitler, and he was trying to convince Hopkins and Bohlen that Hitler's corpse had not been found. With such lies in the forefront of his mind, it may be supposed that he was attempting to give the appearance of candor by mentioning as many recovered Nazi corpses as he could. As a result, his mind, taxed with maintaining the deception with respect to Hitler, manifestly played a trick on him. Two recent relatively

detailed accounts of Poland in Soviet and inter-Allied diplomacy during the war, by Pastusiak and Ślusarczyk, take a more favorable view of Stalin than I give here. But they supply useful details and put complicated matters in chronological order effectively.

57. For example, Stalin told his PKWN Poles in December 1944 that Hungary, by then hardly half "liberated" by the Red Army, should soon establish a government similar to Poland's (which had a "government" only in his eastern eyes). It would, he said, undertake a land reform similar to Poland's: in "Protokół z posiedzenia Biura Politycznego . . . 14 December 1944," AAN, KC PPR, 295/V/1. This uncannily accurate prediction of what a yet unformed Hungarian government might do might have been joined to a similar prediction about what the "Government" (in all but the name) he would soon fix on his part of Germany would do—but perhaps he did not want to give away too much of the future, or was still not sure how much of Germany would come into his grasp. On Soviet electoral manipulations in Hungary, see Lukacs, pp. 304–6.

58. Mikołajczyk and the new government, see "Protokół drugiego plenarnego posiedzenia przedstawicieli Rządu Tymczasowego RP . . . 16 June 1945," in Góra and Kochański, eds., "Rozmowy polityczne," p. 108. The Soviet Union and the new Polish government signed an alliance on April 21, 1945, some weeks before Mikołajczyk was taken into it (Wheeler-Bennett and Nicholls, p. 308).

CHAPTER 5

1. Just after the German attack on the Soviet Union, Soviet Ambassador Maiskii, in London, was hinting to Czech President Beneš that postwar Germany would be "revolutionary and socialist," exactly what the Comintern's Kremlin-originated plans had in black and white during the period of the Pact. See Beneš notes, "Rozhovor s velvysl. Majskim," Aug. 28, 1941, AÚTGM, BA, EB/L 101. Klement Gottwald, The Czech Communist Party chief then resident in Moscow, told Beneš in December 1943 that the Soviets were planning to bring about a "revolution" in Hungary once the Red Army arrived there; see "Poznamky k zápisu o rozmluvách s presidentem Benešem," fifth conversation, Dec. 16, 1943, SÚA, KSC, 100/24, 172, 1526. (Stalin had said the same to his PKWN Poles in December 1944; see Chap. 4, n. 57). It is very interesting that Beneš, even by 1941 in Stalin's tow, unaccountably did not bring these bits of information back to his London hosts in the Foreign Office. Key British policy planning documents used in the Foreign Office and War Cabinet in the latter years of the war show how little the British understood of Stalin's aims. "Probable Post-War Tendencies in Soviet Foreign Policy as Affecting British Interests," Apr. 29, 1944 (PRO, FO371, 43335, N1008), comments: "After Stalin's victory over Trotsky . . . the aim of spreading bolshevism or of fomenting world revolution for its

own sake was abandoned." This was but one of countless other incorrect evaluations and assessments of past and prospective Soviet behavior, such as the notion that Stalin's Polish policy was dictated by his fears of Germany, that he consistently stood for the dismemberment of Germany, that his program was defensive and that it was doubtful that the "Soviet Union would welcome a communist Germany [which would be] a dangerous rival." The latter idea in general, that Stalin feared the establishment of powerful focal points of Bolshevik power abroad, which potentially could rival Moscow, also prevailed when George F. Kennan wrote his influential book, *Russia and the West Under Lenin and Stalin* (1961). My article of 1993, "Stalin Plans His Post-War Germany," which takes a different point of view, is based on research in recently opened former East Bloc archives.

2. Most sources in the West, including those of Hitler's attendants who saw the corpse, say he shot himself. Hugh Trevor-Roper, *The Last Days of Hitler* (first published in 1947), pp. xxxviii–lxi, reviews the Western evidence and comes to the same conclusion. O'Donnell, *The Berlin Bunker: The History of the Reichschancellery Group* (1978), also accepts the stories of suicide by gunshot. The story of death by cyanide and of the taking of the corpse was first generally made known in the West in the late 1960's by Soviet propagandist and history writer Lev Bezymenskii, in *Der Tod des Adolf Hitler* (1968, also in English-language editions of the same year). The account is incomplete and contains many incorrect details, and it offers only feeble excuses for the long delay in telling the story. Bezymenskii did not give his story to Russian readers until several years later, first in *Konets odnoi legendy* (1972) and then in *Razgadannye zagadki tret'ego reïkha* (1982), vol. 2, chapter entitled, "The Last Riddle." *Der Tod des Adolf Hitler* relies heavily on two earlier Soviet sources by Elena Rzhevskaia, *Chetyre vesny v shineli* (1961) and "Berlinskie stranitsy" (1965). Although Trevor-Roper's work preceded the Soviet works by many years, he has in later editions, and in an *Encounter* article of 1988, expressed confidence in his original scholarship and he does not mention the Soviet revelations. In the *Encounter* article he does note that the Soviets had a "sinister purpose" in broadcasting the false tale of Hitler's escape to the West, but he does not suggest what that purpose was; see Trevor-Roper, "Hitler Revisited: A Retrospective," pp. 17–19. Photographs of the Goebbels corpses appear in the Soviet victory film *Berlin* (Korean version in USNA, Audio-Visual Division), but they were taken the day after the bunker was opened; see O'Donnell, pp. 366–67. I recently tried to put together the whole strange story and to suggest why it so long remained a mystery and why much confusion still persists, in "With *Smersh* in Berlin: New Light on the Incomplete Histories of the *Führer* and the *Vozhd'*."

3. Hitler's designated successor, Admiral Karl Dönitz, did not know the story as of May 2, 1945, and perhaps even later (according to Joachim

Schulz-Maymany, television interview on Zweites Deutsches Fernsehen, May 8, 1985). Had he known, it surely would have led him to question his orders to carry on the war.

4. See O'Donnell, pp. 369–72, on the Soviet's backtracking on the original story; see also, Werth, pp. 985, 987. For Stalin and the military, see Bohlen memo, May 28, 1945, U.S. Department of State, *The Conference at Berlin*, 1: 51, and Bohlen, p. 220.

5. *Pravda*, June 26, 1945; *Tägliche Rundschau*, Sept. 11, 1945 (dispatch from TASS).

6. Rzhevskaia, "V tot den'," p. 168; Bohlen, p. 220. The stories were repeated at Potsdam in July to Clement Attlee, Harry Truman, and others; see Fischer, ed., *TJP* (July 31, 1945), p. 358. See also, O'Donnell, pp. 369–70; Werth, pp. 985, 997–98. Recently, stories have emerged that Hopkins was a Soviet agent; see Crozier, pp. 1–3.

7. Rzhevskaia, "V tot den'," pp. 163–68. Rzhevskaia's incomplete account was first published in her *Chetyre vesny v shineli* then more openly published in *Znamia* in 1965. Bezymenskii's account (in English translation) was the first to be noticed by Western readers. For some explanation for this, and more on Bezymenskii, see my article, "With *Smersh* in Berlin." Only recently has it emerged that the Soviets carried Hitler's body all over Soviet-occupied Germany before finally disposing of it. See Raack, "With *Smersh* in Berlin," p. 55; "Hitlers letzte Reise," in *Der Spiegel* (1992).

8. The corrupt ambiance around Stalin suggests the real nature of the Kremlin court. See, for example, Burlatskii, "Khrushchev," and the article, "Beriia," in *Nedelia*, p. 11.

9. See *Berliner Zeitung*, May 26, 1945; Werth, p. 1001.

10. See *The Times* (London), May 26, 1945 (p. 4); for references to "Russia" at Teheran, Dec. 1, 1943, and references to "ice-free ports" in the official documents at Yalta, "Agreement on Far Eastern Questions" (Feb. 11, 1945: "Restoration of the rights of Russia . . . to Port Arthur"), see Fischer, ed., *TJP*, p. 196.

11. The Foreign Office had caught the turn in Soviet propaganda early on, Orme-Sargent noting to Churchill, May 2, 1945, that ever since the Westerners had crossed the Rhine, the Eastern organs had begun to suggest that the Germans were making no resistence to the West, and that it was the Red Army alone that was breaking the back of the German Wehrmacht (PRO, FO371, 46748, C2038). The film of the parade, *Den' pobedy* (copy of the film in the collection of the author), showed as effectively as Soviet cameras and editors could work, Stalin's hopes and plans for the future and his remaking of the past. The Soviet newsreel *Novosti Dnia*, June 30, 1945, showed victory parades in Bratislava, Vienna, Helsinki, and Budapest (all but one under occupation), as if only the Communists were on hand to celebrate, and

only Stalin was to be praised. It seems quite apparent that Zhukov did not know the political line. Stalin's agent, Vyshinskii, is noticeably present at Zhukov's side, as he was at the signing of the surrender in Karlshorst and later at June ceremonies in Frankfurt/Main, where Zhukov collected Western medals, and in Berlin (when he took back his admission of the finding of Hitler's body). Even at the Frankfurt ceremony, Zhukov ungenerously claimed for the Soviet people before his Western hosts the main burden of the war, and allowed as how the Red Army "finally routed the armed forces of Fascist Germany and hoisted the banner of victory over Berlin." British Field Marshal Bernard Montgomery, in his toast on the occasion, said mildly, "The Russian and British peoples have contributed their share to the achievement of victory." See the report of TASS correspondent B. Afanasiev, June 10, 1945, in PRO, FO371, 47939, N70151. Stalin even then had Zhukov routed toward provincial obscurity, or even worse (see Rzhevskaia, "V tot den'," pp. 163–68, 172–74). Stalin's quest for glory later became even more obvious in the postwar journalistic and cinematographic hagiographies, such as Chiaurelli's film *Padenie Berlina*; in that film, Zhukov is notably absent from the scene of victory.

12. Doernberg, *Die Geburt*, pp. 84–85. The best analysis of the background of the Stalinist-controlled and organized Moskali wing of the exiled German Communist Party, including the fate of members in the purges of the late 1930's and Stalin's delivering many members to the Gestapo during the period of the Hitler-Stalin Pact, is Hermann Weber, "Die deutschen Opfer Stalins."

13. This account is based in part on Schulz, pp. 14–15; von Buttlar, p. 42; Krisch, pp. 10–74; with additional material gleaned by the author in the former party archive, the ZPA. For the local color and historical enthusiasm for the course of bolshevization, see K. Urban, "Die Herausbildung der Aktionseinheit der Arbeiterklasse und der demokratischen Selbsverwaltungsorgane unter Führung der KPD," pp. 881–82, 886–93; and S. Thomas, "Der Wiederbeginn des politischen Lebens in Berlin und die Aktionseinheit der Arbeiterparteien (Mai–Juli 1945)," p. 1316. For activities outside Berlin, see Vosske, *Die Vereinigung*, pp. 14–18; S. Thomas, *Entscheidung in Berlin*, pp. 24–74; and Bobek, pp. 427–36. All the above were written before the opening of the archives of the Central Committee of the [East] Germany Socialist Unity Party. From these archives I put together "Stalin Plans His Post-War Germany," cited earlier. All evidence supports the idea that Ulbricht, then Stalin-true, was already considered to be in charge by the Muscovites.

14. Krisch, p. 1; Schulz, pp. 8–21; Geyer, pp. 53–54; Fischer, "Die Sowjetunion und die 'Deutsche Frage' 1945–1949," pp. 45–46; Institut für Zeitgeschichte, Munich, ed., *Der Weg nach Pankow*, p. 17. Pieck's notes of a conversation with Stalin on June 4, 1945, record Stalin's direct expression

of his June 1945 plans for Germany: Pieck Nachlass 36/629, ZPA. The best background (published before the ZPA was opened to independent researchers) is in H. Weber, "Die sowjetische Militäradministration in Deutschland und das Parteisystem der SBZ/DDR"; the most recent, Raack, "Stalin Plans His Post-War Germany." The June 4 notes, deriving from Wilhelm Pieck's meeting with Stalin, were published in 1993, along with many other extremely valuable Pieck notes in facsimile, in Keiderling (the notes of June 4, pp. 468–73). Many of the typescript transcriptions do not accurately reflect Pieck's original handwritten notes, and though Keiderling submits both versions, the reader will likely find it necessary to return to the originals in case of inconsistency. Keiderling's edition has now been followed by another collection (1994) by Loth and Badstübner, eds. This similarly valuable edition, though it includes only documents on the *Deutschlandpolitik* theme, to which there are many other references in the Pieck Nachlass as well as elsewhere in the archive, is useful both to the archivists who must provide scholars with the original documents and keep them intact for future users, and to scholars, who can now use these copies in the libraries. Scholars should still refer to the original handwritten notes, however, in case of any possibility of a misreading of Pieck's sometimes engimatic notes. I should add that Bodensieck, I think incorrectly, believes that Pieck's June 4 notes were from discussions he had with Ulbricht and others, who had previously met with Stalin; see Bodensieck, pp. 29–56. One may ask why Stalin solidified his plans with respect to Germany at such a late date. One reason certainly had to have been that he was very busy; a second might have been that he was originally planning to march much farther west in Germany than the allotted Soviet Zone to take over the entire country but was balked by the amazing successes of the Allied invasion and the quick advance of the Western Allied armies east all the way into the allotted Soviet Zone. This is the argument suggested by Tokaev, pp. 74–78, a great many of whose stories from inside Soviet institutions can be independently confirmed by other sources. To accept this line of argument would, of course, require an overhauling of even the most recent accounts, including this one, of Stalin's European policy during World War II. For Djilas's comment, see Djilas, p. 114.

15. USNA films, 111ADC 4920, 5035, and 5043.

16. "Besprechung[en] mit Dimitrov," Apr. 25 and May 25, 1945, ZPA, Pieck Nachlass 36/500.

17. USNA film, 111ADC 4190; Zhukov, *Erinnerungen und Gedanken*, p. 610, gives Stalin's alleged reasons for repeating the surrender, but it is unlikely that Zhukov really knew about them.

18. The Reims scenes are in the USNA film, 111ADC 5766; those of Karlshorst are in the Soviet film *Berlin* (USNA). Zhukov, who also became persona non grata under Khrushchev, was all but banished from later prints of *Ber-*

lin. See also, Raack, "Film as Historical Fantasy." There was understandable confusion in the Western press about the second "surrender." The *News Chronicle* (London), May 9, 1945 (p. 2), shows pictures of Eisenhower with his Russian liaison at Reims, but on page 1 of the same issue the Berlin ceremony is announced as "ratifying the surrender." The *Times* (London), May 10, 1945 (p. 4), unable to get the story straight, has "Last Act of Surrender Ratified in Berlin" following its May 9, 1945, headline, "Final Act of Surrender at Rheims" (p. 4).

19. Stalin himself was in all likelihood the original author of the East-West dichotomy. He evidently conveyed it to Wilhelm Pieck, who passed it along as a news report to his party helpers ("Germany is divided into two zones, Soviet and Allied"); see Pieck's speeches of June 27, 1945, "Information der Parteimitgliedern," and of June 28, 1945, given to the Moscow German "Betriebsversammlung," in zpa, Pieck Nachlass 36/500. Earlier, Wiesław Gomułka had brought the new line to the Polish Workers' (Communist) Party Central Committee, almost surely getting the line from Bolesław Bierut, who made regular visits to Moscow to get it from the vozhd' himself. See Kochański, ed., *Protokół obrad* KC PPR, pp. 11–12, 43. For the cameraman's recollections of the Karlshorst celebration, see Tsitriniak, pp. 85–88.

20. Werter, p. 966; von Buttlar, pp. 43–47; Krisch, pp. 31–33. On Soviet misbehavior in Yugoslavia, see Banac, p. 28. Nichols (Prague) to C. Warner, Foreign Office, May 23, 1945, notes that Russian behavior in Czechoslovakia includes rape and looting and "requisitioning," PRO, FO371, 47077, N5953; see also, Nichols to Foreign Office, June 4, 1945: Soviets stripping Czech factories and shipping contents to the Soviet Union, ibid., N6532; Zarański-Hankey conversation, Mar. 23, 1945: Soviets in Poland stealing everything, including farm implements and livestock, is, A12. 49/15 III; Soviets behaving in Poland as they do in ex-enemy countries: British Military Attaché to H.M. Ambassador in Poland, Oct. 1, 1945, PRO, FO371, 47954, N13520; ibid., 47129, N14734, Cavendish-Bentinck (Warsaw) to Bevin, Oct. 10, 1945: Soviets wantonly destroy equipment, sink barges because they were once German, rape and plunder; ibid., 47954, N15322, RAF Officer Commanding at Schwechat (Vienna): Red Army soldiers conduct themselves arrogantly. They have even wrecked the facilities turned over to the RAF, still rape and steal; ibid., 46933, C4610, 21st Army Group Weekly Political Survey, Aug. 4, 1945, on German civilians' fear of the Russians and their disdain for Red Army looting. See also, Mautner, pp. 231–34, and Herz, pp. 163–64. Stalin's henchmen in Germany had abundant reports of the Red Army's bestialities but evidently could do nothing about them: "Kurzer Bericht über die Tätigkeit der Berliner Bezirksleitung," Oct. 30, 1945, zpa, Ulbricht Nachlass 182/852; and "Genosse Pieck von Hoernle" (July 1945), zpa, Pieck Nachlass 36/631, and "Erste demokratische Frauen-

versammlung," Aug. 3, 1945, ibid., 36/731, the last one of many such records in this file.

21. USNA film, 111ADC 4539.

22. Military and civil planning for the Communists' descent into Germany: "Vereinbarung von Vorschlägen auf der Sitzung von 6. Februar mit Genossen Chwostow," and another meeting with the same person on Apr. 12, "Besprechung mit Paniushkin (ZK)," Feb. 17, 1945; also "Besprechungen" with Dimitrov on Feb. 17 and Apr. 1, 1945; and "Richtlinien für die Arbeit der deutschen Antifaschisten in dem von der Sowjetarmee besetzten deutschen Gebiet," Apr. 5, 1945, ZPA, Ulbricht Nachlass, 182/851; Adler, pp. 23–27, 50, 64; Vosske, *Die Vereinigung*, pp. 8–9, 91, 95, 104; Vosske, "Dokumente aus der programmatischen Tätigkeit der KPD"; Laschitza, pp. 91–104; Antipenko; Zhukov, "Berlinskaia operatsiia i kapitulatsiia Germanii," pp. 106–11; also, Zhukov, *Erinnerungen*, pp. 615–20; Sandford, p. 25; Fischer, *Die Sowjetische Deutschlandpolitik*, p. 153; Schulz, pp. 8–20; Faisst et al., p. 319.

23. Even acting alone, without their faithful intermediaries, the Soviets could hardly have exercised closer control over their zone. For details of the planning, see Dimitrov-Pieck letters, 1943–45, ZPA, Pieck Nachlass, 36/544, 36/734, esp. Ulbricht to Pieck, May 26, 1945 (36/629), and Ulbricht Nachlass, 182/1180–83. See also, Ruch and Schürer, p. 29; Scheel, ed., pp. 203–6; Ziemke, *The Battle for Berlin*, p. 74.

24. By July 9, 1941, *Pravda* was using such expressions as "fascist barbarians," "Beat the enemy to complete annihilation," "Fascism is the cruel enemy of mankind," and "fascist reptiles." After specific orders for the early anti-German propaganda format were issued, *Pravda* pulled out all stops. On July 17 (p. 1), for example, one article used the phrase, "the unheard of bestialities of the fascists" (quoted by Rodionov, p. 8). *Kino*, on Sept. 5, 1941, quoted *Pravda* of the day before: "Fascist dogs and executioners . . . will be paid back in blood drop for drop . . . death for death!" Much of the language recalled the Soviet propaganda campaign against the Finns in 1939–40: see Thompson, "Nationalist Propaganda in the Soviet Russian Press, 1939–1941."

25. IWM, Film Division, *Soiuz kinozhurnal*, RND34-01; this is but one example among thousands.

26. *Pravda*, May 8, 1945; Tjulpanow (Tiulpanov), pp. 15, 20, 28; Werth, pp. xvii, 965–68; for a slightly different interpretation, see von Buttlar, pp. 28–30, 35–36.

27. Kettenacker, *Krieg zur Friedenssicherung*, p. 501; Ruch and Schürer, p. 28; Foschepoth, p. 691. On the discussions of dismemberment at Yalta, see Fischer, ed., *TJP*, pp. 109–12, 139. Stalin (perhaps following Maiskii's discussion with Churchill in London Dec. 5, 1941, reported by Maiskii to the Narkomindel: *Sovetsko-angliiskie otnosheniia*, p. 182) had proposed to

dismember Germany at his first meeting with Eden in December 1941, just after the German army had been driven away from the gates of Moscow: see Eden to Foreign Office, Dec. 17, 1941, PRO, FO371, 29655, N7463; and "Minutes of a Meeting Attended by Strang, etc. (notes by Dews of 23 April 1942," ibid., 32880, N2182. The Polish PPR leaders noticed the Stalinist volte-face on the issue in the spring of 1945; see Kochański, ed., pp. 11–12.

28. Weiss (Vais), pp. 40–41, quoting Zhukov. The behavior was justified as "revenge" by Marshal Vasili Sokolovskii (Werth, p. 986). See also the citations from the *Nachlässe* in note 20 above.

29. Mikoian's report was also quoted in the *Berliner Zeitung*, May 22, 1945. Ulbricht, writing about Mikoian's visit in *Zur Geschichte der neuesten Zeit* (1: 66) ten years later, omitted Mikoian's unusual testimony to the virtues of free enterprise. But he was quite aware of the plan to avoid all mention of socialism, and he knew that the original dissimulation came from Stalin. See A. Ackermann, "Wissenschaftliche Planung und Leitung wies den Weg," ZPA, 1291/2. See also 21st Army Group Weekly Political Intelligence Summary, July 21, 1945, PRO, FO371, 46933, C4235. Mikoian's, and the KPD's, approach was the same one proclaimed (and likewise later ignored) by the PKWN Poles and reported from them at the time as credible by many Western opinion makers (as note, again, Winterton, in the *News-Chronicle*, London, Aug. 31, 1944). Kennan, in Moscow, shrewdly analyzed Mikoian's business, in Kennan, telegram to Secretary of State, Moscow, May 10, 1945, in USNA, RG59, Lot 55D371, box 5. Dimitrov notified Finder, in Warsaw, Mar. 1, 1943: "Preaching the establishment of the power of the workers and peasants . . . *na dannom etape* . . . is politically incorrect"; see AAN, PPR, 190/I-14; also, Dimitrov to Finder, Apr. 2, 1943, ibid. Later, during discussions between Stalin and the PKWN about parceling out the cabinet posts in the new Warsaw government, Stalin said, in regard to an aged Polish general he thought Mikołajczyk might put up for a cabinet job, that he might be acceptable because (1) the aged fellow might not last long, and (2) he was old, and perhaps could be easily persuaded. See "Protokul [*sic*] z posiedzenia KC . . . 22 October 1944," AAN, KC PPR, 295/V/1.

30. Kovalev and Medvedev, p. 38; Fischer (quoting Wolfgang Leonhard), *Die Sowjetische Deutschlandpolitik*, pp. 152–53; Ulbricht, 1: 62; Vosske, *Die Vereinigung*, p. 14; Zhukov, "Die Kronung des Sieges," p. 4; Stern, pp. 58–59. Stalin's Poles had also been told to keep important matters in their hands when doling out the ministries to Mikołajczyk's group; see Grzędziński, ed., p. 150.

31. The Moscow correspondent of *The Times* of London (May 23, 1945, p. 4) identified Maron as a "worker" named Moran; evidently he garbled the English-language translation of the TASS dispatch.

32. According to *Vechernaia Moskva*, Aug. 25, 1945, the scenes appeared

in the Soviet newsreel *Novosti Dnia*, 15/1945. See also, Scheel, ed., pp. 204–6.

33. Weiss (Vais), pp. 40–41; Zhukov, *Erinnerungen*, pp. 614–19; Fischer, *Die Sowjetische Deutschlandpolitik*, p. 152; Mautner, p. 233.

34. Schulz, pp. 8–20; Schöpflin, pp. 65–69.

35. K. Urban, p. 886; Haacker, pp. 122–26.

36. Schulz, p. 20; Vosske, *Die Vereinigung*, pp. 31–33. The Soviets were not able to force the Communists in Saxony and Thuringia to submit to Ulbricht's discipline until those areas passed from American to Red Army control. Under the Americans, these political parties had been illegal; see Sandford, pp. 32, 73, 268. The appeal to party authority and discipline was, of course, more readily enforced when joined to a *paiok*, the monthly food supplement packages that Red Army officers also received. For chosen Germans, especially as the winter wore on, these special rations were often the difference between hunger and satisfaction. See Riess, 4: 73; Müller and Müller, p. 67. There was noticeable opposition among former Communists in the Western zones of occupation (where opposition could be expressed) to the domineering behavior of Ulbricht and his backers in the East. One described the situation there as *"saumässig"* (filthy); another said he was no Muscovite, others rejected the Soviet brand of communism; see 21st Army Group Political Intelligence Survey on Germany, Aug. 11, 1945, PRO, FO371, 46934, C4772; similar in C3951. For the Soviet role in Antifa in the British Zone, see Political Intelligence Summary no. 7, ibid., C4937 and C4772.

37. Haacker, pp. 123–26; Laschitza, p. 91; S. Thomas, "Der Wiederbeginn," p. 1321.

38. On the meetings of June 4–5, 1945, see Raack, "Stalin Plans His Post-War Germany," pp. 62–64; and Sandford, p. 48. Although Dimitrov had the special qualification of having lived in Germany, the range of his advice surely took in most of the countries for which Stalin had plans. His contact from early on was directly with Warsaw (see his wartime dispatches to Marceli Nowotko and Pawel Finder in AAN, PPR, 190/I-14, by which the Polish Communists were sent the Moscow line). Later, in Moscow, his contact was with Jakób Berman (Ważniewski, pp. 9–10, 14). For more on the Polish case, see Syzdek, "Sprawa połowanie PKN w Moskwie," pp. 91–92.

39. S. Thomas, "Der Wiederbeginn," pp. 1321–23. Ulbricht's notes indicate that in the early days in Berlin he was still thinking in terms of a single workers' party; see his notes (untitled, probably from May 1945) in ZPA, Ulbricht Nachlass 182/853; and "Besprechung mit Dimitrov," May 30, 1945, ZPA, Pieck Nachlass, 36/500. For Stalin's requirement of the two parties, see Pieck notes, June 4, 1945, Pieck Nachlass, 36/629, ZPA. On the Moscow-guided unification of the two parties, see Pieck notes, "Besprech-

ung am 26.12.1945 in Babelsberg," Pieck Nachlass, 36/740; and Pieck notes, "Report of W. U.," Feb. 6, 1946, ZPA, Pieck Nachlass 36/631.

40. S. Thomas, "Der Wiederbeginn," pp. 1316–40; Wheeler-Bennett and Nicholls, pp. 281–82; Sandford, p. 78; Leonhard, p. 391.

41. Fischer, *Die Sowjetische Deutschlandpolitik*, p. 135. The point was noted by British military intelligence: see 21st Army Group Political Intelligence Summary, July 28, 1945, PRO, FO371, 46933, C4635. The importance of Berlin as political capital of Germany was also recognized by the German Socialist Party, SPD; see Schulz, pp. 15, 23.

42. Schulz, p. 33; Scheel, ed., p. 208; H. Weber, ed., *Parteiensystem*, pp. 16–27; Geyer, p. 57. American intelligence reported the obvious Berlin connections of the local Communists in their areas of the Soviet Zone before their withdrawal in early July. They quite correctly reported the Communists' goals as deemphasis of the traditional Communist-socialist economic goals, the Bloc policy, and underground organizational work—forbidden, as were all politics, in American areas of occupation. See USNA, RG226, Field Intelligence studies, no. 10, "Communist political activities in Leipzig before the Russian occupation," July 16, 1945.

43. Geyer, p. 53; H. Weber, ed., *Parteiensystem*, p. 16. For Stalin's plans according to insider A. Ackermann, see "Wissenschaftliche Planung und Leitung wies den Weg," ZPA, 1291/2. See also Eisenhower, chap. 9.

44. Faisst et al., pp. 315–28.

45. Riess, 4: 22.

46. On the success of Berlin radio in duping the Westerners as well as the locals (who complained of "a trickle of news from the Russian front"), see: "SHAEF G-5 Political Intelligence Letter number 10" (June 19, 1945), PRO FO371, 46933, C3485; "Twelfth Army Intelligence Summary number 6" (May 29, 1945), ibid., C3007; "Weekly Background Notes number 3" (June 26, 1945), ibid., C3329; "21st Army Group Intelligence Surveys on Germany" (Aug. 11, 1945), ibid., 46934, C4772; Strang to Bevin (July 26, 1945), ibid., C4937; "Interview with Brigadier Hinde (transmitted by William Strang to Bevin)," Aug. 8, 1945, ibid., C4792. It is easy to perceive the gradual shift in the Soviet line in the changing treatment of subjects bearing on the Western states in the Polish, Soviet, and Soviet-controlled, German presses, especially after Potsdam and the end of the Pacific war. This shift is perhaps most obvious in the newspaper of the German Communist Party, *Deutsche Volkszeitung*.

47. Ulbricht's lack of information is inferred here on the basis of the list of places (exclusively in Silesia) he provided (Apr. 5, 1945) for the procuring of workers to appeal publicly to the Germans to lay down their arms (see Fischer, *Die Sowjetische Deutschlandpolitik*, p. 143). He surely could not have expected a favorable response from workers in territories where the population knew it was going to be turned over to Poland and forcibly

evacuated. I conclude from this that, even at that late date, Ulbricht did not know of Stalin's assignment of Silesia south and west of the Oder to Poland. Likewise, Moscow's state radio, *Inoradio*, in its German-language broadcasts, was still speaking in May of Glatz being in Germany; see the report of various TRJN decrees with respect to Poland's new western border in AAN, 1621, Ambasada RP in Londynie. Ulbricht seems to have got the border at Stettin straight when he went to Moscow for the meeting with Stalin on June 4, 1945 (ZPA, Pieck notes, Pieck Nachlass, 36/629; Vosske, *Die Vereinigung*, pp. 23–26). Ulbricht noted very circumlocutorily in a speech in mid-June the eastern range of his political interest by leaving out the territories east of Frankfurt an der Oder ("Weekly Background Notes number 4," July 4, 1945, PRO, FO371, 46933, C3329). By the end of June, Ulbricht was justifying the Oder-Neisse line as a punishment for German misdeeds (Krisch, p. 40).

48. Fischer, ed., *TJP*, p. 188. The British and Americans soon learned that the Soviets were collaborating with the Poles in driving out the eastern German population. The British were upset enough to let the Soviets know that they did not view these activities as compatible with the Yalta agreements. See USNA, RG59, Lot 55D371, box 5, "Daily Summary," May 16, 1945; and ibid., RG226, E90, folder 85, file "Amzon in and out Berlin-Salzburg 1945," OSS official dispatch, July 21, 1945.

49. Riess, 4: 23; *Der Morgen*, Aug. 11, 1945, p. 4. On the Oder-Neisse line, see *Tägliche Rundschau*; also *Deutsche Volkszeitung* and *Das Volk*, July 7, 1945; Pieck, "Information für Parteimitgliedern," June 27, 1945, ZPA, Pieck Nachlass, 36/500.

50. Stalin had earlier told his Western allies that all he wanted from the Finns was the restoration of the frontiers reflecting his conquests of 1940. See "Memorandum" (dated, in pencil, Dec. 15, 1943), Bohlen Correspondence, USNA, RG59, box 3.

51. *Berliner Zeitung*, June 9, 1945; map for Soviet soldiers.

CHAPTER 6

1. Stalin is said to have remarked in March 1945, regarding the occupation of Germany, "Steal as much as you can"; quoted by Loth, *Stalins ungeliebtes Kind*, p. 20. See also, A. Phillips, p. 32. But should Stalin's economic program surprise us? The Soviets were doing the very same with what they described as "Nazi" possessions in their true satellite, People's Poland (see "Wiadomości krajowe," no. 40, June 6, 1945, IS, A10, 4, 23), as well as in "neutral" Austria; and they would later loot that part of their Chinese ally's territory they occupied as liberators in their coming Asian war with Japan. On Austria, see Rauchensteiner, pp. 78–79, 115; on China: Mineo, p. 209, and Gallicchio, p. 69. Stalin's economic adviser in 1945, E. (Jenö) Varga, may have encouraged the development of the rapacious reparations policy by arguing that exhausting other nations by taking repara-

NOTES TO PAGES 137 – 43 225

tions would lead to the development of the conditions for revolution in those nations; see Duda, p. 217.

2. One British correspondent who had the unusual experience of being given an early trip to the front in 1941 by the Soviet authorities found little evidence of "scorched earth." See the report of Vernon Bartlett, Nov. 26, 1941, in PRO, FO371, 29587, N5603.

3. For popular views of the prewar arms cartels, see Woito, "Between the Wars"; for historians' views, see Baldwin, pp. 13–19. A recent article dealing with the subject of cartel plots, imagined and real, is Anderson, esp. pp. 7–9.

4. The major thefts and dismantlings were outside the control of the SMAD and were directed from Moscow—Doernberg, then a member of the Soviet forces, says by Beria ("Zum Zusammenwirken," p. 312); this attribution would fit with the statement attributed to Stalin and the views of Varga (see note 1 above), since Beria and Stalin were at the time in frequent touch, Beria being a regular in Stalin's evening cabinet. Like the savage behavior of the Red Army, the dismantlings were often an embarrassment to Ulbricht and company: Sandford, p. 41. See also: Schöpflin, p. 66; Benz, p. 158; "Germany: Weekly Background Notes," no. 1 (June 8, 1945), PRO, FO371, 46933, C3215, and no. 2 (June 15, 1945), C3329; also "21st Army Group Political Intelligence Summary" (July 21, 1945), C4235. Many of the dismantled works were simply hauled away to rust on a railroad siding, the fate of so many once productive plants the Soviets had been hauling off from their conquests since 1939. A recent work dealing with the reparations question is Fisch, *Reparationen nach dem Zweiten Weltkrieg*.

5. Leahy, p. 397.

6. Bohlen, p. 222.

7. Ferrell, ed., p. 520. Truman described the Russians as "looters" (*Memoirs*, 1: 522, also 518).

8. Benz, pp. 85–86, 89.

9. Fischer, ed., *TJP*, p. 277; H. Thomas, pp. 122–28.

10. Stalin's insistence on the establishment of a German central government was obviously connected with his insistence on getting a hand on the Ruhr industrial area, which, after earlier suggestions that it be internationalized, had been assigned to the British Zone: see Fischer, ed., *TJP*, pp. 107, 321. Stalin was still pushing this issue at Potsdam (ibid., pp. 352–53). His failure to gain this goal there is a measure of how completely the other powers had by then turned against him.

11. See, for example, Truman, 1: 388. De Santis (pp. 204–8) points out how encounters with the Soviets in eastern Europe hardened American diplomatic attitudes from the lower ranks up to Washington.

12. "21st Army Group Weekly Political Intelligence Summary" (July 14, 1945), and interview with Brigadier Hinde transmitted by William Strang to

Bevin, Aug. 8, 1945, in PRO, FO371, 46933, C4198 and 46934, C4972, respectively. On Soviet behavior in Germany, see: Fischer, *Die Sowjetische Deutschlandpolitik*, pp. 155–56; Benz, pp. 75–76, 90; "Weekly Background Notes number 4" (July 4, 1945), PRO, FO371, 46933, C3215.

13. USNA, RG59, Lot 55D371, box 5, George F. Kennan telegram (from Moscow) to Secretary of State, May 10, 1945, reports stories of Soviet misbehavior that had even got that far, noting: a "hysterical outbreak of destruction, pillage and brutality" which even the Soviets admit, has put the Germans in "a state of utter terror and shock." President Truman, in Potsdam, had direct communication with United States military headquarters in Frankfurt/Main and with Washington, but not with the United States occupation forces just across the Havel in Berlin.

14. Ferrell, ed., pp. 518, 521.

15. Fischer, ed., *TJP*, pp. 187–88. Góra and Kochański, p. 119, note that Ambassadors Harriman and Archibald Clark-Kerr, who with Molotov constituted a special commission in Moscow to deal with Polish issues, had already in June made clear their governments' determination to hold strictly to the Yalta agreements on the Polish frontier. The gist of those agreements, insofar as they pertained to the western frontiers, was to delay all agreement until a peace conference.

16. Churchill noted during the Potsdam proceedings that the success of the conference would depend on the successful resolution of the Polish question (Fischer, ed., *TJP*, p. 320). Although Churchill at Teheran had referred to Stalin as "Stalin the Great," he was by the spring of 1945 generally, but not consistently, very anti-Soviet; see Bohlen, p. 229; Joseph Davies to Truman, June 12, 1945, in U.S. Department of State, *FRUS*, *The Conference at Berlin*, 1: 67–76; Douglas, *From War to Cold War*, pp. 76, 84, 87, 92; Harbutt, pp. 50, 77–78. T. Romer report: 2 Nov. 1944, IS, A12, 49/15, III.

17. Truman was astonished by the unilateral Soviet arrangement of the Oder-Neisse line ("without so much as a 'by your leave'"), and its consequences; see Mark, "Today Has Been a Historical One," esp. Truman's entries of July 25 and 26, 1945. For the growth of British and American doubts about the friendly intentions of Stalin, see Graml, pp. 64–65, 70–71.

18. See the report of Polish Ambassador Raczyński on his conversation with Eden, July 13, 1945, in IS, A12, 49/16. Attlee's optimism is also noted in Williams, *A Prime Minister Remembers*, pp. 76–77. Since Yalta, where Polish issues, according to American Secretary of State Edward Stettinius, had been the most controversial and difficult (Pastusiak, p. 30), the Soviets had disputed with the Western powers through their ambassadors in Moscow the nature and composition of the Polish government: would it be an entirely new entity as the Westerners thought the Yalta agreements had required, or a reorganization of the group Stalin had already invested? Ob-

viously, Stalin won. See Góra and Kochański, pp. 96–99. Recently one Polish writer has suggested that the Western Allies ought to have tied the issue of recognition of the Oder-Neisse border to a Soviet specific guarantee to hold free elections in Poland by a specific date (see Kamiński, pp. 69–82). But, in fact, the Western Allies refused to recognize the Oder-Neisse border at Potsdam, just as their predecessors had at Yalta, hence they really had nothing to trade to Stalin for yet another promise of his good political behavior in Poland. Truman, like Roosevelt, simply could not grasp the complexities of Polish diplomatic life—in the service of preserving the existence and independence of a nation "between the hammer and the anvil." This fact, his haste, and again, the concept of "a faraway place of which we know little," probably account for his not fighting for the Poles at Potsdam. Also like Roosevelt, he disliked the Poles, and like Roosevelt and most of the British, thought the London group deserved their fate. He had missed most of the events of wartime diplomacy during which he might have gathered the information to arrive at another conclusion. Truman was, of course, well known for being strongly opinionated. He likewise disliked de Gaulle, thought Churchill's time had passed, and, early on, was suspicious of the "Russians." In the latter two cases his notions seem hardly improper. His dislike of de Gaulle was shared with almost every anglophone; see Liebovich, p. 72.

19. Benz, pp. 132–34; Fischer, *Die Sowjetische Deutschlandpolitik,* pp. 130, 135. At Yalta, Stalin was evidently playing for a weak center for postwar Europe (that is, dismemberment of Germany), where his Soviet-controlled eastern empire would wield a strong influence from the outset. He later reversed this, perhaps with a view to presenting himself to the Germans as the savior of their nation and also to gaining even more control there by means of the Control Council. He also thought that by establishing popular parties and unions, which the KPD would dominate, he would get a hand over all of what remained of the former Reich; see Pieck notes (conversation with Stalin, etc.), June 4, 1945, ZPA, Pieck Nachlass, 36/629. For background of the "central governments" issue, see Welsh and Zank, p. 201; H. Weber, *Geschichte der DDR,* pp. 97–101; Vogelsang, pp. 511–12; Niedbalski, pp. 457–58. The latest on the central governments (but evidently written before the East German archives were opened): Kraus, pp. 34–60.

20. The Soviet approach to government creation was temporarily, and propagandistically, pluralistic in some of the Red Army–occupied nations (see Gati, p. 43), as we have seen in Germany and Poland, but only persons whom the Soviets considered reliable or easily influenced were kept in the key ministerial slots; each government to one degree or another was patterned along the lines of the Soviet governments that were set up in the Baltic nations. The Soviets were urging the Renner government in Austria,

228 NOTES TO PAGES 146 - 47

totally their own creation, as the one that ought to be recognized by the West (Rauchensteiner, pp. 66–77; Fischer, ed., *TJP*, pp. 300, 316). With, perhaps, the models of Soviet government creation in Bulgaria, Romania, and Poland in mind, the Western conferees held back (*TJP*, p. 400). One of the best accounts of a contemporary manipulation of local elements behind the Red Army front toward effecting a Soviet-desired conclusion is in Němec and Moudrý, pp. 89–124. American intelligence advisers soon grasped the revolutionary nature of Soviet economic changes in its zone; see USNA, RG226, OSS Field Intelligence Studies (no box number), no. 33, "Observations on the Berlin political scene in October 1945," Oct. 19, 1945. But, in an evident effort to keep Westerners as far as possible from what he was doing, Stalin even made certain that the Allied Control Council would not sit in his sector of Berlin.

21. Fischer, ed., *TJP*, pp. 204–5; James, *Anthony Eden*, pp. 306, 307; Assistant Secretary Dunn to Assistant Secretary Grew, July 14, 1945, *The Conference at Berlin*, 1: 245. Molotov had brought up the central governments issue the day before at the meeting of the foreign ministers ("Tenth meeting of the Foreign Ministers, July 30, 1945," in *Conference at Berlin*, 1: 502.

22. Geyer, pp. 54–55, 57–58; *TJP*, pp. 204–5, 351–53; Acting Secretary Grew to Truman, May 30 and June 18, 1945, *Conference at Berlin*, 1: 159, 172, and 178–79; Staff Paper, June 22, 1945, *Conference at Berlin*, 1: 188–89. Early in the conference, Truman erroneously thought the German government problem already solved, presumably by the creation of the Control Council; see Ferrell, ed., p. 521. On the suspicion of Stalin's Austrian government, see De Santis, p. 152.

23. Fischer, ed., *TJP*, pp. 204–5; Leahy, pp. 405–6; Truman, 1: 346; Grew to Truman, May 30, 1945, *Conference at Berlin*, 1: 158–66; U.S. Delegation Position Paper, July 13, 1945, *Conference at Berlin*, 1: 240; Dunn to Secretary of State, July 14, 1945, *Conference at Berlin*, pp. 505–6. American intelligence some months later reported the nature of the Soviet-organized political system in the SBZ, and compared it with the system originally conceived and organized for their zone. See USNA, RG226, OSS Field Intelligence Studies (no box number), no. 33, "Observations on the Berlin political scene in October 1945," Oct. 19, 1945, and E90, folder 85, file "Amzon in and out Berlin-Salzburg 1945," OSS official dispatch, Aug. 2, 1945 (on recruiting of reliable Germans as help). See also, Fischer, *Die Sowjetische Deutschlandpolitik*, p. 134.

24. On the Control Council, see Benz, pp. 68–72; Truman, 1: 345. On the history of the establishment of the Western zonal states and governments, see Benz, pp. 121–28, 140. American State Department advisers had been quick to detect the divisive drift of Soviet policy: USNA, RG59, Lot

55D371, box 5, Robert Murphy, Paris, to H. Freeman Mathews (State Department Director of European Affairs), Apr. 25, 1945.

25. Indeed, the existence of the Zentralverwaltungen went unpublished until September 1945 (Benz, p. 133). Pieck's notes of his meetings with Stalin reveal how Stalin persisted in running the scheme to advance Soviet zonal power westward in Germany for the first three and a half postwar years; see Badstübner, "'Beratungen' bei J. W. Stalin. Neue Dokumente." See also, Raack, "Stalin Plans His Post-War Germany," pp. 66–68.

26. The Americans had by this time learned that the Soviets were ardently pursuing intelligence information on American military units. See USNA, RG226, E90, folder 85, "Amzon in and out Berlin-Salzburg 1945," OSS official dispatch, July 10, 1945. On Potsdam and the "central governments" (or "administrations"): the Soviets brought the central government issue up in the context of discussions about four-power control of the Ruhr. And they were still openly pushing for all-German political parties and a unified Germany in 1948. Indeed, the unification theme dominated SBZ propaganda even in 1948; see Willis, pp. 27, 35; and, draft of "An die Regierung . . . Grossbritanniens z. Hd. Herrn Ministerpräsident Attlee" and comments (of the same day) of Gribanov to the same (the Soviet representative tells Pieck to sharpen his attack, that the British are standing in the way of the unification of Germany, etc.), in Russian and German, ZPA, Pieck Nachlass 36/740, Mar. 15, 1948.

27. Fischer, ed., TJP, p. 261. On the refugees: the Conference, including Stalin, went on to provide in its final resolutions, that is to say, in phrases quietly ignored by those doing the actual work, for the "orderly resettlement" of the Germans being moved out of the states to the east, including a good many who, in spite of Stalin's denials, were still east of the Oder-Neisse line (ibid., pp. 261, 403). Leahy's comment to Truman about the allegedly voluntarily departed Germans was that, if none were now to be found where so many had once lived, it was because "the Bolshies had killed all of them" (Leahy, p. 369). The British, overwhelmed by the refugees they were having to feed in their own zone out of the slim rations then available, began complaining that same August about the Poles' continuing to push the mass of Germans remaining in the eastern areas westward; see Fuchs, pp. 280–81. The Westerners at Potsdam knew that Stalin had annexed eastern Czechoslovakia in June 1945 (in spite of a 1943 treaty with the exiled Czech government that guaranteed Czechoslovak territory), part of the very same state that Stalin's supporters had so much reproached the Western powers for sacrificing, in part, to annexation by Hitler in 1938. Stalin, who also took that territory without so much as a "by your leave," argued that the territory held people ethnically akin to a Soviet people—the same argument that Hitler used in 1938 when he made his demands on Prague (see

Davis, pp. 160–61). It is important to record that the annexation of Czecho-slovakian Ruthenia was planned well before 1945. Molotov in October 1944 allowed it to slip out that "Hungary bordered on *Russia*" (see Siracusa, pp. 45–48; my emphasis), though this was quite untrue at the time and was only a fact after the Soviets annexed eastern Czechoslovakia in 1945. This is one more proof that Stalin had his map worked out long in advance. See also, Taborský, pp. 180–90, 204–5.

28. One near East-West collision occurred when Stalin called Churchill's complaints about the situation of the virtually Soviet-immured British mission in Bucharest "fairy tales"; Truman, 1: 385. Back in 1940, when Stalin was at full tilt toward Hitler, Molotov had termed Attlee and Bevin "lackeys of capitalism" because of their support of the Finns; cited from *Die Welt* (Stockholm), Apr. 5, 1940, p. 372.

29. See Ulam, *The Rivals*, p. 72. For some of Truman's and Admiral Leahy's well-targeted suspicions of the Soviets at Potsdam, see Truman, 1: 351, 360, 364, 369, 410; Truman's realistic assessment of Stalin is on pp. 411–12; see also, Gallicchio, p. 57. De Santis, chap. 6, describes some of the reactions and reports of contemporary American diplomats confronting the new Soviet order in eastern Europe. On the British, see Foschepoth, pp. 686–709; and the documents supplied by members of the Foreign Office between May and July 1945, printed by Ross, ed., nos. 38 and 39. The British had received testimony about the Soviet mechanisms of control in the Soviet Zone (see Schwabe, p. 317), and they had multiple reports of Soviet fast play, as well as thievery and murder, elsewhere in east central Europe. Attlee then got it right characterizing the Soviets as "ideological imperialists" (H. Thomas, p. 197); see also Williams, *Ernest Bevin*, pp. 241, 255, 262; and Williams, *A Prime Minister Remembers*, pp. 76–78, 171. Attlee had been convinced long before he became P.M. that the Soviets were behaving in a "bloody way." So had Bevin. See Douglas, *From War to Cold War*, pp. 88, 92–93, 115, 123.

30. United States Army Air Force cinematographers caught the scenes in Czechoslovakia, as well as in many parts of destroyed Germany, in color in the summer of 1945. See the USAAF Collection in USNA, Audio-Visual Division.

31. An example of the tightening of the reparations rules: the Soviets were to take their reparations out of their zone, as well as from relevant foreign German assets, and were to receive only carefully defined reparations from the Western zones, some in exchange for foodstuffs. See Fischer, ed., *TJP*, pp., 397–98; Leahy, pp. 426–28; and Feis, p. 322. The ad hoc component in the resolution of the reparations issue is described by Nübel, pp. 203–4.

32. By far the best description of a local Soviet political takeover, that in Berlin, and the Soviets' ultimate failure to retain its total power there, is

Faisst et al., pp. 319–46. For some of the reaction to it, see S. Thomas, *Entscheidung in Berlin*, pp. 111–14.

33. Sommer, *Das Memorandum*, p. 121.

34. Benz, p. 104; De Santis, p. 157.

35. Similarly, the Russians, at Potsdam, obviously were still hoping for a large role in the management of the Rhine-Ruhr industrial areas in the British Zone. This would serve their twin purposes of extracting more reparations and getting a valuable industrial and political foothold farther west in Germany. In spite of previous wartime talk about internationalizing these Western industrial regions, the Americans and British at Potsdam firmly closed down Soviet hopes for extending a meddlesome hand into the operation of their zones. See also: Benz, pp. 110, 112, 135; Fischer, *Die Sowjetische Deutschlandpolitik*, pp. 157–58; De Santis, p. 156.

36. The line of demarcation in Berlin followed arbitrary district administrative borders.

37. For later history of the central governments, see Hurwitz, 3: 58–65. Many of the intellectuals already had a propensity to embrace leftist systems, but they nonetheless had significant influence in traditional European society, in this case one particularly guilt-ridden. Jan T. Gross, in "Social Consequences of War," offers some interesting thoughts about the postwar success of the Communists in setting aside the opposition in east central Europe. One is that a "displaced" people (and displacement in Germany, as well as in Poland, was unarguably almost omnipresent) are more dependent on authority (p. 204); the second is that the "democratic majority . . . feel isolated internationally" whereas the Communists have the support of all local power (p. 207). But in Germany this was the case only where the Red Army was absolutely in charge. This was not the case in western Germany (or in Finland, which, evidently for local reasons, also escaped bolshevization). For years the Germans in the sbz had a way out to the West; and over the years, until 1961, millions of the most mobile left.

38. Geyer, p. 63; for Stalin's system, see Mastny, pp. 306, 307–13. On Stalin's need to take charge, see Raack, "Stalin Plans His Post-War Germany," p. 67; and Goncharov, Lewis, and Litai, p. 32. The Soviet failure in Germany was not simply a fluke; the Soviets also failed in Austria, where, as in Germany, the Red Army lacked, for Soviet purposes, the all-important exclusive control of the national center.

39. The early Soviet political and cultural successes in Berlin alerted Sir William Strang to suggest necessary changes in Western behavior: see Strang to Eden, July 13, 1945, PRO, Fo371, 46933, C3858; and Strang's report to Bevin of his interview with Brigadier Hinde in Berlin, Aug. 8, 1945, ibid., 46934, C4972.

40. Foschepoth, pp. 705–9; Benz, p. 187. The French, in the Control Council, ultimately vetoed the establishment of all-German parties on Oct.

26, 1945 (Willis, p. 27). For Communist fears of the local elections in the U.S. Zone, see "Stenographische Niederschrift über die Funktionärvkonferenz am 4. Januar 1946," ZPA I2/5/39, p. 4.

41. Winterton, in the *News-Chronicle* (London), Sept. 14, 1944, in PRO, FO371, 43377 (7565).

42. Geyer, pp. 63–65; Hurwitz, 4: 1348–70.

43. On the American correspondents, but uncritical, see Bassow, chaps. 5 and 6. Paul Winterton, one of the journalists long in Moscow during the war, reflected on the journalistic malfeasance during the war, as well as on its causes, in his *Report on Russia* (1945). For evidence that journalists as a group have missed Winterton, which ought to be mandatory reading for them, and have taken few steps to overcome the past, see Sikorski, "Coda to the Russo-Afghan War," pp. 21–24.

SUMMARY AND EPILOGUE

1. Tadashi, p. 70.

2. Slusser, pp. 132–33, 136–37; Benz, p. 112. Some British writers have had a propensity to blame the Americans, and not Churchill (see, for example, James, *Anthony Eden*, p. 307), for the failure to confront Stalin directly at Potsdam. But whatever Truman's weaknesses there, he quickly drew the necessary conclusions with respect to holding the line against Stalin in Asia.

3. La Feber, p. 52. For an excellent general analysis of American public opinion, see Lukacs, chap. 7. By the end of the war, the American right-wing press of the variety then published by Henry Luce (*Time, Life, Fortune*) had begun to veer away from its wartime wild enthusiasm for the "Russians"; see Liebovich, p. 29. For an analysis of how the slow development of public opinion affected diplomatic behavior, see De Santis, p. 207.

4. Mineo, p. 208; Slusser, pp. 125, 132–33, 136; Benz, p. 112. Marc S. Gallicchio, *The Cold War Begins in Asia*, characterized the American status in Asia after the first few months of the effort to deal with the eye-opening at Potsdam, the atomic bomb, the Soviet attack on Japan, and the Japanese surrender as "the end result of an interconnected system of unexpected events, improvised responses and unintended consequences" (p. 137); a similar characterization could be made of the American status in Europe at about the same time. President Truman said at the time of the German surrender, in May 1945, reflecting his admiration of his predecessor, "What a pity that Franklin D. Roosevelt did not live to see this day." Six months later, after all the changes and the new light on the Soviets, Truman might well have had some questions about Roosevelt's diplomatic skills. See also, Truman, *Memoirs*, 1: 412. On the revival of the doctrine of world revolution, see Crozier, p. 4.

5. Gaddis, "Korea in American Politics," p. 278.

6. Stalin had apparently relied on the local Communist parties in France and Italy as effective fifth columns, prepared to deliver those nations over to a Soviet-united Europe, "like ripe fruit," when the proper time arrived. We know that V. G. Dekanozov, who must have got his coaching from Stalin and Molotov, had some years earlier proclaimed that the French were already in Moscow's power owing to the power and influence of the 50,000 Communist teachers, who were bringing over the younger generation (U.S. Congress, *Third Interim Report*, p. 463; Sommer, *Das Memorandum*, p. 119–21; Raack, "Stalin's Plans for World War II," p. 220). That Dekanozov's pledge to organize teachers vs. the French bourgeois democratic order and government reflected a full-fledged Bolshevik design is reflected in "Quelles données sur la propagande communiste en Tchéchoslovaquie" (c. 1937), which says, commenting on the Czechoslovak Communist party, "on suit l'example français et l'on tâche de mettre en premier lieu les professeurs et les maîtres d'écoles dans les intérêts bolchevistes" (They follow the French example and try first to draw professors and schoolteachers into Bolshevik interests); in AAN, MSZ, Poselstwo w Pradze, 5427. Marshal Tito, who obviously believed that the Western European CP's were in a strong position to take action after the war, later maintained that Stalin had been "too cautious in pushing the Communists in France and Italy" (quoted by Gati, p. 18). Although Stalin had taken even more territory from the Finns after their second surrender in 1944, the nation was not occupied by the Red Army, and its peace treaty was organized by the Big Three at Potsdam (Mastny, p. 303). Stalin was worried about how the Americans might respond in 1944 and 1945 (Miner, p. 262) if he took over all Finland with the help of an occupying Red Army, as he had planned in 1939, and he was again apparently relying on the local Communist party to bring in the "ripe fruit." The Americans, still vaguely remembering their longtime prewar admiration of the Finns (who "paid their war debts"), had never declared war on them. The British had, but only because Moscow demanded it.

7. Collier, pp. 94–96, 140–41, 145–48, 164.

8. Kramar, p. 34; Chen, pp. 10, 18–31; Weathersby, pp. 23–32; Goncharov, Lewis, and Litai, pp. 136–202.

9. On the development of the resolute anti-Soviet state of mind in the U.S. Foreign Service in 1946–47, see De Santis, p. 211.

10. On Stalin and his gardens, see Medvedev, p. 173; Stalin and Tsar Alexander: Khrushchev, p. 144; W. Averill Harriman, quoted in G. Urban, p. 55; also see, Burlatskii, "Khrushchev," p. 18. See also the reported suspicions of one of Stalin's sons that Stalin was put to death by Beria, in Kolesnik, p. 66. On Stalin's continuing hope for the final thrust to the west, see Wettig, pp. 163–64. John Lewis Gaddis tells a story illustrative of the abundant insanities at Kremlin center in Stalin's later years, from the British Foreign Office collections (in "Intelligence, Espionage, and Cold War

Origins," p. 202): Stalin told Italian Socialist Pietro Nenni in 1952 that New York's Cardinal Spellman had been at the Yalta Conference in disguise in order, at the command of the Vatican, to turn Roosevelt against the Russians. For more on Stalin's preoccupation with the Cardinal, see Rollet, "Un nouveau serpent du Mer," pp. 303, 314.

BIBLIOGRAPHY

ARCHIVES VISITED

Archiv Ministerstvo Zahraničních Věcí České Republiky, Prague
Archiv Ústava Tomasa G. Masaryka, Benešův Archiv, Prague
Archive of the Hoover Institution, Stanford, California
Archiwum Akt Nowych, Warsaw
Bundesarchiv: Berlin: Stiftung der Parteien und Massenorganisationen der
  DDR im Bundesarchiv; Koblenz and Berlin, film archive
Imperial War Museum, Film Archive, London
Library of Congress, Manuscript Division, Washington, D.C.
Public Record Office, London
Rossiiskii Gosudarstvennyi Arkhiv Kinofotodokumentov, Krasnogorsk
Sikorski Institute and Polish Museum, London
Státní Ústřední Archiv, Archiv Ústřední Kommunistická Strana Českoslo-
  venska, Prague
United States National Archives, Written Documents and Motion Picture
  Divisions, Washington, D.C.
Wytwórnia Filmów Dokumentalynych, Warsaw

FILMS AND FILM SERIES

Berlin. Soviet Union, 1945; rev. version, 1967.
Boevye budni. Soviet Union, 1940 (?); USNA 111M52911R, reel 6.

Den' pobedy. Soviet Union, 1945.
Die Deutsche Wochenschau, no. 566/1941. Germany.
Esli zavtra voina. Soviet Union, 1938.
The First of May. Soviet Union, 1941; USNA 111M52939R.
Jewish Life in Lwów. Poland (?), 1938 (?).
Liniia Mannergeima. Soviet Union, 1940.
Mechta. Soviet Union, 1941; first issued 1943.
Novosti Dnia, no. 30/1945. Soviet Union.
Osvobozhdenie. Soviet Union, 1940.
Padenie Berlina. Soviet Union, 1949.
Siege. United States, 1939.
Soiuz kinozhurnal nos. 20, 40–41/1943 and 34/1944. Soviet Union.
The Soviet-Finnish War. United Kingdom, 1978.
Soviet Lithuania. Soviet Union, probably 1941.
Spanish Earth. Netherlands, 1937.
In addition: various untitled, archived films in the USNA 111ADC collection:
   4190, 4920, 5035, 5043, 5766; and from the United States Army Air Force
   Collection (for Germany, Austria, and Czechoslovakia, 1945).

NEWSPAPERS CITED AND MENTIONED

Berliner Zeitung
Deutsche Volkszeitung (Berlin)
Frankfurter Allgemeine Zeitung
Izvestiia (Moscow)
Kino (Moscow)
Manchester Guardian
Der Morgen (Berlin)
New York Herald-Tribune
New York Times
News-Chronicle (London)
Nowe Widnokręgi (Moscow, Kuibyshev)
Pravda (Moscow)
Polityka (Warsaw)
Rzeczpospolita (Lublin, Warsaw)
Tägliche Rundschau (Berlin)
The Times (London)
La Tribune de Genève
Vechernaia Moskva
Das Volk (Berlin)
The Washington Post
The Washington Star
Die Welt (Stockholm)
Wolna Polska (Moscow)

BOOKS AND ARTICLES CITED

Adler, Hans. *Berlin in jenen Tagen. Berichte aus der Zeit 1945–1948.* Berlin, 1959

Akademiia nauk SSSR. Institute of Marxism-Leninism of the Central Committee of the Communist Party of the Soviet Union. *Sotsialisticheskie revolutsii 1940 g. v Litve, Latvii i Estonii.* Moscow, 1978.

Anderson, David. "British Rearmament and the 'Merchants of Death,' The 1935–36 Royal Commission on the Manufacture of and Trade in Armaments." *Journal of Contemporary History* 29 (1994): 5–37.

Anfilov, Viktor. "Samye tiazhkie gody. Letopis' desiatiletii 1937–1946." *Literaturnaia gazeta,* Mar. 22, 1989: 11.

Antipenko, Nikolai. "Tyl v Berlinskoi operatsii." In V. D. Voznesenskii and D. B. Rubezhnyi, eds., *9 Maia 1945 goda. Vospominaniia,* pp. 722–50. Moscow, 1970.

Antosiak, A. V. "Osvobozhdenie Zapadnoi Ukrainy i Zapadnoi Belorussii." *Voenno-istoricheskii zhurnal,* 1989, no. 9: 51–60.

Babiński, Witold. "Sprawa granic Polski w okresie II wojny światowej." *Niepodległość* 11 (1978): 245–88.

Bacia, Horst. "Merkwürdigkeiten beim Eingeständnis über die Massaker von Katyn." *Frankfurter Allgemeine Zeitung,* Apr. 17, 1990: 3.

Badstübner, Rudolf. "'Beratungen' bei J. W. Stalin. Neue Dokumente." *Utopie kreativ,* 1991, no. 7: 99–116.

Baldwin, Peter. "Social Interpretations of Nazism: Renewing a Tradition." *Journal of Contemporary History* 25 (1990): 5–37.

Banac, Ivo. *With Stalin Against Tito: Cominformist Splits in Yugoslav Communism.* Ithaca, N.Y., 1988.

Baryshnikov, N. and V. "Zimnaia voina." *Avrora,* 1990, no. 2: 24–45. 1992, no. 3: 83–90.

Bassow, Whitman. *The Moscow Correspondents: Reporting on Russia from the Revolution to Glasnost.* New York, 1988.

Batowski, Henryk. *Polska dyplomacja na obczyźnie 1939–1941.* Cracow, 1991.

Bell, P. M. H. *John Bull and the Bear: British Public Opinion, Foreign Policy, and the Soviet Union, 1941–1945.* London, 1990.

Ben-Moshe, Tuvia. *Churchill: Strategy and History.* Boulder, Colo., 1991.

———. "Winston Churchill and the 'Second Front': A Reappraisal." *Journal of Modern History* 62 (1990): 503–37.

Beneš, Edvard. *Memoirs of Dr. Eduard Benes: From Munich to New War and New Victory.* Trans. from the Czech. Boston, 1954.

———. *Mnichovské dny.* Prague, 1968.

Bennett, Edward M. *Franklin D. Roosevelt and the Search for Security: American-Soviet Relations, 1933–1939.* Wilmington, Del., 1985.

Benz, Wolfgang. *Potsdam 1945. Besatzungsherrschaft und Neuaufbau in Vier-Zonen-Deutschland.* Munich, 1986.

"Beriia." *Nedelia,* no. 8 (1988): 11.

Bethel, Nicholas. *The War Hitler Won: The Fall of Poland, September 1939.* New York, 1972.

Bezymenskii, Lev. *The Death of Adolf Hitler.* London, 1968.

———. *Konets odnoi legendy.* Moscow, 1972.

———. *Razgadannye zagadki tret'ego reĭkha 1941–1945.* Vol. 2. Moscow, 1982.

———. *Der Tod des Adolf Hitler.* 2d ed. Munich, 1982.

Bilmanis, Alfred, ed. *Latvian-Russian Relations: Documents.* 2d ed. Lincoln, Nebr., 1978.

Binion, Rudolph. *Hitler Among the Germans.* New York, 1976.

Bobek, Gertrud. "Schwerer Anfang in der befreiten Heimat." In Ilse Schiel and Erna Milz, eds., *Im Zeichen des roten Sternes. Erinnerungen an die Traditionen der deutsch-sowjetischen Freundschaft,* pp. 427–40. Berlin, 1974.

Bodensieck, Heinrich. "Wilhelm Piecks Moskauer Aufzeichnungen von '4/6.45'—ein Schlüsseldokument für Stalins Deutschlandpolitik?" In Alexander Fischer, ed., *Studien zur Geschichte der SBZ/DDR,* pp. 29–56. Berlin, 1993.

Bohlen, Charles. *Witness to History, 1929–1969.* New York, 1973.

Boyle, Andrew. *The Climate of Treason.* Rev. ed. London, 1987.

Bracher, Karl Dietrich, and Hans-Adolf Jacobsen, eds. *Dokumente zur Deutschlandpolitik.* Erste Reihe, Bd. 1, *3 September 1939 bis 31 Dezember 1941: Britische Deutschlandpolitik.* Comp. by Rainer A. Blasius. Frankfurt/Main, 1984.

Brandes, Detlef. *Grossbritannien und seine osteuropäische Allierten 1939–1943.* Munich, 1988.

Bregman, Aleksander. *Najlepszy sojusznik Hitlera.* 5th ed. London, 1980.

Buber-Neumann, Margarete. *Als Gefangener bei Hitler und Stalin.* Munich, 1949.

Bullitt, Orville H., ed. *For the President: Personal and Secret: The Correspondence Between Franklin D. Roosevelt and William C. Bullitt.* Boston, 1972.

Burlatskii, Feodor. "Ispoved' reformatora." *Literaturnaia gazeta,* July 19, 1989: 11.

———. "Khrushchev. Shtrikhi k politicheskomu portretu." *Literaturnaia gazeta,* Feb. 24, 1988: 18.

Butler, J. R. M. *History of the Second World War.* Vol. 2, *Grand Strategy.* London, 1957.

Buttlar, Walrab von. *Ziele und Zielkonflikte der Sowjetischen Deutschlandpolitik 1945–1947.* Stuttgart, 1980.

Carley, Michael J. "Down a Blind Alley: Anglo-French-Soviet Relations, 1920–1939." Review article. *Canadian Journal of History* 29 (1994): 147–72.

Cecil, Robert. "The Cambridge Comintern." In Christopher Andrew and David Dilks, eds., *The Missing Dimension: Governments and Intelligence Communities in the Twentieth Century*, pp. 169–88. Urbana, Ill., 1984.

Chen, Jian. "The Sino-Soviet Alliance and China's Entry into the Korean War." Cold War International History Project, Working Paper no. 1. Washington, D.C., 1992.

Churchill, Winston S. *Great Contemporaries*. Rev. ed. London, 1938.

———. *The Second World War*. Vol. 1, *The Gathering Storm*. Boston, 1948. Vol. 2, *The Hinge of Fate*. Boston, 1949.

Cienciała, Anna M. *Polska polityka zagraniczna w latach 1926–1932 [1939] na podstawie tekstów ministra Józefa Becka*. Paris, 1990.

———. "Polska w polityce brytyskiej i francuskiej w 1939 roku: wola walki czy próba uniknięcia wojny?" *Zeszyty historiczne*, no. 75 (1986): 152–83.

———. "The Question of the Polish-Soviet Frontier in British, Soviet, and Polish Policy in 1939–1940: The Litauer Memorandum and Sikorski's Proposal." *Polish Review* 33 (1988): 295–324.

Cohen, Michael T. *Churchill and the Jews*. London, 1985.

Collier, Richard. *Bridge Across the Sky: The Berlin Blockade and Airlift, 1948–1949*. New York, 1978.

Colville, John. *The Fringes of Power: Downing Street Diaries, 1939–1955*. Vol. 1, *1939–1941*. London, 1986.

Conquest, Robert. *Stalin: Breaker of Nations*. New York, 1990.

Coulondre, Robert. *De Staline à Hitler. Souvenirs de deux ambassades 1936–1939*. Paris, 1950.

Crowl, James William. *Angels in Stalin's Paradise: Western Reporters in Stalin's Russia, 1917–1937*. Washington, D.C., 1982.

Crozier, Brian. *Free Agent: The Unseen War, 1941–1991*. London, 1993.

Czajkowski, Bogdan. "Soviet Policies in the Literary Sphere [in eastern Poland, 1939–1941]: Their Effects and Implications." Paper read at a School of Slavonic and East European Studies conference, London University, Apr. 13, 1989.

Dallin, Alexander. "Stalin and the German Invasion." *Soviet Union* 18 (1991): 19–37.

The Dark Side of the Moon. London, 1947.

Darman, Thomas. *Diplomatic Correspondent*. New York, 1968.

Dashichev, V. I. "Der Pakt der beiden Banditen." *Rheinischer Merkur*, Apr. 24, 1989: 3–4.

———. "Planungen und Fehlschläge Stalins am Vorabend des Zweiten Weltkrieges." In Karl Dietrich Bracher et al., *Deutschland zwischen Krieg und*

Frieden. Beiträge zur Politik und Kultur im 20. Jahrhundert. Festschrift für Hans-Adolf Jacobsen, pp. 66–73. Bonn, 1990.

Davis, Lynn E. *The Cold War Begins: Soviet-American Conflict over Eastern Europe*. Princeton, N.J., 1974.

De Mowbray, Stephan. "Soviet Deception and the Onset of the Cold War." *Encounter* 63 (1984), no. 2: 16–24.

De Santis, Hugh. *The Diplomacy of Silence: The American Foreign Service, the Soviet Union, and the Cold War, 1933–1947*. Chicago, 1983.

Derwiński, Zdzisław. "Rząd rzeczypospolitej Polskiej na Obczyźnie wobec utworzenia Komitetu Narodowego 'Wolne Niemcy'." *Dzieje najnowsze* 18 (1986): 225–34.

Dilks, David. "Great Britain and Scandinavia in the Phoney War." *Scandinavian Journal of History* 2 (1977): 33–51.

———, ed. *The Diaries of Sir Alexander Cadogen, 1938–1945*. New York, 1972.

Djilas, Milovan. *Conversations with Stalin*. Trans. from the Serbo-Croat. New York, 1962.

Doernberg, Stefan. *Die Geburt eines neuen Deutschland (1945–1949)*. Berlin, 1959.

———. "Zum Zusammenwirken von SMAD und KPD bzw. SED." In Hans-Joachim Krusch, ed., *Zum deutschen Neuanfang 1945–1949. Tatsachen—Probleme—Ergebnisse—Irrwege. Die Arbeiterbewegung und die Entstehung der beiden deutschen Staaten*, pp. 309–26. Bonn, 1993.

Douglas, Roy. "Chamberlain and Appeasement." In Wolfgang J. Mommsen and Lothar Kettenacker, eds., *The Fascist Challenge and the Politics of Appeasement*, pp. 79–88. London, 1983.

———. *From War to Cold War, 1942–48*. London, 1981.

Drechsler, Karl. "Germany and Its Allies and the War Against the Soviet Union." *Soviet Union* 18 (1991): 39–58.

Duda, Gerhard. *Jenö Varga und die Geschichte des Instituts für Weltwirtschaft und Weltpolitik in Moskau 1921–1970*. Berlin, 1994.

Duroselle, Jean-Baptiste. *La Décadence 1932–1939*. Paris, 1979.

Dushyck, Walter. *Death and Devastation on the Curzon Line: The Story of the Deportations from the Ukraine*. New York, 1948.

Eden, Anthony. *The Reckoning*. Boston, 1965.

Eisenhower, David. *Eisenhower at War, 1943–1945*. London, 1986.

Faisst, Michael, et al. "Die Berliner Sozialdemokratie und die Personalpolitik der Besatzungsmächte 1945/1946." *IWK: Internationale wissenschaftliche Korrespondenz zur Geschichte der deutschen Arbeiterbewegung* 16 (1980): 313–46.

Feis, Herbert. *Between War and Peace: The Potsdam Conference*. Princeton, N.J., 1960.

Ferrell, Robert H., ed. *Dear Bess: The Letters from Harry to Bess Truman, 1910–1959*. New York, 1983.

Firsov, F. N. "Arkhivy Kominterna i vneshnaia politika SSSR v 1933–1941 gg." *Novaia i noveishaia istoriia*, 1992, no. 6: 12–35.

———. "Stalin und die Komintern." In Institut für die Geschichte der Arbeiterbewegung, ed., *Die Komintern und Stalin. Sowjetische Historiker zur Geschichte der Kommunistischen Internationale*, pp. 65–132. Berlin, 1990.

Fisch, Jörg. *Reparationen nach dem Zweiten Weltkrieg*. Munich, 1992.

Fischer, Alexander. *Die Sowjetische Deutschlandpolitik im Zweiten Weltkrieg 1941–1945*. Stuttgart, 1975.

———. "Die Sowjetunion und die 'Deutsche Frage' 1945–1949." In Göttinger Arbeitskreis, ed., *Die Deutschlandfrage und die Anfänge des Ost-West Konflikts 1945–1949*, pp. 451–57. Berlin, 1984.

———, ed. *Teheran, Jalta, Potsdam. Die sowjetischen Protokolle von den Kriegskonferenzen der "Grossen Drei."* Cologne, 1968.

Fitzpatrick, Sheila. "New Perspectives on Stalinism." *Russian Review* 45 (1986): 357–74.

Fleischhauer, Ingeborg. *Diplomatischer Widerstand gegen "Unternehmen Barbarossa": Die Friedensbemühungen der Deutschen Botschaft Moskau 1939–1941*. Berlin, 1991.

———. *Der Pakt. Hitler, Stalin und die Initiative der deutschen Diplomatie 1938–1939*. Berlin, 1990.

Foschepoth, Josef. "Britische Deutschlandpolitik zwischen Yalta und Potsdam." *Vierteljahrshefte für Zeitgeschichte* 30 (1982): 675–714.

Frei, Norbert. "'Wir waren blind, unglaubig und langsam.' Buchenwald, Dachau und die amerikanischen Medien im Frühjahr 1945." *Vierteljahrshefte für Zeitgeschichte* 35 (1987): 385–401.

Friedman, Filip. *Zagłada żydów lwówskich*. Łódź, 1945.

Fuchs, Konrad. "Grossbritannien und die polnisch verwaltete deutsche Ostgebiete im Jahre 1945." *Jahrbuch der Schlesischen Friedrich-Wilhelms Universität* 25 (1986): 273–94.

Gaddis, John Lewis. "Intelligence, Espionage, and Cold War Origins." *Diplomatic History* 13 (1989): 191–212.

———. "Korea in American Politics, Strategy and Diplomacy, 1945–50." In Yonosuke Nagai and Akira Iriye, eds., *The Origins of the Cold War in Asia*, pp. 277–98. Tokyo, 1977.

———. *The United States and the Origins of the Cold War, 1941–1947*. New York, 1972.

Gafençu, Grigore. *Prelude to the Russian Campaign: From the Moscow Pact (August 23rd 1939) to the Opening of Hostilities in Russia (June 22nd 1941)*. London, 1945.

Gallicchio, Marc S. *The Cold War Begins in Asia: American East Asian Policy and the Fall of the Japanese Empire.* New York, 1988.

Garliński, Józef. *Polska w drugiej wojnie światowej.* London, 1982.

Garrett, Christer S., and Stephan A. Garrett. "Death and Politics: The Katyn Forest Massacre and American Foreign Policy." *East European Quarterly* 20 (1986): 429–46.

Gati, Charles. *Hungary and the Soviet Bloc.* Durham, N.C., 1986.

Germany. Auswärtiges Amt. *Documents on German Foreign Policy, 1918– 1945.* Series D, vols. 1 and 2, Washington, D.C., 1949.

Geyer, Dietrich. "Deutschland als Problem der sowjetischen Europapolitik am Ende des zweiten Weltkrieges." In Josef Foschepoth, ed., *Kalter Krieg und Deutsche Frage. Deutschland im Widerstreit der Mächte 1945– 1952,* pp. 50–65. Göttingen, 1985.

Gilbert, Martin. *Winston S. Churchill.* Vol. 5, *1932–1939.* Boston, 1976. Vol. 6, *The Finest Hour. 1939–1941.* Boston, 1983. Vol. 7, *The Road to Victory.* Boston, 1986.

Glees, Anthony. *Exile Politics During the Second World War: The German Social Democrats in Britain.* Oxford, 1982.

———. *The Secrets of the Service: British Intelligence and Communist Subversion, 1939–1951.* London, 1987.

Goerlitz, Walter, ed. *General Feldmarschall Keitel. Verbrecher oder Offizier Erinnerungen. Briefe. Dokumenten des Chefs OKW.* Göttingen, 1961.

Goncharov, Sergei N., John W. Lewis, and Xue Litai. *Uncertain Partners: Stalin, Mao, and the Korean War.* Stanford, Calif., 1993.

Góra, Władysław, and Aleksander Kochański, "Rozmowy polityczne w sprawie utworzenia Tymczasowego Rządu Jedności Narodowej," *Archiwum ruchu robotniczego* 9 (1984): 95–155.

[Gorbachev, Mikhail S.]. *Inteligencja wobec nowych problemów socjalizmu. Spotkanie Michaila Gorbaczowa z przedstawicielami polskiej inteligencji.* Warsaw, 1988.

Gor'kov, Iu. A. "Gotovil li Stalin uprezhdaiushchii udar protiv Gitlera v 1941 g.?" *Novaia i noveishaia istoriia,* 1993, no. 3: 29–45.

Gorlov, S. A. "SSSR i territorial'nye problemy Litvy." *Voenno-istoricheskii zhurnal,* 1990, no. 7: 20–28.

Gorodetsky, Gabriel. *Sir Stafford Cripps' Mission to Moscow, 1940–1942.* Cambridge, Eng., 1984.

———. "Stalin und Hitlers Angriff auf die Sowjetunion." In Bernd Wegner, ed., *Zwei Wege nach Moskau. Vom Hitler-Stalin Pakt bis zum "Unternehmen Barbarossa,"* pp. 347–66. Munich, 1991.

Graml, Hermann. *Die Teilung Deutschlands.* Frankfurt, 1985.

Gross, Jan T. *Revolution from Abroad: The Sovietization of the Western Ukraine and Western White Russia, 1939–1941.* Princeton, N.J., 1988.

———. "Social Consequences of War: Preliminaries to the Study of the Imposition of Communist Regimes in East Central Europe." *Eastern European Politics and Societies* 3 (1989): 198–214.

———. "Wybory." *Aneks. Kwartalnik polityczny*, nos. 45 (1987): 129–60; and 46/7 (1987): 171–210.

———. "Wywózki do Rosji" *Aneks. Kwartalnik politiczny*, no. 51/2 (1988): 43–91.

Gross, Jan T., and Irena Grudzińska Gross. *War Through Children's Eyes: The Soviet Occupation of Poland and the Deportations.* Stanford, Calif., 1981.

Grzędziński, Edward, ed. "Sprawozdanie Bolesława Bieruta z pobytu delegacji PKWN w Moskwie (październik 1944)." *Z pola walki*, R. 30 (1987): 147–58.

Haacker, Carl. "Aussprache vor der Tobis-Belegschaft am 12. 6. 1945." *Filmwissenschaftliche Beiträge* 21 Jg. (1980): 122–26.

Hanak, H. "Sir Stafford Cripps as British Ambassador in Moscow, May 1940 to June 1941." *English Historical Review* 94 (1979): 48–70.

Harbutt, Fraser J. *The Iron Curtain: Churchill, America, and the Origins of the Cold War.* New York, 1986.

Haslam, Jonathan. *The Soviet Union and the Struggle for Collective Security in Europe, 1933–39.* New York, 1984.

Hass, Gerhard. *23. August 1939. Der Hitler-Stalin Pakt.* Berlin, 1990.

Heider, Paul. "Die Gründung des National-Komitees 'Freies Deutschland' und des Bundes Deutscher Offiziere—alleiniger Verdienst der Führung der KPD oder Sowjetischer Entschluss." *BzG*, 1992, no. 3: 4–28.

Herndon, James S. "British Perceptions of Soviet Military Capabilities, 1935–1939." In Wolfgang J. Mommsen and Lothar Kettenacker, eds., *The Fascist Challenge and the Politics of Appeasement*, pp. 297–319. London, 1983.

Herz, Martin F. "The View from Austria." In Thomas T. Hammond, ed., *Witnesses to the Origins of the Cold War*, pp. 161–85. Seattle, 1982.

Historicus. "Stalin on Revolution." *Foreign Affairs* 27 (1949): 175–214.

"Hitlers letzte Reise." *Der Spiegel*, 1992, no. 30: 110–16.

Hochman, Jiri. *The Soviet Union and the Failure of Collective Security, 1934–1938.* Ithaca, N.Y., 1984.

Hofer, Walther. *Die Entfesselung des Zweiten Weltkrieges. Darstellung und Dokumente.* Düsseldorf, 1984.

Hoffmann, Joachim. "Die Angriffsvorbereitungen der Sowjetunion 1941." In Bernd Wegner, ed., *Zwei Wege nach Moskau. Vom Hitler-Stalin-Pakt bis zum "Unternehmung Barbarossa,"* pp. 367–89. Munich, 1991.

Hooker, J. R. "Lord Curzon and the Curzon Line." *Journal of Modern History* 30 (1958): 137–38.

Hurwitz, Harald. *Demokratie und Antikommunismus in Berlin nach 1945.*

Vol. 3, *Die Eintracht der Siegermächte und die Orientierungsnot der Deutschen 1945–1946*. Cologne, 1984. Vol. 4, *Die Anfänge des Widerstandes*, part 2, *Zwischen Selbsttäuschung und Zivilcourage: Der Fusionkampf*. Cologne, 1990.

Ikonnikov, Aleksandr. "Pust' skazat' tovarishch Molotov." *Raduga*, 1990, no. 8: 49–54.

Institut Marksizma-Leninizma pri TsK KPSS. "Komintern i sovetsko-germanskoi dogovor o napadenii." *Izvestiia TsK KPSS*, 1989, no. 12: 202–10.

Institut für Zeitgeschichte, Munich, ed. *Der Weg nach Pankow. Zur Gründungsgeschichte der DDR*. Munich, 1980.

Irving, David. *Hitler's War*. London, 1977.

Ivashov, L. G. "V poslednie predvoennye." *Voenno-istoricheskii zhurnal*, 1989, no. 11: 12–19.

Jacobsen, Hans-Adolf. *Zur Konzeption einer Geschichte des Zweiten Weltkrieges 1939–1945*. Frankfurt/Main, 1964.

———, ed. *1939–1945. Der Zweite Weltkrieg in Chronik und Dokumenten*. Darmstadt, 1959.

James, Robert Rhodes. *Anthony Eden*. London, 1986.

———. "The Epic Concluded: Martin Gilbert's 'Churchill.'" *Encounter* 71 (1988), no. 2: 40–41.

Jordan, Nicole. *The Popular Front and Central Europe: The Dilemmas of French Impotence, 1918–1940*. Cambridge, Eng., 1992.

Kacewicz, George. *Great Britain, the Soviet Union, and the Polish Government in Exile (1939–1945)*. The Hague, 1979.

Kalenychenko, Pavlo M. *Pol'ska prohresyvna emigratsiia v SRSR v roky Drohoi Svitovoi Viini*. Kiev, 1957.

Kamiński, Marek K. "Sprawa wyborów w Polsce a kwesti zachodniej granicy państwa polskiego na konferencji w Poczdamie." *Dzieje najnowsze*, R. 21 [1989]: 69–82.

Kaplan, Karel. *The Short March*. Trans. from the German. London, 1987.

Karski, Jan. "Tajna diplomacja Churchilla i Roosevelta w sprawie Polski (1940–1945)." *Zeszyty historyczne*, no. 78 (1986): 16–20.

Kaslas, Bronis J. *The Baltic Nations*. Pittston, Pa., 1976.

———. "The Lithuanian Strip in Soviet-German Secret Diplomacy, 1939–1941." *Journal of Baltic Studies* 4 (1973): 211–25.

———. *La Lithuanie et la seconde guerre mondiale*. Paris, 1981.

———. *The USSR-German Aggression Against Lithuania*. New York, 1973.

Keiderling, Gerhard, ed. *"Gruppe Ulbricht" in Berlin April bis Juni 1945. Von der Vorbereitungen im Sommer 1944 bis zur Wiedergründung der KPD im Juni 1945. Eine Dokumentation*. Berlin, 1993.

Kennan, George F. "Comment" to the articles, "World War II: 30 Years After. Allied Leadership in World War II [sections on Churchill, Roosevelt and Stalin]." *Survey* 21 (1974): 29–36.

————. Interview of May 30, 1972, with J. K. Zawodny. Published as Appendix C in J. K. Zawodny, *Nothing But Honour: The Story of the Warsaw Uprising, 1944*, pp. 217–28. Stanford, Calif., 1978.

————. *Russia and the West Under Lenin and Stalin*. New York, 1961.

————. "Russia—Seven Years Later." In Joseph M. Siracusa, ed., *The American Diplomatic Revolution: A Documentary History of the Cold War*, pp. 62–70. Milton Keynes, 1978.

————. "The View from Russia." In Thomas T. Hammond, ed., *Witnesses to the Origins of the Cold War*, pp. 27–33. Seattle, 1982.

Kersten, Krystyna. *Repatriacja ludności polskiej po II wojnie światowej (Studium historyczne)*. Wrocław, 1974.

Kettenacker, Lothar. "The Anglo-Soviet Alliance and the Problem of Germany, 1941–1945." *Journal of Contemporary History* 17 (1982): 435–58.

————. *Krieg zur Friedenssicherung. Die Deutschlandplanung der britischen Regierung während des Zweiten Weltkriegs*. Göttingen, 1989.

Khrenov, Ivan A., et al., eds. *Dokumenty i materialy po istorii sovetsko-pol'skikh otnoshenii*. Vol. 7 Moscow, 1974.

Khrushchev, Nikita S. *Khrushchev Remembers: The Glasnost Tapes*. Trans. and ed. by Jerrold S. Schecter and Vyacheslav V. Luchkov. Boston, 1990.

Kimball, Warren. *Swords or Ploughshares*. Philadelphia, 1976.

————, ed. *Churchill and Roosevelt: The Complete Correspondence*. Vol. 1, *Alliance Emerging, October 1933–November 1942*. Vol. 2, *Alliance Forged, November 1942–February 1944*. Vol. 3, *Alliance Declining, February 1944–April 1945*. Princeton, N.J., 1984.

Kisielewski, Tadeusz. "W odpowiedzi historykowi czeskiemu. Polemika z Jaroslavem Valentą w sprawie stosunków polsko-czeskich w latach 1938–1945." *Dzieje najnowsze* 25 (1993): 91–100.

Kitchen, Martin. *British Policy Toward the Soviet Union During the Second World War*. New York, 1986.

Kobrin, Vladimir. "Stalin as an Historian." *Encounter* 72 (1989), no. 2: 5.

Kochański, Aleksander, ed. *Protokół obrad KC PPR w maju 1945 roku*. Warsaw, 1992.

Kolesnik, A. N. "Vzlet i padenie Vasiliia Stalina." *Voenno-istoricheskii zhurnal*, 1989, no. 2: 65–69.

Kolski, Witold. "O wojnach sprawiedliwych i nie sprawiedliwych." In *Nowe Widnokręgi*, 1941, no. 4: 129–45.

————. *W służbie ludu pod sztandarem KPP*. Warsaw, 1955.

Kovalev, V. I., and N. E. Medvedev. "Pomoshch Sovetskoi Armii naseleniiu Germanii april'-iiul' 1945 g." *Voenno-istoricheskii zhurnal* 23 (1981): 38–44.

Kowalski, Włodzimierz T. "Zachodni sojuszniszy Polski wobec niemieckiej agresji na Polskę." *Wojskowy przegląd historyczny* 34 (1989): 42–59.

Kramar, Mark. "Archival Research in Moscow: Progress and Pitfalls." *Cold War International Historical Project Bulletin*, no. 3 (fall 1993): 1, 18–39.

Kraus, Elizabeth. *Ministerien für ganz Deutschland. Der allierte Kontrollrat und die Frage gesamtdeutscher Zentralverwaltungen.* Munich, 1990.

Krisch, Henry. *German Politics Under Soviet Occupation.* New York, 1974.

Krosby, Peter. *Finland, Germany, and the Soviet Union, 1940–1941: The Petsamo Dispute,* Madison, Wis., 1968.

Kumanev, Georgii. "Istoriia sovetskogo obshchestva. Kratkii ocherk (1917–1945). Glava shestaia. V ogne tiazhelykh ispytanii (iiun' 1941–noiabr' 1942 g.)." *Istoriia SSSR*, 1991, no. 2: 3–31.

Kuznetsov, I. I. "Generaly 1940 goda." *Voenno-istoricheskii zhurnal*, 1989, no. 10: 29–37.

La Feber, Walter. "American Policymakers, Public Opinion, and the Outbreak of the Cold War, 1945–50." In Yonosuke Nagai and Akira Iriye, eds., *The Origins of the Cold War in Asia*, pp. 43–65. Tokyo, 1977.

Lane, Thomas. "The Soviet Occupation of Poland Through British Eyes." In John Hiden and Thomas Lane, eds., *The Baltic and the Outbreak of the Second World War*, pp. 142–64. Cambridge, Eng., 1992.

Langner, Władysław. "Ostatnie dni obrony Lwowa." *Niepodległość* 11 (1978): 193–96.

Laqueur, Walter. *Stalin: The Glasnost Revelations.* New York, 1990.

———. *The Terrible Secret.* Boston, 1980.

Larson, Deborah Welch. *The Origins of Containment: A Psychological Explanation.* Princeton, N.J., 1983.

Laschitza, Horst. *Kämpferische Demokratie gegen Faschismus. Die programmtische Vorbereitung auf die antifaschistisch-demokratische Umwälzung in Deutschland durch die Parteiführung der KPD.* Berlin, 1969.

Latviešu Tautas Palidziba. *These Names Accuse: Nominal List of Latvians Deported to the Soviet Union, 1940–1941.* Stockholm, 1951.

Lawlor, Sheila. "Britain and Russian Entry into the War." In R. T. B. Langhorne, ed., *Diplomacy and Intelligence During the Second World War*, pp. 175–81. Cambridge, Eng., 1985.

Leahy, William D. *I Was There.* New York, 1950.

Lehmann, Hans-Georg. *Der Oder-Neisse Konflikt.* Munich, 1979.

Lenin, V. I. "Ia proshu zapisyvat' menshe: eto ne dol'zhno popadat' v pechat'." *Istoricheskii arkhiv* 1992, no. 1: 12–30.

Leonhard, Wolfgang. *Die Revolution entlässt ihre Kinder.* Cologne, 1956.

Létourneau, Paul. "Évaluation canadienne des perspectives ouvertes à l'Allemagne." *Guerres mondiales et conflits contemporains*, 40ième année (1990): 49–66.

Lewin, Kurt I. "Archbishop Andreas Sheptytsky and the Jewish Community in Galicia During the Second World War." *Unitas* (English ed.) 12 (1960): 133–42.

Liebovich, Louis. *The Press and the Origins of the Cold War.* New York, 1988.

Liszewski, Karól. *Wojna Polsko-Sowiecka 1939 r.* London, 1986.

The editors of *Lituanus.* "The Molotov-Ribbentrop Pact: The Documents." *Lituanus* 35 (1989): 47–74.

Łossowski, Piotr. *Litwa a sprawa polska.* Warsaw, 1982.

Loth, Wilfried. *Stalins ungeliebtes Kind: warum Moskau die DDR nicht wollte.* Reinbeck, 1994.

Loth, Wilfried, and Rolf Badstübner, eds. *Wilhelm Pieck—Aufzeichnungen zur Deutschlandpolitik 1945–1953.* Berlin, 1994.

Lubachenko, Ivan S. *Belorussia Under Soviet Rule, 1917–1957.* Lexington, Ky., 1972.

Lukacs, John. *1945: Year Zero.* Garden City, N.Y., 1978.

Lukas, Richard. *The Strange Allies: The United States and Poland, 1941–1945.* Knoxville, Tenn., 1978.

Lukes, Igor. "Benesch, Stalin und die Komintern 1938/1939. Vom Münchener Abkommen zum Hitler-Stalin Pakt." *Vierteljahrshefte für Zeitgeschichte,* Jg. 1993, Heft 3: 325–53.

———. "Stalin and Benes in the Final Days of September 1938." *Slavic Review* 52 (1993): 29–48.

Lundestad, Geir. "Moralism, Presentism, Exceptionalism, and Other Extreme Usages in American Writing on the Early Cold War Years." *Diplomatic History* 13 (1989): 327–46.

Łuszkiewicz, Grazyna. "Rodowód historyczny manifestu PKWN." In Grazyna Łuszkiewicz, ed., *Materiały na konferencję naukową n. t. "Idee manifestu PKWN i ich realizacja w Polsce Ludowej,"* pp. 9–40. Warsaw, 1984.

Mal'kov, V. L. "Pribaltiki glazami amerikanskikh diplomatov (iz arkhivov SShA)." *Novaia i noveishaia istoriia,* 1990, no. 5: 41–52.

Manne, Robert. "The British Decision for Alliance with Russia, May 1939." *Journal of Contemporary History* 9 (1974): 3–26.

———. "Some British Light on the Nazi-Soviet Pact." *European Studies Review* 9 (1981): 83–102.

Mark, Eduard. "American Policy Toward Eastern Europe." *Journal of American History* 68 (1981): 313–36.

———. "'Today Has Been a Historical One': Harry S Truman's Diary of the Potsdam Conference." *Diplomatic History* 4 (1980): 317–26.

Mastny, Vojtech. *Russia's Road to the Cold War, 1941–1945.* New York, 1979.

Mautner, Kurt. "The View from Germany." In Thomas T. Hammond, ed., *Witnesses to the Origins of the Cold War,* pp. 231–48. Seattle, 1982.

May, Ernest. *American Cold War Strategy: Interpreting NSC 68.* Boston, 1993.

Mazur, Zbigniew. "Niemiecko-radzieckie poruzumienia z sierpnia i września 1939 r." *Przegląd zachodni*, 1989, no. 4: 125–50.

Medvedev, Roi. "O Staline i Stalinizme." *Znamia*, 1989, no. 4: 165–203.

Millman, Brock. "Toward War with Russia: British Naval and Air Planning for Conflict in the Near East, 1939–1940." *Journal of Contemporary History* 29 (1994): 261–83.

Mineo, Nakajima. "The Sino-Soviet Confrontation in Historical Perspective." In Yonosuke Nagai and Akira Iriye, eds., *The Origins of the Cold War in Asia*, pp. 203–23. Tokyo, 1977.

Miner, Stephen M. *Between Churchill and Stalin: The Soviet Union, Great Britain, and the Origins of the Grand Alliance*. Chapel Hill, N.C., 1988.

Ministère des Affaires Étrangères. Commission de publication des documents relatifs aux origines de la guerre 1939–1945. *Documents diplomatiques françaises*. Deuxieme série, *1936–1939*, vols 10–12. Paris, 1976–78.

Ministerstvo Inostrannykh del SSSR. *Sovetsko-angliiskie otnosheniia vo vremia Velikoi Otechestvennoi voiny 1941–1945*. Vol. 1, *1941–1943*. Moscow, 1983.

Misiunas, Romuald, and Rein Taagepera. *The Baltic States: Years of Dependence*. London, 1983.

Mon allié, Staline. Ce qu'en pense Winston Churchill. n.p., n.d.

Mroczkowski, Władysław, and Tadeusz Sierocki, eds. "Rozmowy delegacji PKWN i KRN z przedstawicielami rządu RP na emigracji (sierpień 1944)." *Z pola walki*, R. 27 (1984): 109–53.

Müller, Marianne, and Egon Erwin Müller. "*Stürmt die Festung Wissenschaft!*" *Die Sowjetisierung der mitteldeutschen Universitäten seit 1945*. Berlin, 1953.

Myllyniemi, Seppo. *Die Baltische Krise 1938–1941*. Trans. from the Finnish. Stuttgart, 1979.

Nadzhadov, D. G. "Diplomatiia SShA i Sovetsko-germanskie peregovory 1939 goda." *Novaia i noveishaia istoriia*, 1992, no. 1: 43–58.

Nazarewicz, Ryszard. "Więź PPR z międzynarodówką komunistyczną i ośrodkiem lewicy polskiej w ZSRR." In Wyższa Szkoła nauk społecznych przy KC PZPR, ed. *40-lecie Polskiej Partii Robotniczej*, pp. 66–90. Warsaw, 1983.

Nekrich, Aleksandr M. "*June 22, 1941*." *Soviet Historians and the German Invasion*. Ed., trans., and with an appendix by Vladimir Petrov. Columbia, S.C., 1969.

———. "Perestroika in History. The First Stage." *Survey* 30 (1989): 22–43.

Nekrich, Aleksandr M., and Mikhail Heller. *Utopia in Power: The History of the Soviet Union from 1917 to the Present*. New York, 1986.

Němec, František, and Vladimir Moudrý. *The Soviet Seizure of Carpathian Ruthenia*. Reprint ed. Westport, Conn., 1981.

Niedbalski, Bernd. "Deutsche Zentralverwaltungen und Deutsche Wirtschaftskommission (DWK)." *Vierteljahrshefte für Zeitgeschichte* 33 (1985): 456–77.

Nies, Susanne. "Die Stalin(ismus)-Kontroverse in der Sowjetunion." *Osteuropa Forum Aktuell*, 1989, no. 24: 11–14.

Nordling, Carl O. *Defense or Imperialism: An Aspect of Stalin's Military and Foreign Policy, 1933–1945.* Uppsala, 1984.

Noskov, A. M. "Severnyi uzel." *Voenno-istoricheskii zhurnal*, 1990, no. 7: 7–19.

Nübel, Otto. *Die amerikanische Reparationspolitik gegenüber Deutschland 1941–1945.* Frankfurt/Main, 1980.

O'Donnell, James. *The Berlin Bunker: The History of the Reichschancellery Group.* Boston, 1978.

Osóbka-Morawski, Edward. "Moskowskie spotkanie i rozmowy." *Pobrzeże*, 1985, no. 3: 10–11.

Ozimek, Stanisław. *Film Polski w wojennej potrzebie.* Warsaw, 1974.

Pagel, Jürgen. *Polen und die Sowjetunion 1938–1939.* Stuttgart, 1992.

Parker, R. A. C. "Britain, France, and Scandinavia, 1939–1940." *History* 61 (1976): 371–87.

Parsadanova, Valentina S. *Sovetsko-pol'skie otnosheniia v gody Velikoi Otechestvennoi voiny 1941–1945.* Moscow, 1982.

Pastusiak, Longin. *Dramatyczne sześć miesięcy. Od rządu tymczasowego RP do tymczasowego rządu jedności narodowej (styczeń-czerwiec 1945 r.).* 2d ed. Toruń, 1991.

Penkower, Monty Noam. *The Jews Were Expendable.* Urbana, Ill., 1983.

Perechnev, U. G. "O nekotorykh problemakh podgotovki strany i vooruzhennykh sil k otrazheniiu fashistkoi agressii." *Voenno-istoricheskii zhurnal*, 1988, no. 4: 42–50.

Petropoulos, Jonathan. "Saving Culture from the Nazis." *Harvard Magazine* 92 (1990), no. 4: 34–42.

"Petrow." In the *Lithuanian Bulletin* 8 (1950), no. 7–12: 11–14.

Pfaff, Ivan. "Prag und der Fall Tuchatschewskii." *Vierteljahrshefte für Zeitgeschichte* 35 Jg. (1987): 95–134.

Phillips, Ann L. *Soviet Policy Toward East Germany Reconsidered: The Postwar Decade.* New York, 1986.

Phillips, Hugh D. *Between the Revolution and the West: A Political Biography of Maxim M. Litvinov.* Boulder, Colo., 1992.

Piekalkiewicz, Janusz. *Polenfeldzug. Hitler und Stalin zerschlagen die Polnische Republik.* Bergish Gladbach, 1982.

Pietrow-Ennker, Bianka. "Stalinistische Aussenpolitik 1939–1941. Ein Beitrag zur Vorgeschichte des deutschen Angriffs auf die Sowjetunion am 22. Juni 1941." *BzG*, 1991, no. 6: 811–17.

Pinchuk, Ben-Cion. "Jewish Refugees in Soviet Poland, 1939–1941." *Jewish Social Studies* 40 (1978): 141–58.

———. *Shtetl Jews Under Soviet Rule: On the Eve of the Holocaust.* Oxford, 1990.

Platonov, S., ed. *Vtoraia mirovaia voina, 1939–1945.* Moscow, 1958.

Pobóg-Malinowski, Władysław. *Najnowsza historia polityczna Polski 1864–1945.* Vol. 3, *1939–1945.* London, 1960.

"Polacy znad Wilii, Niema, Narwi, i Bugu w łagrach sowieckich 1944–47." *Zeszyty historyczne,* no. 67 (1984): 155–87.

Polonsky, Anthony, ed. *The Great Powers and the Polish Question, 1941–45.* London, 1976.

Polonsky, Anthony, and Bolesław Drukier. *The Beginnings of Communist Rule in Poland.* London, 1980.

Poźarskas, Myoklas. *Stosunki Litwy Radzieckiej i Polski Ludowej.* Kaunas, 1974.

Prus, Edward. "Utworzenie kolaboracyjnego rządu ukraińskich nacjonalistów i ogłoszenie we Lwowie w 1941 r. 'samostijnej derzhavy' pod protektoratem Trzeciej Rzeszy." *Z dziejów stosunków polsko-radzieckich* 9 (1972): 107–38.

Raack, R. C. "Film as Historical Fantasy. The Red Army Beflags the Reichstag." In Stephen Dolezel and K. R. M. Short, eds., *Hitler's Fall: The Newsreel Witness,* pp. 57–69. London, 1988.

———. "History as Past and Current Politics: The *Gensek,* Stalin, and the Beginnings of the Cold War." *East European Quarterly* 23 (1989): 129–144.

———. "Nazi Film Propaganda and the Horrors of War." *Historical Journal of Radio, Film, and Television* 6 (1986): 189–96.

———. "Nazi Newsreels for the General Gouvernement." *Studia historica slavo-germanica* 13 (1984): 163–80.

———. "Poor Light on the 'Dark Side of the Moon': Soviet Actuality Film Sources for the Early Days of World War II." *Film and History* 20 (1990): 3–15.

———. "Stalin Fixes the Oder-Neisse Line." *Journal of Contemporary History* 25 (1990): 467–88.

———. "Stalin Plans His Post-War Germany." *Journal of Contemporary History* 28 (1993): 53–73.

———. "Stalin's Plans for World War II." *Journal of Contemporary History* 26 (1991): 215–27.

———. "When Plans Fail: Small-Group Behavior and Decision-Making in the Conspiracy of 1808 in Germany." *Journal of Conflict Resolution* 14 (1970): 1–14.

———. "With *Smersh* in Berlin: New Light on the Incomplete Histories of the *Führer* and the *Vozhd'.*" *World Affairs* 114 (1991): 47–55.

Rann, Toivo. *Estonia and the Estonians.* Stanford, Calif., 1987.

Rauchensteiner, Manfred. *Der Sonderfall. Die Besatzungszeit in Oester-reich 1945 bis 1955*. Graz, 1981.

Resis, Albert. "Spheres of Influence in Soviet Wartime Diplomacy." *Journal of Modern History* 53 (1981): 417–39.

———, ed. *Molotov Remembers: Inside Kremlin Politics. Conversations with Felix Chuev*. Chicago, 1993.

Riess, Curt. *Das gab es nur einmal. Der deutsche Film nach 1945*. Vol. 4. Vienna, 1977.

Rodionov, O. A. "Geroicheskii trud kinooperatorov na frontakh Velikoi Otechestvennoi voiny 1941–1945 godov." Diss., Vse-soiuznyi Gosudar-stvennoi Institut Kinomatografii, Moscow, 1967.

Rollet, Henri. "Un nouveau serpent du Mer. La note soviétique du 10 mars 1952 et la visite de Pietro Nenni à Staline." *Revue d'histoire diploma-tique*, 102e année (1988): 279–318.

Rosenfeld, Gunter. "Anbahnung und Abschluss des Hitler-Stalin Paktes. Er-gebnisse der Historiographie und einige überlegungen zum Thema." *BzG*, 1991, no. 3: 291–309.

Ross, Graham, ed. *The Foreign Office and the Kremlin. British Documents on Anglo-Soviet Relations, 1941–1945*. Cambridge, Eng., 1984.

Rothwell, Victor. *Britain and the Cold War, 1941–1947*. London, 1982.

Rotundo, Louis. "Stalin and the Outbreak of War in 1941." *Journal of Con-temporary History* 24 (1989): 277–300.

Ruch, Siegfried, and Hans Schürer. "Die Rolle der Sowjetarmee bei der Ent-stehung eines neuen Deutschlands." *Theorie und Praxis* 11 (16) Jg. (1965): 27–33.

Rupnik, Jacques. *Histoire du parti communiste tchécoslovaque. Dès ori-gines à la prise de pouvoir*. Paris, 1981.

Ryerson, André. "Questions of Bias: How Eight College Courses Teach American Foreign Policy." *Academic Questions* 1 (1988): 5–34.

Rzhevskaia, Elena. *Berlin, Mai 1945*. Moscow, 1986.

———. "Berlinskie stranitsy." *Znamia*, 1965, no. 5: 154–98.

———. *Chetyre vesny v shineli*. Moscow, 1961.

———. "V tot den', pozdnei osen'iu." *Znamia*, 1986, no. 12: 157–77.

Salmon, Patrick. "Great Britain, the Soviet Union, and Finland at the Begin-ning of the Second World War." In John Hiden and Thomas Lane, eds., *The Baltic and the Outbreak of the Second World War*, pp. 95–123. Cambridge, Eng., 1992.

Sandalov, L. M. *Perezhitoe*. Moscow, 1966.

Sandford, Gregory W. *From Hitler to Ulbricht: The Communist Recon-struction of East Germany, 1945–46*. Princeton, N.J., 1983.

Scheel, Klaus, ed. *Die Befreiung Berlins 1945*. Berlin, 1975.

Schlesinger, Jr., Arthur. "The Origins of the Cold War." *Foreign Affairs* 46 (1967): 22–52.

Schöpflin, George. "The Pattern of Political Takeovers: How Eastern Europe Fell." *Encounter* 64 (1985), no. 2: 65–69.

Schroeder, Hans-Henning. "Die Lehren von 1941. Die Diskussion um die Neubewertung des 'Grossen Vaterländischen Krieges' in der Sowjetunion." In Wolfgang Michalka, ed., *Der Zweite Weltkrieg. Analysen—Grundzüge—Forschungsbilanz*, pp. 608–25. Munich, 1989.

"Schukows Angriffsplan." *Der Spiegel*, 1991, no. 24: 140.

Schulz, Klaus Peter. *Auftakt zum Kalten Krieg. Der Freiheitskampf der SPD in Berlin 1945/6*. Berlin, 1965.

Schwabe, Klaus. "Die Amerikanische Besatzungspolitik in Deutschland und die Entstehung des 'Kalten Krieges' (1945/1946)." In Alexander Fischer, et al., eds., *Russland-Deutschland-Amerika. Festschrift für Fritz T. Epstein zum 80. Geburtstag*, pp. 311–42. Wiesbaden, 1978.

Schwartz, Andrew J. *America and the Russo-Finnish War*. Washington, D.C., 1960.

Seaton, Albert. *The Russo-German War, 1941–1945*. London, 1971.

Semidetko, V. I. "Istoki porazheniia v Belorussii." *Voenno-istoricheskii zhurnal*, 1989, no. 4: 22–31.

Semiriaga, M. I. "Eshche raz o krizisnom gode, 1939 . . ." *Mirovaiia ekonomika i mezhdunarodnaia otnosheniia*, 1989, no. 12: 118–23.

———. "17 sentiabria 1939 goda." *Sovetskoe Slavianovedenie*, 1990, no. 5: 3–16.

———. "Sovetskii soiuz i predvoennyi politicheskii krizis." *Voprosy istorii*, 1990, no. 9: 49–64.

———. "Voina kotoruiu stydno vspominat'." *Molodoi kommunist*, 1990, no. 3: 72–79.

Sikorski, Radek. "Coda to the Russo-Afghan War: A Correspondent Reports." *Encounter* 71 (1988), no. 1: 20–30.

Simon, Gerhard. *Nationalismus und Nationalitätenpolitik in der Sowjetunion*. Baden-Baden, 1986.

Siracusa, Joseph M. "The Meaning of *Tolstoy*: Churchill, Stalin, and the Balkans. Moscow, October, 1944." *Diplomatic History* 3 (1979): 443–63.

Skrzypek, Andrzej, ed. "Czwarta podróż S. Mikołajczyka do Moskwy." *Dzieje najnowsze* 17 (1985): 185–95.

Ślusarczyk, Jacek. *Stosunki polsko-radzieckie 1939–1945*. Warsaw, 1991.

Slusser, Robert M. "Soviet Far Eastern Policy, 1945–50: Stalin's Goals in Korea." In Yonosuke Nagai and Akira Iriye, eds., *The Origins of the Cold War in Asia*, pp. 123–46. Tokyo, 1977.

Smith, C. Jay. *The Russian Struggle for Power, 1914–1917*. New York, 1956.

Sokolov, V. V. "Narkomindel Viacheslav Molotov." *Mezhdunarodnaia zhizn'*, 1991, no. 5: 99–112.

Sommer, Erich F. *Botschafter Graf Schulenberg. Der letzte Vertreter des Deutschen Reiches in Moskau*. Asendorf, 1987.

———. *Das Memorandum. Wie der Sowjetunion der Krieg erklärt wurde.* Munich, 1981.

Sontag, Raymond J., and James S. Beddie. *Nazi-Soviet Relations, 1939–1941.* Washington, D.C., 1948.

"Les Souvenirs d'un agent soviétique." *La Tribune de Genève*, Dec. 25, 1949–Jan 2, 1950.

Speer, Albert. *Inside the Third Reich.* New York, 1971.

Spirin, L. M. "Stalin i voina." *Voprosy istorii KPSS*, 1990, no. 5: 90–105.

Spring, Derek. "The Soviet Decision for War Against Finland." *Soviet Studies* 38 (1986): 207–26.

Spychalski, Marian. "Powołanie PKWN—wspomnienia." *Z pola walki* 12 (1979): 195–222.

Stalin, Joseph. *The Foundations of Leninism.* 1924 (published in many editions).

———. "Tov. Stalin o perspektivakh GKP i o bol'shevizatsii." *Pravda*, Feb. 3, 1925, p. 1.

Stanisławska, Stefania, ed. *Sprawa polska w czasie II wojny światowej na arenie międzynarodowej. Zbiór dokumentów.* Warsaw, 1965.

Stehle, Hans-Jacob. "Der Lemberger Metropolit Šeptyćkyj und die Nationalsozialistische Politik in der Ukraine." *Vierteljahrshefte für Zeitgeschichte* 34 (1986): 407–26.

Stern, Frank. *Dogma und Widerspruch: SED und Stalinismus in den Jahren 1946 bis 1958.* Munich, 1992.

Stettinius, Edward. *The Diaries of Edward Stettinius, Jr., 1943–1946.* New York, 1975.

Stone, Daniel. "The Economic Origins of the Soviet Famine of 1932–1933: Some Views from Poland." *Polish Review* 37 (1992): 167–83.

Strang, William. *Home and Abroad.* London, 1956.

———. *The Moscow Negotiations.* Leeds, 1968.

Strong, Anna Louise. *The Soviets Expected It.* New York, 1942.

Suda, Zdenek. *Zealots and Rebels: A History of the Ruling Communist Party of Czechoslovakia.* Stanford, Calif., 1980.

Suvorov, Viktor. *Der Eisbrecher. Hitler in Stalins Kalkül.* Trans. from the Russian. Stuttgart, 1989.

———. "Yes, Stalin Was Planning to Attack Hitler in June 1941." *Journal of the Royal United Services Institute for Defence Studies*, no. 131 (1986): 73–74.

Suziedelis, Saulis. "The Ribbentrop-Molotov Pact and the Baltic States: An Introduction and Interpretation." *Lithuanus* 35 (1989): 8–46.

Sword, Keith. "The Division of Poland, September 1939." In David W. Pike, ed., *The Opening of the Second World War*, pp. 107–17. New York, 1991.

———. In *Polityka* (Warsaw), 1989, no. 3 (Jan. 21): 14.

Syzdek, Eleonora. "Sprawa powołania Polskiego Komitetu Narodowego w

Moskwie (grudzień 1943–styczeń 1944)." *Archiwum ruchu robotniczego* 9 (1984): 36–94.

———, ed. *Wanda Wasilewska we wspomnieniach.* Warsaw, 1982.

Szaz, M. *Die deutsche Ostgrenze.* Munich, 1961.

Taborský, Edvard. *President Edward Benes.* Stanford, Calif., 1981.

Tadashi, Aruga. "The United States and the Cold War: The Cold War Era in American History." In Yonosuke Nagai and Akira Iriye, eds., *The Origins of the Cold War in Asia*, pp. 66–88. Tokyo, 1977.

Takayuki, Ito. "The Genesis of the Cold War: Confrontation over Poland, 1941–44." In Yonosuke Nagai and Akira Iriye, eds., *The Origins of the Cold War in Asia*, pp. 147–202. Tokyo, 1977.

Tennenbaum, Joseph. *In Search of a Lost People: The Old and the New Poland.* New York, 1948.

Terry, Sarah Meiklejohn. *Poland's Place in Europe: General Sikorski and the Origins of the Oder-Neisse Line.* Princeton, N.J., 1983.

Thomas, Hugh. *Armed Truce: The Beginnings of the Cold War, 1945–46.* New York, 1987.

Thomas, Siegfried. *Entscheidung in Berlin. Zur Entstehungsgeschichte der SED in der deutschen Hauptstadt 1945/46.* Deutsche Akademie der Wissenschaften zu Berlin. Schriften des Instituts für Geschichte, Reihe 1, Bd. 27. Berlin, 1964.

———. "Der Wiederbeginn des politischen Lebens in Berlin und die Aktionseinheit der Arbeiterparteien (Mai–Juli 1945)." *Zeitschrift für Geschichtswissenschaft* 8 Jg. (1960): 1310–41.

Thompson, Ewa M. "Nationalist Propaganda in the Soviet Russian Press, 1939–1941." *Slavic Review* 50 (1991): 385–99.

Tiulpanov, Sergei. *Deutschland nach dem Kriege (1945–1949). Erinnerungen eines Offiziers der Sowjetischen Armee.* Berlin, 1986.

Tokaev, Grigorii A. *Stalin Means War.* London, 1951.

Topitsch, Ernst. *Stalin's War: A Radical New Theory on the Origins of the Second World War.* Trans. from the German. London, 1987.

Trevor-Roper, Hugh. "Hitler Revisited: A Retrospective." *Encounter* 71 (1988), no. 5: 17–19.

———. *The Last Days of Hitler.* 5th ed. London, 1978.

Truman, Harry S. *Memoirs by Harry S Truman.* Vol. 1. Garden City, N.Y., 1955.

Tsakaloyannis, Panos. "The Moscow Puzzle." *Journal of Contemporary History* 21 (1986): 37–56.

Tsitriniak, Grigorii. *Ne zabyto! Rasskazy frontovykh kinooperatov i kinorezhisserov.* Moscow, 1986.

Tucker, Robert C. *Stalin as Revolutionary, 1879–1929: A Study in History and Personality.* New York, 1973.

————. *Stalin in Power: The Revolution from Above, 1928–1941.* New York, 1990.

Tusiński, Piotr A. "Sytuacja międzynarodowa PKWN (lipiec-grudzień 1994." In Grazyna Łuszkiewicz, ed., *Materiały na konferencję naukową n. t. "Idee manifestu PKWN i ich realizacja w Polsce Ludowej,* pp. 41–66. Warsaw, 1984.

Tych, Felix, ed. "Wanda Wasilewska. Wspomnienia (1939–1944)." *Archiwum ruchu robotniczego* 8 (1982): 383–408.

Übershär, Gerd. "'Der Pakt mit dem Satan, um den Teufel auszutreiben.' Der deutsch-sowjetische Nichtangriffsvertrag und Hitlers Kriegsabsicht gegen die UdSSR." In Wolfgang Michalka, ed., *Der Zweite Weltkrieg. Analysen—Grundzüge—Forschungsbilanz,* pp. 568–85. Munich, 1989.

Ulam, Adam. *The Rivals: America and Russia Since World War II.* New York, 1971.

————. *Stalin: The Man and His Era.* New York, 1973.

Ulbricht, Walter. *Zur Geschichte der neuesten Zeit.* Vol. 1, erster Halbband. Berlin, 1955.

Umiastowski, Roman. *Russia and the Polish Republic, 1918–1941.* London, n.d.

United States Congress, House of Representatives. Select Committee on Communist Aggression. *Third* and *Fourth Interim Reports.* Washington, D.C., 1954.

United States Department of State. *Foreign Relations of the United States. Diplomatic Papers. The Conference at Berlin, 1945.* Vol. 1. Washington, D.C., 1960.

————. *The Conferences at Cairo and Teheran.* Washington, D.C., 1961.

————. *The Conferences at Malta and Yalta.* Washington, D.C., 1955.

Urban, G. R. *Stalinism: Its Impact on Russia and the World.* London, 1982.

Urban, Karl. "Die Herausbildung der Aktionseinheit der Arbeiterklasse und der demokratischen Selbsverwaltungsorgane unter Führung der KPD in der Provinz Brandenburg (Ende April bis Anfang Juni 1945)." *Beiträge zur Geschichte der deutschen Arbeiterbewegung* 5 Jg. (1963): 818–97.

Ushakov, Aleksandr. *Die Erbe Stalins in den deutsch-polnischen Beziehungen.* Cologne, 1970.

USSR. Ministerstvo inostrannykh del, *God krizisa (sentiabr' 1938–sentiabr' 1939). Dokumenty vneshnei politiki SSSR 1938–1939 gg.* Vol. 2. Moscow, 1990.

Vardys, V. Stanley, ed. *Lithuania Under the Soviets: Portrait of a Nation, 1940–1965.* New York, 1965.

Vashchenko, P. F. "Esli by Finliandiia i SSSR . . ." *Voenno-istoricheskii zhurnal,* 1990, no. 1: 27–34.

Vengerov, L. *Vanda Vasilevskaia. Kritiko-biograficheskii ocherk.* Moscow, 1955.

Venkov, I. N. "Dopustit' razmeshchenie voisk . . ." *Voenno-istorichiskii zhurnal*, 1990, no. 4: 31–42.

Vihavainen, Timo. "The Soviet Decision for War Against Finland: A Comment." *Soviet Studies* 39 (1987): 314–17.

Vogelsang, Theophile. "Die Bemühungen um eine deutsche Zentralverwaltung 1945/46." *Vierteljahrshefte für Zeitgeschichte* 18 (1970): 510–28.

Volkogonov, Dimitri A. "Drama reshenii 1939 goda." *Novaia i noveishaia istoriia*, 1989, no. 4: 3–27.

Vosske, Heinz. "Dokumente aus der programmatischen Tätigkeit der KPD für den Aufbau eines neuen antifaschistisch-demokratischen Deutschlands." *Beiträge zur Geschichte der Arbeiterbewegung* 10 Jg. (1968): 473–92.

———. *Die Vereinigung der KPD und der SPD in Mecklenburg-Vorpommern. Mai 1945 bis April 1946.* Rostock, 1966.

Wandycz, Piotr. *Czechoslovak-Polish Confederation and the Great Powers, 1940–1943.* Westport, Conn., 1979.

Watt, Donald C. "Britain and the Historiography of the Yalta Conference and the Cold War." *Diplomatic History* 13 (1989): 67–98.

Ważniewski, Władysław. *Walka polityczna w kierownictwie PPR i PZPR 1944–1964.* Toruń, 1991.

Weathersby, Kathryn. "Soviet Aims in Korea and the Origins of the Korean War, 1945–1950: New Evidence from Russian Archives." Cold War International History Project. Working Paper no. 8. Washington, D.C., 1993.

Weber, Hermann. "Die deutschen Opfer Stalins." *Deutschland-Archiv*, 1989, no. 4: 412–16.

———. *Geschichte der DDR.* Munich, 1985.

———. "Die sowjetische Militäradministration in Deutschland und das Parteisystem der SBZ/DDR." *Deutschland-Archiv* 15 Jg. (1982): 1064–79.

———, ed. *Parteiensystem zwischen Demokratie und Volksdemokratie. Dokumente und Materialen zum Funktionswandel der Parteien und Massenorganisationen in der SBZ/DDR 1945–1950.* Cologne, 1982.

Weber, Reinhard W. *Die Entstehungsgeschichte des Hitler-Stalin Paktes.* Frankfurt/Main, 1980.

Węgierski, Jerzy. *Lwów pod okupacją sowiecką 1939–1941.* Warsaw, 1991.

Weiler, Peter. *British Labour and the Cold War.* Stanford, Calif., 1988.

Weinberg, Gerhard. *Germany and the Soviet Union, 1939–1941.* Leiden, 1954.

———. "The Nazi-Soviet Pacts: A Half-Century Later." *Foreign Affairs* 68 (1989): 175–189.

Weinstein, Jan. "Dokumenty w sprawie zamordowania przez Gestapo b. Premiera Profesora Kazimierza Bartla." *Zeszyty historyczne*, no. 11 (1967): 92–94.

Weiss, Grigori. *Am Morgen nach dem Kriege. Erinnerungen eines sowjetischen Kulturoffiziers.* Berlin, 1981.

Welsh, Helga A., and Wolfgang Zank. "Zentralverwaltungen. Einleitung." In Martin Broszat and Hermann Weber, eds. *SBZ Handbuch. Staatliche Verwaltungen, Parteien, gesellschaftliche Organisationen, und ihre Führungskräfte in der Sowjetischen Besatzungszone Deutschland 1945–1949,* pp. 201–6. Munich, 1990.

Werth, Alexander. *Russia at War, 1941–1945.* London, 1964.

Wettig, Gerhard. "Die Stalin-Note vom 10. März 1952 als geschichtswissenschaftliches Problem." *Deutschland-Archiv,* 1992, no. 2: 157–67.

Wheeler-Bennett, Sir John, and Anthony Nicholls. *The Semblance of Peace: The Political Settlement After the Second World War.* London, 1972.

Williams, Edward Francis. *Ernest Bevin: Portrait of a Great Englishman.* London, 1952.

———. *A Prime Minister Remembers: The War and Post-War Memoirs of the Rt. Hon. Earl Attlee.* London, 1961.

Willis, F. Roy. *The French in Germany, 1945–1949.* Stanford, Calif., 1968.

Winterton, Paul. *Report on Russia.* London, 1945.

Wittfogel, Karl August. "Einleitung zu Marx' 'Enthüllungen zur Geschichte der Diplomatie im 18. Jahrhundert.'" In Karl Marx, *Enthüllungen zur Geschichte der Diplomatie im 18. Jahrhundert,* pp. lxiv–lxxix. Frankfurt, 1981.

Wohlforth, William C. *The Elusive Balance: Power and Perceptions During the Cold War.* Ithaca, N.Y., 1993.

Woito, Robert. "Between the Wars." *Wilson Quarterly* 11 (1987): 108–21.

Woodward, E. L., et al. *Documents on British Foreign Policy, 1919–1939.* 3d series, vol. 7. London, 1954.

Wright, Peter. *Spycatcher.* New York, 1988.

Zabiełło, Stanisław. *O rząd i granice. Walka dyplomatyczna o sprawę polską.* 3d ed. Warsaw, 1970.

Zaks, Zofia. "Stosunki polsko-radzieckie w 1943r. w świetle franzuskiej dokumentów diplomaticznych." *Dzieje najnowsze* 19 (1987), no. 2: 127–43.

———. "Stosunki polsko-radzieckie w świetle franzuskiej dokumentacji diplomatycznej 1944 roku (styczeń-lipiec 1944 r.)." *Dzieje najnowsze* 19 (1987), no. 3: 111–39.

———. "'Wolna Francja' i Czechosłowacja (1940–1944). *Dzieje najnowsze* 20 (1988), no. 2–3: 109–29.

———. "'Wolna Francja' i Polska w latach 1943–1944 (październik 1943–lipiec 1944)." *Kwartalnik historyczny* 94 (1988), no. 2: 99–130.

Zaremba, Piotr. "Szczecin 1945. Dziennik wydarzeń i dokumenty historyczne." Ms., 13 vols. (c. 1960). In the Biblioteka główna PAN, Warsaw.

———. "Wyzwolenie Szczecina w 1945 r. na tle sytuacji międzynarodowej." *Zycie i myśl*, R. 22 (1972): 71–80.

Zawodny, Janusz. *Nothing but Honour: The Story of the Warsaw Uprising, 1944*. Stanford, Calif., 1978.

Zhukov, Georgii. "Berlinskaia operatsiia i kapitulatsiia Germanii." In V. D. Voznesenskii and D. B. Rubezhnyi, eds., *9 Maia 1945 goda. Vospominaniia*, pp. 66–121. Moscow, 1970.

———. *Erinnerungen und Gedanken*. Stuttgart, 1969.

———. "Die Kronung des Sieges." *Neues Deutschland*, Apr. 25, 1970, p. 4.

Ziemke, Earl. *The Battle for Berlin*. London, 1969.

———. "Stalin as Strategist, 1940–1941." *Military Affairs*, 1983, no. 4: 173–80.

Zoria, Iu., and N. Lebedeva. "1939 god v Niurnbergskom dos'e." *Mezhdunarodnaia zhizn'*, 1989, no. 9: 124–37.

Zyblikiewicz, Lubomir. *Polityka Stanów Zjednoczonych i Wielkiej Brytanii wobec Polski 1944–1949*. Warsaw, 1984.

INDEX

In this index an "f" after a number indicates a separate reference on the next page, and an "ff" indicates separate references on the next two pages. A continuous discussion over two or more pages is indicated by a span of page numbers, e.g., "57–59." *Passim* is used for a cluster of references in close but not consecutive sequence. Entries are alphabetized letter by letter, ignoring word breaks, hyphens, and accents.

Library of Congress Cataloging-in-Publication Data

Raack, R. C. (Richard C.)
    Stalin's drive to the West, 1938–1945 : the origins of the Cold
  War / R. C. Raack.
        p.   cm.
Includes bibliographical references and index.
ISBN 0-8047-2415-6 (alk. paper)
  1. Soviet Union—Foreign relations—1917–1945.   2. Stalin, Joseph,
1879–1953.   3. World War, 1939–1945—Diplomatic history.   4. World
War, 1939–1945—Soviet Union. 5. Europe, Eastern—Politics and
government—1918–1945.   I. Title.
DK273.R33   1995
947.084′2—dc20
95-4990   CIP

∞This book is printed on recycled, acid-free paper.
It was designed by Omega Clay, and typeset by
G&S Typesetters, Inc. in 10/13 Trump Medieval.